R0061623054

01/2012

SEEING REDS

Arsenal Pulp Press | Vancouver

SEEING REDS

The Red Scare of 1918–1919,
Canada's First War on Terror

DANIEL FRANCIS

ARSENAL PULP PRESS
#101-211 East Georgia St.
Vancouver, BC
Canada V6A 1Z6
arsenalpulp.com

The publisher gratefully acknowledges the support of the Canada Council for the Arts and the British Columbia Arts Council for its publishing program, and the Government of Canada through the Canada Book Fund and the Government of British Columbia through the Book Publishing Tax Credit Program for its publishing activities.

Efforts have been made to locate copyright holders of source material wherever possible. The publisher welcomes hearing from any copyright holders of material used in this book who have not been contacted.

Editing by Susan Safyan
Design by Shyla Seller
Author photograph by Patrick Francis

Printed and bound in Canada

Library and Archives Canada Cataloguing in Publication

Francis, Daniel
    Seeing reds : the red scare of 1918-1919, Canada's first war on terror / Daniel Francis.

Includes index.
Also issued in electronic format.
ISBN 978-1-55152-373-6

    1. Canada—History—1918-1939. 2. Anti-communist movements—Canada. 3. General Strike, Winnipeg, Man., 1919. 4. Soviet Union—History—Revolution, 1917-1921—Influence. I. Title.

FC555.F73 2010   971.061   C2010-904249-2

Contents

FIGURE 1 A crowd of protestors works at tipping over a streetcar on Main Street in Winnipeg, June 21, 1919, known as "Bloody Saturday." Moments later, the RCMP made their appearance. *Photo: Foote Collection, Manitoba Archives, SIS N2762*

The View from the Third Floor

"... the only way to deal with Bolshevism is to hit it and to hit it hard, every time it lifts its ugly head."
—*A.J. Andrews, Citizens' Committee of 1,000 leader, July 10, 1919*

It is 2:30 on the afternoon of Saturday, June 21, 1919. Lewis Foote is crouched in a window on the third floor of a building on Main Street, north of the intersection with Portage Avenue in downtown Winnipeg. Foote, a forty-six-year-old commercial photographer who has been documenting the life of the city since he and his wife arrived to live here in 1902, has heard there is trouble brewing, and he does not want to miss it. He points his camera across Main at a crowd of people who are milling around an empty street-railway car. The men in the crowd are dressed in dark suits and wear white straw hats, felt fedoras, or soft cloth caps, the costume of the respectable working class. The women, of whom there are only a few, wear stylish hats and long skirts with hems that brush the dusty street. Everyone seems slightly dressed up, as if they are going to a company picnic.

In fact, in a few minutes they will find themselves in the middle of the most famous riot in Canadian history.

The street-railway tram is tilted at an angle and some of its windows are smashed. The stronger men in the crowd have their hands pressed up against the tram, which they are rocking back and forth, trying to push it over onto its side. They are part of a larger crowd of 5–6,000 marchers, mainly returned veterans of the Great War and their supporters, who are proceeding along Main Street to the Royal Alexandra Hotel where they hope to meet with the federal Minister of Labour, Gideon Robertson, who has come out from Ottawa to try to resolve the crisis. It is day thirty-six of the Winnipeg General Strike, and 30,000 workers are off the job, bringing business in the city to a halt.

It is not by accident that marchers have targeted the street railway. Streetcar service has been a bone of contention since the strike began. Transit workers joined the work stoppage back in May and the trolleys had remained in their barns since that time. But three days ago, management rounded up enough railway men who were willing to defy the strike to resume limited service. The angry veterans want to send a message that the strike will not so easily be broken. When they cannot knock the car off the tracks, they smash the windows and set it on fire in frustration.

Snap. Lewis Foote takes his picture. And almost as if it was his fault, all hell breaks loose. Suddenly the clatter of horses' hooves can be heard. "Here come the bloody soldiers," someone shouts as a troop of red-coated Mounted Police on horseback, armed with clubs, bursts from Portage Avenue onto Main and trots briskly north into the crowd. Defiant marchers pelt the horsemen with rocks, bricks, bottles—whatever they can find lying on the pavement. The Mounties wheel and come back down Main past City Hall, using their truncheons to drive protestors from the street back onto the sidewalks. Mayor Charles Gray, who has been watching from the roof of City Hall and who has already banned all public parades, descends to the front steps to read the Riot Act ordering the crowd to disperse. At almost this precise moment, gunfire breaks out. A police horse has fallen in the street, taking down its rider, who is being beaten by one of the marchers. The officer in command of the mounted force has ordered his men to shoot into the crowd.

Witnesses report hearing three volleys, one of which is aimed at the people surrounding the streetcar. A tinsmith named Mike Sokolowiski dies instantly. He is "shot through the heart while heaving a brick at a policeman," according to Toronto's *Globe* newspaper. (Other sources say the bullet struck him in the head.) Others fall wounded to the ground; one of them, Steve Schezerbanowes, will die from gangrene poisoning. Up in his third-floor perch, still taking photographs, Lewis Foote comes under fire. "Someone was shooting at me from across the street..." he later claims. "Three bullets were fired—one went through the window above my head and the other two struck the building."[1] Foote presumes he is being fired on by a striker, but it is only the police who possess guns that afternoon.

Later generations come to know June 21, 1919 as "Bloody Saturday." (The phrase is thought to have been coined by Fred Dixon, one of the strike's martyrs, who used it to headline his account of the events in the workers' own newspaper, the *Strike Bulletin*. Perhaps Dixon meant it to be a reference to the "Bloody Sunday" of January 1905, when the army of Tsar Nicholas II fired on unarmed demonstrators in Leningrad, killing hundreds of them.) People flee in a panic to get away from the gunfire, only to run into cordons of special police wearing white armbands and wielding clubs. These "specials" have replaced members of the regular police force who have been fired for failing to sign loyalty oaths. Brawls break out along Main and up the adjacent streets and alleyways. During the melee, the "specials" arrest as many protestors as they can. At the same time, the militia arrives on horses and in motorized transport armed with machine guns and fan out across the downtown, bayonets fixed to their rifles, making further arrests. Authorities take a total of ninety-four people into custody. The armed occupation of the largest city in western Canada lasts long into the night.

Five days later, the Winnipeg General Strike ends.

+ + +

"The boil broke in Winnipeg on Saturday," Senator George Foster wrote in his diary when he heard about the violence. "Some blood was shed but law and order was maintained and probably the issue as to that point was settled for all Canada. It has been an anxious and serious time and is not yet all over."[2] Lewis Foote's photograph, and others he took showing the Mounted Police charging up and down Main Street, captures the moment when, in Foster's phrase, "the boil broke," when the violence that had been bubbling just below the surface not only in Winnipeg but in the whole of Canada for the past year burst into the open.

In retrospect it is not surprising that Winnipeg should have been at the eye of the storm. The "Gateway to the West," home to so many immigrants from Britain and Eastern Europe, was awash with free-thinkers and radical ideas. Theories of social change infused the air like the aroma of spring flowers. Single-taxers, phrenologists, social democrats, atheists, feminists, social gospellers, table bumpers, cooperators, syndicalists, Marxists, impossibilists, pacifists, and theosophists: Winnipeg was a potent brew of intoxicating notions about the true nature of mankind and society. If radicalism was going to confront authority anywhere in Canada, it was logical that it be in Winnipeg.

At the same time, the city was not unique. From the coal mines of Cape Breton to the logging camps of Vancouver Island, from the factory floor to the company boardroom, from the House of Commons in Ottawa to the neighbourhood labour hall, Canadians were debating the future. The Great War, though just ended, had already been a transformative event, setting in motion changes that looked to be overturning the old, familiar society. One historian of the period has written that "1919 represented the greatest opportunity for significant social change ever to occur in Canada."[3] Many people who lived through the tumultuous period agreed with Stephen Leacock when he warned that "this is a time such as there never was before."[4]

Where Canadians disagreed was in the value of that change and who was going to control it. Were the traditional elites going to preserve their positions of influence and authority in the new Canada? Or was an insurgent class of socialist labour leaders and social activists going to transform the country in a radical new image? The larger issue that Senator Foster thought was being settled in Winnipeg was simply this: who would rule Canada? Was it going to be the respectable forces of established authority or the angry voices stirring from below demanding a new social order?

FIGURE 2 *Armistice Day, Munitions Centre* by the British artist Frederick Etchells captures the exuberance of a crowd celebrating the end of World War I. Etchells was one of the painters recruited into the official war art program initiated by Lord Beaverbrook to make a visual record of the conflict. *Source: CWM 19710261-0139, Beaverbrook Collection of War Art, © Canadian War Museum*

CHAPTER ONE

Roots of Unrest

"The Spirit of Revolt is Everywhere Apparent"
—*Joseph Marks,* Industrial Banner, *August 25, 1916*

If you were an ordinary person living in Canada in the winter of 1918–19, you might well have thought that the world was coming down around your ears.

World War I had ended at 11 a.m. on Monday, November 11, 1918. Word of the armistice reached Canada in the early hours of the morning. As people heard of it, they spilled from their houses into the streets, some of them still in their pyjamas and nightgowns, congregating on street corners to toast the peace. After more than four years of war, there was a passion to celebrate. In Toronto, a pre-dawn procession of munitions workers, mainly women, paraded down Yonge Street, beating on pots and pans and blowing whistles. Towns and cities erupted in a noisy jubilee: sirens began wailing, factory whistles blew, church bells rang. Bonfires crackled on street corners and fireworks exploded. In the prairies, haystacks burned brightly in the fields. When daybreak came, work was forgotten as downtown thoroughfares filled with celebrants. Effigies of the German Kaiser were strung up and set ablaze. Civic officials hastily organized victory parades where Canadians expressed their relief that the war was finally over. Churches held special services of thanksgiving. The acting prime minister, William Thomas White (Prime Minister Robert Borden was already in England preparing for peace talks), dashed off a telegram to Arthur Currie, commander of the Canadian forces, commending their "courage, endurance, heroism and fortitude."

But the euphoria did not last for long. Once the hangover of celebration wore off, Canadians woke up to the realization that there was no peace. Instead, everywhere in the world there seemed to be violence and turmoil: revolution in Germany and Hungary; civil war in Russia; uprisings in China and India; war in Afghanistan; general strikes in major cities across the United States. It was the Bolsheviks, people said; they seemed to be everywhere, overturning governments, seizing private property, and imposing their radical ideas. For some, these foreign "Reds" represented hope for a more just society; for others, they were a dangerous evil let loose to prey upon mankind.

If unrest was the rule around the world, why not in Canada? The war had left many Canadians disappointed and anxious about the future. The cost of living had been rising at three times the pace of wages. Working people found themselves poorer off than before the conflict began. As demobilized veterans returned home looking for jobs, a looming unemployment crisis threatened the economy. Returning soldiers were angry to find recent immigrants and people who had not put their lives at risk during the war occupying positions that they thought should belong to themselves. Conscription had opened an ugly division between French and English Canada. Under Borden's Conservative government, political life seemed to have achieved unprecedented levels of corruption. The government and the press were engaged in a full-blown panic about the threat to the Canadian way of life posed by foreign agitators and labour radicals. "The strain of war has produced a reckless and desperate temper," Professor O.D. Skelton wrote in the *Queen's Quarterly*. "The world cannot be torn up by the roots for five years without destroying much of the old stability and acquiescence in the established order."[1]

Canadians wondered what the war had been all about if the result was so much uncertainty, so much turmoil. They were proud of their country's contribution to the conflict, but unsure about how to make it count for something. Surely more than 60,000 young Canadians had not given their lives just to preserve the status quo. The sacrifice seemed to demand a better way of doing things. A thirst for significant change cut across all stratas of society, from factory workers to farmers, from church ministers to returned soldiers to politicians. The federal cabinet minister Newton Rowell summed it up: "We cannot go back to old conditions, if we would, and we ought not to, even if we could."[2]

But there was little agreement about what a new, improved Canada might look like. At a conference on reconstruction organized by the federal government in Ottawa, business leaders revealed their suspicion of even the most basic reforms, preferring instead a return to "normalcy," by which they meant the way things had always been. That was the conservative, go-slow approach to postwar policy making: change if necessary but not necessarily change. What was the point of winning the war against Kaiserism, they wondered, if it led to Red revolution at home? More assertive voices for change emanated from the Protestant churches, which before the war had organized the Social Service Council to advocate for progressive social reform. The Council threw its support behind "industrial democracy" and a wide-ranging set of social welfare policies, including mothers' allowances, unemployment insurance, and old-age pensions. The Methodists went farther still, calling for "nothing less than a complete social reconstruction" of post-war Canada.[3]

Yet even this clarion call did not go far enough for political activists in the labour movement and the various socialist parties. They adopted the rhetoric of world revolution. Nothing would satisfy these radicals short of an overhaul of the structure of economic ownership in the country. "Are we in favour of a bloody revolution?" asked Calgary labour organizer Jean MacWilliams, appearing before a government commission in the spring of 1919. "Why any kind of revolution would be better than conditions as they are now."[4] In other words, what was the point of winning the war in Europe if it *did not* lead to Red revolution at home?

Fundamentally the debate was about the future of Canada. Who would control the means of production? What should be the role of working people in the new economy? How might a true democracy function? But if these questions had their answers in the future, they had their roots in the recent past in the wartime experiences of Canadians.

+ + +

While the Great War was a momentous struggle that united most Canadians in support of their armed troops, it was also a divisive force, revealing and intensifying deep fractures in Canadian society. Native-born Canadians doubted the loyalty of the foreign-born. Imperialists, who thought the war was about defending the British Empire against the barbaric Hun, could not agree with nationalists, who thought it was about Canada's independent role in the world. As the cost of living rose and wages failed to keep pace, working people wondered if their employers were bearing a fair share of the war's economic burden. There was widespread cynicism about a government which had asked for so much sacrifice yet seemed to be corrupting the electoral process to cling to power. English and French were redrawing the linguistic battle lines that had kept them at odds since Confederation. When the prominent Presbyterian clergyman Charles Gordon (who also wrote hugely popular novels under the pen name Ralph Connor) returned home in early 1917 from France where he had been serving as a front-lines chaplain to the 79th Cameron Highlanders, he was deeply discouraged by the public mood that he encountered. "What had come over the Canadian people?" he wondered. "I remembered how my heart had been filled with a new hope for a new national unity that would wipe out forever from true Canadian hearts all the racial and religious jealousy and hate that had darkened the future of our Canadian life. Now all was back again, and in a more disgraceful and dangerous form."[5] As long as the war continued, serious dissatisfaction was confined to a small number of malcontents on the fringes of political life. Nonetheless, these divisive issues bubbled away beneath the surface, gaining strength as the war progressed and preparing to burst to the surface when it ended.

For two decades prior to the war, Canada had flung its doors wide open to immigration from around the world. The Prairie West needed settlers, and the government sought them wherever they could find them: in the United States, in Great Britain, in

Scandinavia and Italy, and in Germany and the Austro-Hungarian and Russian empires. As Clifford Sifton, minister of the interior from 1896 to 1905 and chief architect of this policy, told the House of Commons: "I don't care what language a man speaks, or what religion he professes. If he is honest and law-abiding, if he will go on that land and make a living for himself and his family, he is a desirable settler."[6] (Sifton did not mean to include Asians in his open invitation, but that is a different matter.) Millions of newcomers flooded into the country. In 1896, the year the Laurier government came to office, 16,835 immigrants arrived. By 1901 that number had tripled, and in 1913, the last pre-war year, the total exceeded 400,000. (By comparison, in 2008 Canada welcomed somewhere around 247,000 immigrants.)

When the war began in August 1914, Canadians had to decide what to do about the half-million people living among them who traced their origin to countries with which Canada was now in conflict. Many of these people were residents of long standing, many were not. Initially the public was not hugely concerned with these "enemy aliens." After all, it was conventional wisdom that the war would be over by Christmas. When it wasn't, when fighting dragged on and casualties began to mount, the public rethought its approach to the foreigners living among them. In April 1915 Canadian soldiers went into combat at the Second Battle of Ypres, where the enemy deployed deadly chlorine gas for the first time. This battle was followed early in May by the sinking of the British passenger liner RMS *Lusitania* off the Irish coast by a German u-boat, killing 1,198 people, many of them children. Canadians began to understand that the war was not some schoolbook adventure story; it was going to be a brutal, drawn-out affair that the enemy would do anything to win. For the prominent feminist Nellie McClung, as

FIGURE 3 New recruits, shown here leaving Winnipeg for Europe in 1915, were swept up in the excitement of the war and expected the fighting to be over soon. When it wasn't, the Borden government felt obliged to introduce conscription, a policy that divided the country. *Photo: Manitoba Archives, Edith Rogers Chapter (IODE), 82, N22276*

for many others, the *Lusitania* was the last straw. It transformed her from a pacifist to a supporter of the war. "It was the *Lusitania* that brought me to see the whole truth," she wrote. "Then I saw that we were waging war on the very Prince of Darkness. [...] I knew that no man could die better than in defending civilization from this ghastly thing which threatened her!"[7]

In Toronto, Montreal, and Winnipeg, German-owned businesses came under attack from angry mobs. When word reached Victoria, BC, that fifteen local people were among the *Lusitania* victims—including the son of James Dunsmuir, a former premier—a crowd of liquor-fuelled patriots smashed up the German Club. Armed guards were posted at Government House for fear that the mob might take out its anger on the wife of the lieutenant-governor who was a member of a German family, albeit one with deep roots in the province. When a mysterious fire destroyed the Centre Block of the Parliament Buildings in Ottawa early in February 1916, killing seven people, it was widely believed that the Kaiser's saboteurs were responsible. Three months later the town of Berlin, Ontario, changed its name to Kitchener, after the British War Minister. (A year later, when someone suggested switching back, protest riots erupted.) All these incidents were evidence that the tide of public opinion had turned against the enemy alien, a trend that only grew stronger as the weeks and months passed and the cost of the war, in terms of Canadian lives lost, became more obvious.

At the outset, even though most Canadians believed the war would end by Christmas in a glorious Allied victory, Members of Parliament decided it was necessary to grant emergency powers to the prime minister and his cabinet. At the request of Justice Minister Charles Doherty, one of his department officials, W.F. O'Connor, a lawyer from Halifax, came up with draft legislation literally overnight. Much to Doherty's surprise, Liberal MPs, without even knowing what the bill contained, let it be known that they would have no objections to it. Parliament met in a special war session on August 18, and on August 22, with almost no debate in the House of Commons, the Senate, or the press, the War Measures Act (1914) received final approval.[8]

The War Measures Act ("An Act to confer certain powers upon the Governor in Council and to amend the Immigration Act") gave open-ended and unprecedented authority to Prime Minister Borden and his cabinet to rule through orders-in-council, unconstrained by Parliament. (The exact wording in Section 6 of the Act was: "The Governor in Council shall have power to do and authorize such acts and things, and to make from time to time such orders and regulations, as he may by reason of the existence of real or apprehended war, invasion or insurrection deem necessary or advisable for the security, defence, peace, order and welfare of Canada.") There was no provision for terminating the Act; it was left up to the government to decide when the perceived threat was over.

With regard to enemy aliens resident in Canada, the authorities initially used the Act with discretion. Police forces and the military had the authority to detain Germans and Austrians who might be preparing to return home to fight for their native countries or who seemed likely to engage in fifth-column work inside Canada. Instead, Ottawa simply ordered all aliens to begin reporting monthly to registration centres at the end of October 1914. If they wished to leave the country, they could do so if a registrar was satisfied that they had no intention of joining the enemy army. Otherwise they were expected to carry identity papers with them at all times. (One notorious German who managed to slip out of the country was Joachim von Ribbentrop, a wine merchant in Ottawa and one of the most eligible bachelors in the pre-war capital. He fled by train to New York from where he made his way home to Germany and into uniform. Ribbentrop survived the war and later served as Adolf Hitler's foreign minister.) In extreme cases, registrars could intern individuals suspected of harbouring anti-Canadian sentiments, but initially most people who were identified as enemy aliens were left at liberty.

As public opinion hardened, however, more and more Germans, Austrians, and other central Europeans were rounded up and placed in internment camps. Many of the internees were labourers who had been enticed to Canada before the war to take unskilled work in the mines, logging operations, and construction camps of the resource hinterland. During the pre-war economic downturn, many had lost their jobs, and now they found themselves the victims of

wartime paranoia. Large numbers congregated in the cities, causing local officials to fear outbreaks of civil unrest if nothing was
done. The internment camps seemed like a convenient dumping
ground for these economic refugees. By the end of 1915 there were
fourteen camps across the country holding more than 7,000 men,
the majority of them civilians who posed no threat to the country.
They were herded like animals into tents and makeshift barracks,
confined behind barbed wire, and guarded by armed soldiers. In
some cases they were joined by their wives and children who had
no other means of support. Most of these men were set to work as
cheap labour on land and road clearing projects, in mines, and on
railway construction.[9]

As the internment operation progressed, anti-alien sentiment
among Canadians continued to grow. In Toronto, city council
voted to fire any employee of German, Austrian, or Turkish background who was not a naturalized citizen. Calls to strip aliens of
their jobs or to deport them without cause became common currency in political debate. Under the pressures of war, Canadians
drew an increasingly strict line between "us" and "them." Enemy
aliens were demonized and victimized, no matter how long they
had been in Canada. By the end of the war, after years of hostility
and fear-mongering on the part of Anglo-Canadians against "bohunks" and "Huns," it was not surprising that public opinion could
also be aroused against another group of "foreigners," the Reds,
who seemed to threaten the Canadian way of life every bit as much
as the enemy alien had during the war.

+ + +

The most notorious internee held in any of the Canadian camps was

Leon Trotsky.[10] When news reached North America in March 1917 that the Russian tsar, Nicholas II, had abdicated, Trotsky was living in exile in New York City. He immediately arranged to return to his homeland. On March 27 he boarded the Norwegian freighter *Christianiafjord* with his wife and two sons, bound for Petrograd. Trotsky had been under surveillance in New York where British authorities took note of his departure. The situation in Russia was confused, but the Allies knew that socialists like Trotsky wanted to withdraw Russian troops from the war. It was widely believed that they were enemy agents funded by the Germans to divide the Allied war effort. At Halifax, the British naval commander received orders to board the *Christianiafjord* when it arrived and to detain Trotsky and the other Russians with whom he was travelling.

On April 1 the freighter steamed into Halifax harbour. Naval officers marched Trotsky and his comrades to jail cells in the Citadel, the imposing stone fortification overlooking the city. Then, while Natalia Sedova-Trotskaya and the boys were lodged with a police employee in town, the men were interned in a prisoner-of-war camp, a converted iron foundry at Amherst near the New Brunswick border.

Trotsky was not cowed by his treatment. Quite the opposite: he defiantly petitioned the Russian government and the British prime minister, protesting his illegal detention. Meanwhile, he began to harangue his fellow prisoners with speeches, in fluent German, proclaiming the need for a revolution in Germany. "That month the concentration camp very much resembled a perpetual mass meeting," he later wrote. To the dismay of officials, he became a hero to the 800 other detainees. He was "by far the most popular man in the whole camp," the commander reported. Another officer recalled that Trotsky "gave us a lot of trouble at the camp, and if he had stayed there any longer [...] would have made communists of all the German prisoners."

Trotsky was a citizen of a country with which Great Britain, and therefore Canada, was an ally in the fighting, and he was travelling with perfectly legal permits and visas. His internment was giving Canada a black eye internationally. At rallies in New York and Russia, speakers denounced Canada as a tyranny, no better than the Tsarist autocracy. Finally, after a month in confinement, he won his release. A crowd of cheering prisoners lined his path as he walked to the gate, followed by an impromptu camp band doing its best to play the *Internationale*. And with that, Leon Trotsky's sojourn in Canada ended.

+ + +

The detention of Leon Trotsky indicated that in wartime the Canadian government was not going to distinguish between political and military objectives, especially when it was to its advantage not to do so. All activities which were seen to threaten the war effort were suppressed, and as the fighting wore on, the definition of what constituted such a threat expanded. In particular, ordinary political dissent and labour organizing came to be seen as treasonous.

A case in point was the Industrial Workers of the World (IWW), the famous Wobblies. Founded at a convention in Chicago in 1905, the IWW was a militant socialist group dedicated to the idea of industrial unionism, the organization of workers across an entire industry rather than by craft or trade. The preamble to the IWW constitution made clear how it felt about the employer: "The working class and the employing class have nothing in common. There can be no peace so long as hunger and want are found among millions of working people and the few, who make up the employing class, have all the good things of life." Canadians were active in the creation of the IWW, and on both sides of the border the Wobbly brand of radicalism found particular support among western miners, loggers, and unskilled labourers, many of whom were immigrants. The IWW took an uncompromising stand toward the employer and supported the general strike as a weapon in the war of labour against capital. In the US, Wobblies were linked, however tenuously, to several violent incidents, and authorities took a special interest in their activities.[11]

The peak year for Wobbly agitation in Canada was 1912. Early in the year, Wobblies were active on the streets of Vancouver organizing unemployed workers and holding open-air meetings to spread their radical message. In January the police began arresting transients for vagrancy, and city council passed a law banning outdoor meetings. "The gang of thugs and thieves who have made life a burden here for weeks should be run out of town without delay," editorialized the Vancouver *Province* newspaper. On the last Sunday of the month, police armed with clubs and horsewhips attacked a large meeting convened to test the ban and discuss the jobless situation. Several people received beatings, and more than two dozen wound up in jail. Alarmed at the prospect of further demonstrations, immigration officials closed the border to Wobblies, forcing the most persistent of them to use interior mountain trails to sneak into the country. Police in Vancouver stepped up their arrests of vagrants, dispersing any crowds that looked like "free speech" gatherings. At one point a group of Wobblies and their supporters took to the water, addressing a crowd in Vancouver's Stanley Park from rented boats using megaphones. Eventually, after meetings with

FIGURE 4 Members of the radical labour union the Industrial Workers of the World (IWW), known as the Wobblies, led a strike of railway workers against the Canadian Northern Railway in the Fraser Canyon area of British Columbia in 1912. Authorities considered the Wobblies to be the most dangerous of the Reds and monitored their activities closely. *Photo: BC Archives, E-002300*

the mayor, police officials, and the premier, peace was restored and open-air meetings resumed.[12]

No sooner had the free speech fight ended in Vancouver than a strike began on the Canadian Northern rail line under construction through the Fraser Canyon east of the city. The IWW had been organizing workers on the line since the previous summer, defying the strong-arm tactics of police and construction contractors. Matters came to a head on March 27, 1912, when IWW workers on the line near Lytton, BC, walked off the job to protest conditions in the construction camps. Several thousand workers from Hope to Kamloops joined the strike. IWW organizers erected their own camps where strikers received food, basic lodging, and large doses of political education. One camp was like "a miniature republic run on Socialistic lines," reported the *Province*.[13] Shortly after the strike began, the Wobbly troubadour Joe Hill arrived at the Yale camp. Today, Hill is a famous Wobbly martyr, executed in 1915 for a murder in Salt Lake City, which many people believe he didn't commit. At the time of the Fraser River strike, he was an unknown blanketstiff (i.e., one of the nomadic workers who roamed the US and Canada before the war, riding the rails and picking up jobs in mines, logging camps, and construction projects) with a gift for making inspiring verse out of the desperate lives of the itinerant workers on the western resource frontier.

Most of the strikers were foreign-born, part of the great wave of immigrants that flooded into Canada in the pre-war years. They had no friends in the press or among the business elites in Vancouver and the towns along the rail lines. Public opinion was against them. Rail contractors were essentially free to settle the strike in their own way. They brought in strike breakers to resume the work and hired private detectives to guard them. Pressure mounted on the provincial government to intervene, which it finally did, sending police and health inspectors to tear down the strike camps, close the IWW meeting halls, and forcibly drive the men from the area. Canadians "will not tolerate the red flag of anarchy," warned one magistrate in New Westminster as he convicted Wobblies of trumped-up charges of vagrancy and conspiracy.[14] The strike was effectively broken.

The IWW found its support among the unskilled, the disorganized, the foreign-born. Ideas of industrial unionism and aggressive class warfare were as obnoxious to the mainstream labour movement as they were to employers and government. Even the Socialist Party of Canada kept its distance. During World War I the Wobblies' outlaw status increased along with the growth of anti-alien sentiment. They were seen to be not only dangerous revolutionaries, but traitors as well, giving aid and comfort to the enemy in

Europe by disrupting industrial peace and production at home. In such an atmosphere, it was not difficult for the authorities to intensify their harassment of the movement. In the US the justice department raided IWW offices across the country in September 1917 and indicted major leaders on charges of conspiracy. Inspired by their American counterparts, law enforcement officials in Canada followed suit. As the federal government proceeded with plans to introduce conscription that year, Prime Minister Borden, alarmed at the antagonism of the radicals, ordered various security agencies to step up their activities against the militant labour organizations.[15]

The federal government had several agencies to deploy in its home front war against the Reds. Immigration agents could harass activists who were not yet Canadian citizens, threatening them with internment or deportation, and the military had its own security service. For the most part, however, it was the two national police forces that the government called on to keep tabs on the Reds. The Dominion Police was created in 1868 during the panicky fear of a Fenian invasion from the United States. It was responsible for enforcing federal laws and protecting federal buildings. Technically it was a national force, as its name implied, but by the outbreak of the war it was active mainly in eastern Canada. The force was small and had to call on the services of private detectives such as the Pinkerton Agency and the Theil Detective Service Company to do most of its undercover work. In the West, the Royal North-West Mounted Police (RNWMP) provided policing in Alberta and Saskatchewan and, after 1914, took part in intelligence-gathering activities for the federal government. By 1918 the RNWMP was losing officers to the armed forces and seemed destined to disappear, having completed the role for which it was created, namely the pacification of western Canada in anticipation of settlement. But quite suddenly official concern about radical political activity breathed new life into the force. At the end of 1918, the Borden government decided to divide the country in half at the Lakehead region of Ontario and give responsibility for security and intelligence to a revitalized RNWMP (renamed the RCMP early in 1920) in the West and to the Dominion Police in the East.[16] Canada now had two secret services to combat the Reds. The Dominion Police took an aggressive approach to arresting and prosecuting suspected Reds, principally in Ontario. Out West, the RNWMP tried a different approach. Early in 1919, A. Bowen Perry, the RNWMP commissioner, began recruiting a corps of secret agents to spy on the Reds. These agents were ordered to infiltrate unions, left-wing political groups, and immigrant communities. They were the eyes and ears of the state. "The Government relies on the RNWMP to keep it early advised of any development toward social unrest," Perry wrote. Information gathered by agents was added to files that the force began keeping on "prominent agitators," but for the most part Perry thought it best to watch and wait rather than to create martyrs by arresting activists.[17]

+ + +

Another weapon in the campaign against the Reds was wartime censorship. In chief censor Ernest J. Chambers, the government found a zealous public servant eager to use his wide powers to ban the publication and distribution of information considered useful to the enemy, critical of the Allied war effort, or discouraging to morale on the homefront. Chambers was born in England in 1862 and emigrated to Canada with his parents eight years later. His lifelong

FIGURE 5 Ernest Chambers, shown here in his uniform as the Usher of the Black Rod, was Canada's chief censor. His office took particular interest in spying on people he considered to have radical opinions. *Photo: National Archives of Canada, C-001824*

association with the militia began when, as a boy in Montreal, he joined his school's cadet rifle corps. Following graduation he went to work at the Montreal *Star* as a cub reporter. In 1885 he travelled west to cover the North-West Rebellion for the paper. Not content simply to report on the fighting, he volunteered for the Canadian side and saw action in several skirmishes, including the pivotal battle at Batoche. He remained in the West for several years, working as a journalist in Calgary before returning to Montreal and then Ottawa where, in 1904, he became Gentleman Usher of the Black Rod, the official in charge of protocol at the Senate. At the opening of Parliament it was, and still is, the Usher of the Black Rod who summoned the Commons to the Senate Chamber to hear the Governor General read the Speech from the Throne. (The name derives from the ebony stick that the Usher uses to bang on the door of the House of Commons to gain admission.) Chambers was also editor of the *Canadian Parliamentary Guide* and a major in the militia, promoted to lieutenant-colonel when the war broke out. In short, Chambers' background in the military and in journalism seemed to make him the perfect choice when the government established a Chief Press Censor's office in June 1915.

Chambers attacked his job with relish. He saw it as his contribution to the war effort, working long into the evening every day for no pay whatsoever. (He remained on salary as the Gentleman Usher.) Along with his own stable of editors and translators, he had the power to request telephone operators to listen in on calls, telegraphers to provide copies of all their messages, and postal workers to open all suspicious letters or parcels. The law made it illegal to criticize the war effort in any way, and Chambers was determined to enforce the law. He was especially suspicious of new Canadians and received reports on the contents of publications in thirty-one different languages. He also banned publications from the United States that contained pacifist or anti-British points of view. Most of these were non-mainstream papers and magazines, but in November 1916 he banned fourteen newspapers belonging to the Hearst chain because they were critical of Great Britain.

It was Chambers' view that Canadians had to be protected not just from anti-war points of view but also any news or images that conveyed the horrors of war at the front. He excluded photographs that gave a realistic sense of the human cost of the war, and he censored movies and news reels for the same reason. On one occasion a film that had been seen widely in Great Britain had to be edited for viewing in Canada because Chambers believed the sight of wounded soldiers would cause women in theatres to become hysterical. On another, he ordered several temperance pamphlets suppressed because he felt they gave the impression that Britons were all drunks. His powers extended to the theatre and even to gramophone records. Chambers basically controlled everything Canadians listened to, saw, read, and talked about, right down to the songs they sang and the pictures they looked at.

When the war ended, the office of the Chief Press Censor remained open and active. Chambers simply shifted his emphasis to the enemy within, the political radicals who replaced the Hun as the direst threat facing the nation. He continued to suppress left-wing publications—253 of them had been banned during the war, mostly foreign-language and left-wing—and to tamper with the mail, using the post office to control the flow of published radical material as well as to intercept correspondence between radical leaders. "The secret mail censorship is raising hell with us just now," complained Chris Stephenson, the secretary of the Socialist Party of Canada, in a letter to Winnipeg socialist leader Bob Russell. "Every letter we get is opened. Some letters are held up for three or four weeks and others never reach us at all. Parcels of literature, circulars, leaflets are also held up and never reach their destination. And we get no response to our complaints."[18] In another letter, Stephenson wrote: "A bunch of tinhorn Bismarks [*sic*] in Ottawa are now able to stifle all criticism, censor the mails at their sweet will and manipulate, mutilate and censor all news of what is happening, not alone in Europe, but in this country. The mass of the people are now reduced to the position of school children, spoon fed with fairy tales."[19]

+ + +

More than the censorship or the harassment of radicals or the internment of aliens, none of which affected more than a minority of workers, probably the most divisive wartime issue among working people was the rising cost of living. In 1913, after two decades of uninterrupted expansion, the country had experienced a serious recession. Unemployment skyrocketed as construction ground to a halt and industrial production went into a tailspin. Foreign investors, the source of much of the capital that had fuelled the expansion, withdrew their money from Canada. It took a couple of years for war production to reverse the situation, but by mid-1916 the armed forces and the munitions industries had soaked up most of the unemployed and the economy was humming once again. The downside of wartime expansion, however, was a rising cost of living. Between 1900 and 1914, price inflation measured a modest 1.5 percent per year. But during the war years, this moderate rate escalated dramatically to thirteen percent annually. "Simply put," writes historian Desmond Morton, "purchasing power in the war years was halved."[20]

The problem was that wages did not keep pace with rising living costs. In 1917 the average office worker in Canada's manufacturing sector was making about $1,317 annually; the average industrial worker $760.[21] Women invariably received less than men who did the same jobs. The hourly wage for a carpenter in Halifax was forty cents; for an electrician in Montreal, forty-three cents; for a plumber in Toronto, fifty cents. Unskilled labour earned significantly less, anywhere from twenty-five to forty cents in the same three cities. Wages in the western provinces were higher; for example, an electrician in Winnipeg earned sixty-five cents an hour, and a carpenter in Vancouver fifty-one cents. Still, an average weekly wage across the country was in the neighbourhood of twenty dollars, which amounted to $1,040 a year, and then only if an individual worked the full year, which most did not. If the average office worker was making $1,300 a year, it seems safe to say that the average tradesperson was making less than $1,000.[22] Because this amount did not increase during the war at the same pace as inflation, working people felt a decline in their standard of living. Not only did they have to make do with less, they had to struggle with serious shortages of food and fuel. There was no wartime rationing, but the government did launch advertising campaigns asking Canadians to restrict their consumption voluntarily. Shortages of coal, the main home-heating fuel, were commonplace. In early 1918, for example, coal was in such short supply in Ontario that all businesses shut down over a long weekend to conserve dwindling stocks. Stores and banks closed, along with factories, offices, and schools.

As the war progressed, discontent grew. Support for the war effort did not necessarily decline, but there was a noticeable increase in grumbling about how the burden of fighting the war was being shared. The conventional wisdom among working people was that war profiteering was responsible for much of the economic inequality. While soldiers gave their lives, and workers saw their cost of living soar, manufacturers producing munitions, foodstuffs, uniforms, and other war goods were enjoying windfall profits. It didn't seem right.

The Ross rifle was the most infamous example of the corruption that seemed to accompany the business of war. Sir Charles Ross, a British sportsman and arms manufacturer, began producing his bolt-action rifle early in the century at the request of the Canadian government. The weapon became standard issue for the troops when they went into combat, despite a number of design flaws that showed up almost immediately: it was heavy, the bayonet fell off during firing, the bolt sometimes exploded, and most importantly, the rifle jammed during rapid fire. Soldiers became so frustrated by the rifle that they scavenged on the battlefield for British-made Lee-Enfields or German Mausers whenever they could. "After the first ten rounds with the Ross," one private wrote home, "it is only good to use as a club."[23] Regardless, Sam Hughes, the eccentric minister of the militia, defended what he called "the most perfect military rifle in the World today" and refused to accept its deficiencies. It was mid-1916 before the Ross was withdrawn from use in the front line; a few months later Borden dropped the incompetent and discredited Hughes from cabinet.

Along with the Ross rifle, the government was also publicly embarrassed by boots that disintegrated in the mud and trenching shovels that did not dig properly. Coupled with insistent press stories about suppliers with close ties to the Conservative Party and government inquiries into the way Hughes' department was handing out contracts, it seemed at times like the war was a gigantic patronage opportunity for well-connected equipment makers. "Personally," the Winnipeg anti-war activist Fred Dixon told a protest rally, "I think those responsible for the Ross rifle, defective shells, shoddy clothes, paper boots, and the whole black record of profiteering and graft gave ten thousand times more aid and comfort to the enemy than all the Socialists and conscientious objectors put together."[24]

The fat-cat capitalist who became the face of the profiteer for most Canadians was Joseph Flavelle, president of the William Davies Company, Toronto's largest meat packer. Flavelle was a stiff-backed Methodist, opposed to drinking, smoking, and dancing (he was known as "Holy Joe"). According to his biographer Michael Bliss, he began each day by kneeling in prayer at the breakfast table with his family.[25] He lived in one of the city's most opulent brick mansions and was a leading member of the charmed circle of entre-preneurs-financiers who controlled Toronto's financial life. Part of Flavelle's personal ethic involved a commitment to public service; during the war he put this into practice by taking on the non-pay-ing job of chair of the Imperial Munitions Board (IMB). The Board was the agency that organized the production of munitions in Can-ada for sale to the British. In its original incarnation as the Shell Committee, it had been plagued by incompetence and corruption, and it was widely agreed that Flavelle did an excellent job reforming its operations. It is ironic, therefore, that Flavelle ended up becom-ing in the public's mind the most high profile war profiteer in the country.

Flavelle's reputation first took a nose dive in 1916 when a dispute arose over wages and working conditions in the munitions factories over which he had control. As head of the IMB, Flavelle had re-fused to introduce the fair-wage clauses that were standard in other industries. He had little sympathy with the needs of the munitions workers. As far as he was concerned, they were fortunate to have jobs that gave them an opportunity to contribute to the war effort.

Flavelle was more concerned that higher wages might cause employers to withdraw from the production of badly needed supplies.[26] Union leadership, not wanting to appear anti-war, refused to be drawn into a confrontation with the government or the employers. But the rank and file grew increasingly restive. They wanted a shorter workday (nine hours instead of the customary ten), better wages, and payment for overtime. In April 1916, faced with the threat of a general strike among munitions workers in Toronto, the federal government appointed a royal commission to look into the machinists' grievances. Later that spring the commission reported in favour of the workers' position. The work day should be nine hours, the commission recommended; workers should receive time and a half for overtime, double pay on Sundays and holidays; and hourly wages should be increased to between 27.5 cents and 42.5 cents, depending on the job.

It looked like a victory for the workers, except that employers simply refused to accept the commission report. The result, in Hamilton at least, where much of the war work was centred, was a strike by members of the machinists union. Both Flavelle and the union leadership tried to find a middle path, but the employers were adamant. One of them, Basil Magor, vice-president of the National Steel Car Company, assured Flavelle, in the face of all evidence to the contrary, that: "Our men have got no complaint with regard to wages, conditions or anything else..." The problem, claimed Magor, was the interference of "a few Labour Agitators." Given such intransigence, the workers saw no alternative but to strike, and they did so on June 12, walking off the job at more than thirty plants across the city. Employers responded with an organized publicity campaign accusing strikers of being unpatriotic and blaming "paid outside agitators" for the unrest. In the name of wartime security and to stop sympathy strikes from occurring elsewhere, the federal government banned all reporting about the strike in the daily press. The union leadership itself remained uncommitted to the strike, which not surprisingly lost steam over the summer as employees went back to work or left town to find jobs elsewhere. Flavelle could have played a more decisive role in this affair by requiring the companies to meet the standards recommended by the royal commission, but he chose not to. As a result he appeared to make himself a collaborator in the efforts of capital to suppress the legitimate demands of labour.

But this was only the beginning of Flavelle's fall from grace, at least as far as the labour movement was concerned. Along with the job at the IMB, he continued to be president of the William Davies Company, which was doing very well during war, selling bacon to the British and tinned "bully" beef for the men in the trenches. Company profits more than tripled, and in the summer of 1917 a federal government report seemed to indicate that the Davies Company had made an enormous profit on its sales of bacon. Press reports made the figures seem more damning than in fact they were. Suddenly Flavelle—or "His Lardship" as he came to be called—was tarred as a hypocritical millionaire making a fortune from the sacrifice of others. This time it was more than a few labour rabble rousers who were involved. The public was furious. "I can truly say that I never before met with such widespread *rage* over any other scandal," remarked one Ottawa politician. Flavelle's own church rebuked him. "There is a general feeling abroad in Canada," opined the Methodist *Christian Guardian* newspaper, "that the man or the corporation which comes out of this war richer than when they went into it [...] have failed to exhibit true patriotism." Customers boycotted Davies stores and editorialists vilified Flavelle in the daily press. In the end a government inquiry ruled that the Davies Company was simply conducting legitimate business. By then it didn't really matter. Flavelle was held in contempt for making millions while young Canadians fought, and died, in the trenches for $1.10 a day, and the Toronto entrepreneur came to represent the whole range of manufacturers and financiers whom many people suspected of profiting from war.[27]

Workers responded to the decline in their standard of living by joining unions in unprecedented numbers. At the beginning of the war, 166,000 Canadians were unionized. By the time the Red Scare was at its height, that number had more than doubled to 378,000. Not only did more workers join unions, they did so with much more militant attitudes. Workers had become disaffected by economic conditions and believed the government and employers were not taking their complaints seriously enough. As a result, the number of labour disputes increased. In 1914 there had been only forty-four strikes in the country, affecting just 8,600 workers; in 1919 there were 298 strikes, among them, of course, the General Strike in Winnipeg and all the sympathetic work stoppages associated with it across the country.

As labour turmoil increased, the federal government promised to conciliate labour. In January 1918 labour leaders came to Ottawa to meet with government officials, and Ottawa made promises to include labour representatives on some of the committees and boards that oversaw the war economy. Labour, at least mainstream labour, was optimistic that the government was ready to accept the idea of power-sharing agreements to address their grievances. Joseph Marks, an Ontario labour journalist, wrote in the *Industrial Banner* on February 22: "In Canada, on every hand, may be seen manifestations of the coming resurrection, the throb of the new life, and the hope of future achievements, when the workers of the Dominion will take their rightful place and make their influence felt in shaping the destinies of the Dominion ..." But in the end, the promises made by the Borden government came to nothing. The labour movement remained outside the decision-making process and workers continued to feel ignored by the power structure.

+ + +

At the end of 1914, when the war was just a few months old and everyone expected it would end soon, Prime Minister Borden made a promise about Canadian recruitment: "There has not been, there will not be, compulsion or conscription." For the next two years he honoured that promise, but by the spring of 1917 the prime minister realized he would have to recant. Canada had been wrung dry of young men and women willing to serve voluntarily. In the month of April, less than 5,000 enlisted, compared to 30,000 in one month just a year earlier. Borden travelled to Europe for an Imperial War Conference in London and crossed to the continent to visit the front lines himself. He saw how desperate the situation was in the Canadian Corps—monthly casualties were more than double the number of recruits—and recognized that if Canada was going to live up to its commitment to the war effort, more troops were needed. Back in Canada in May, he announced in the House of Commons a program of compulsory service.

Borden knew how divisive conscription was going to be. And if he didn't, he soon found out. In Vancouver, the Trades and Labour Council voted as a body to oppose the draft and the provincial Federation of Labour considered calling a general strike on the issue. In Winnipeg, gangs of ruffians disrupted a meeting of

FIGURE 6 Robert Borden was the Conservative prime minister between 1911 and 1920. His government encouraged the Red Scare by initiating a series of policies aimed at suppressing dissent during and after the war. *Photo: National Archives of Canada, PA-117658*

the Anti-Conscription League (ACL) and assaulted the outspoken socialist MLA Fred Dixon. Pro-conscription bullies intimidated the ACL from holding any further meetings. The atmosphere was so charged with violence that three leading opponents of the new legislation—Lillian Beynon Thomas, her husband Vernon, and her sister Francis Marion Beynon—all left Winnipeg to live in New York, fearing for their own safety. In April in Toronto, police arrested Isaac Bainbridge, secretary of the Social Democratic Party, and charged him with seditious libel for printing anti-conscriptionist material in the party's newspaper, *Canadian Forward*. The police magistrate who committed him for trial said Bainbridge belonged in a mental hospital for his views, and in May he was convicted and given a suspended sentence.[28]

Initially Borden hoped to co-opt the opposition in Parliament by making conscription a bipartisan issue. He invited Liberal Party leader Wilfrid Laurier to join his Conservatives in a coalition that would push the policy through. Laurier supported the war and acknowledged the recruitment problem, but he refused the invitation. He could not agree to a policy that would see the death of his party in Quebec, where opposition to compulsory enlistment was strongest. French-English relations were already at a low point because of attempts by the Ontario government to limit the teaching of French in its schools. Conscription elevated the unity issue to a crisis point.

For Borden, the war trumped all other considerations. On June 11 he went ahead and introduced the Military Service Act in Parliament. After much debate it was signed into law at the end of August. Several English-speaking Liberal MPs broke with Laurier to vote for the Act. It looked as if a coalition of Conservatives and disaffected Liberals might be possible. First of all, Borden felt he had to consolidate his position for the upcoming federal election,

FIGURE 7 Conscription was particularly unpopular in Quebec, as illustrated by this protest march in Montreal in May 1917. But significant numbers of farmers and members of the labour movement also opposed the policy. *Photo: National Archives of Canada, C-006859*

which would be fought on the issue of conscription. Victory was by no means certain. Anti-government street demonstrations began in Quebec that summer. In August, Borden introduced the Military Voters Act, which gave the vote to all members of the armed forces no matter how long they had lived in Canada, including women and Aboriginals; these were two groups that had not possessed the franchise to that point and still would not if they were civilians. Military voters were allowed simply to select their political party of choice, which could then assign the ballots to any constituency it wanted. (It was estimated that in the ensuing election Borden won at least fourteen parliamentary seats by manipulating the military vote in this way.)

This was followed up in September by the Wartime Elections Act, granting the vote to all female relatives of servicemen while taking away the vote from conscientious objectors and from people who were born in an enemy country and had become naturalized Canadians since 1902. The result was that tens of thousands of people—Canadian citizens—lost the right to vote. Obviously the government was trying to extend the franchise to as many voters as possible who would be expected to support the war, and therefore the Conservative government. It was a blatant and unprecedented manipulation of the vote for partisan purposes. Winnipeg peace activist Francis Marion Beynon vilified the legislation, calling it "a monstrous act of injustice that has already roused bitter race hatreds which will endure for generations."[29] The prime minister's logic seemed to be that in order to unite Canadians behind the war, it was necessary to divide them along ethnic-linguistic lines. Most Canadians agreed with him; aside from elements in the labour movement, the Act aroused little opposition anywhere in the country.

With Borden seizing the political initiative, no matter how cynically, English-speaking Liberal MPs began to abandon their leader and flock to the standard of a Union government. "The racial chasm which is now opening at our feet may perhaps not be overcome for many generations," a despondent Laurier wrote to a colleague.[30] The war did not arouse the same support in Quebec as it did in anglophone Canada, and Quebecers saw conscription as a discriminatory policy aimed directly at them because they had not been signing up at the same rate as other Canadians. They resented their loyalty being called into question. As the nationalist leader Henri Bourassa pointed out, they were loyal to Canada—just not to an Imperial ideal that required them to spill their blood for the Mother Country. For their part, English Canadians resented the fact that Quebec, with twenty-five percent of the population, had contributed just five percent of the men and women in uniform. For many in the English press and public, this was little short of treason. Canada was at war; everyone should fight.

The labour movement was likewise divided. At its September convention, the Trades and Labor Congess of Canada, which had been on record as opposing compulsory service, voted lukewarm support for the policy. The Congress's left-wing was furious. Its view had been expressed at the outset of the war by Winnipeg's Bob Russell: "This is a capitalists' war, so why should we let ourselves be gulled to fight their battle?"[31] For the militant left, there could be no conscription of manpower without conscription of wealth. "If the state had adopted the policy of conscription of money, industry and natural resources," Social Democratic Party stalwart Dick Rigg declared, "there would be absolutely no necessity for the passing and enforcing of any scheme to conscript men."[32] But for the time being at least, this view was in the minority in labour's national organization.

On October 12, 1917, the prime minister unveiled a new cabinet consisting of twelve Conservatives, nine Liberals, and a labour representative, Senator Gideon Robertson. The subsequent election campaign was bitter and disgraceful. The prime minister could not venture into Quebec for fear of a violent reception, and even in Ontario anti-conscription hecklers drove him from the platform. When it looked as though farmers were going to vote against him, he suddenly decided, two weeks before voting day, to exempt their sons from the draft. On the other side, the seventy-six-year-old Laurier was vilified as a traitor and a friend of the Kaiser. "Every Hun sympathizer from Berlin to the trenches ... wishes success to Laurier," warned the Unionist cabinet minister Sir George Foster.

Unionists identified themselves with the soldiers overseas, claiming that a vote for the Liberals was a vote for the enemy. In Toronto, war veterans beat up voters who openly declared their support for the Liberal leader.

It was the most divisive election in Canadian history, and the result was a foregone conclusion: a sweeping victory for Borden and his Unionist coalition and a stunning defeat for French and English unity and the anti-conscription movement. Coalition candidates took 153 seats, of which only three were in Quebec. The Laurier Liberals held on to eighty-two seats, only twenty of which were outside Quebec. In the three Prairie provinces, where Unionist candidates won seventy-one percent of the vote and forty-one of forty-three seats, half of the Liberal candidates did not even keep their deposits.[33] Anti-conscriptionist labour candidates did even worse. Labour parties ran in seven ridings between the Red River and the Rockies; in each one of them the candidate lost his deposit. Despite the outspoken opposition to conscription by many of their left-wing leaders, most working people thought that the patriotic option was to vote Unionist.[34]

The election result by no means ended the opposition to conscription. Many labour activists continued to counsel non-compliance, and in the province of Quebec street demonstrations became a regular feature of daily life. The following March police looking for draft evaders in Quebec City touched off riots that required troops to be called in from Ontario. On April 1, four civilians— a student and three workers—died when the soldiers fired on a crowd. Elsewhere authorities used the provisions of the Military Service Act to get anti-war pacifists and radicals off the streets and into the army, or jail.

The debate over conscription deeply polarized the country. In the most obvious sense, it set French and English against each other. But it also reinforced the growing alienation of the labour movement from mainstream politics. The government's open manipulation of the vote so as to ensure conscription lent support to radical voices who claimed that democracy would always be rigged to work in the interests of the elites. The election was won "by corruption and lies," declared the Manitoba peace activist Gertrude Richardson.[35] Even a moderate Liberal observer like O.D. Skelton had to admit that "Parliament has been seriously out of touch with the masses of the people alike in city and in country. It is not merely that there has been high-handed manipulation of the franchise, and usurpation by the executive of the powers of parliament, through orders-in-council, but that labour has been practically unrepresented."[36]

The 1917 election campaign, with its virulent rhetoric and scurrilous patriotic appeals, tarred left-wingers with the brush of disloyalty. A year later, when the war ended, it was easy for the popular press and mainstream politicians to portray these "Reds" as cowardly traitors who had refused to come to the aid of their country in its time of need. Not only was a significant portion of the labour movement alienated from its moderate leadership, but it was also alienated from the political system itself.

In the end, compulsory enlistment did not mean much to the war effort. First of all, more than ninety percent of the initial call-up applied for exemptions under the legislation, and by the end of 1917 almost three-quarters of these applications had been successful. Second, thousands of draft-resisters simply failed to register. About 100,000 men finally were conscripted into the army, but only slightly more than 24,000 reached the Front before the guns fell silent on November 11, 1918. The fractious debate stirred up by conscription was a heavy price to pay for such small military gain.

FIGURE 8 Torontonians celebrate the end of World War I in November 1918. The armistice did not bring an end to the government's surveillance of political subversives. *Photo: National Archives of Canada, PA-0711980*

+ + +

At the war's end, Canadians displayed mixed emotions. There was unrestrained joy, of course, that the conflict had ended in victory, and there was relief that the years of struggle were finally over. There was sadness at the loss of so many young men and women—sons, daughters, sisters, brothers, neighbours, and friends. There was anger at the enemy for causing the war (and, implicitly, all the disruptions that ensued) and letting it drag on for so long. There was resentment against those who had not done their share. There was guilt that an entire generation of young Canadians had been asked to pay for the mistakes of their elders, and determination that their sacrifice should count for something.

At the end of the war, many Canadians were left feeling a strong sense of injustice as well. Working people had watched their standard of living decline while big business prospered from high profits and special deals with Ottawa. Meanwhile, the government seemed to be ignoring labour's legitimate demands. English-speaking Canadians seethed at the lack of support for the war in Quebec, while Francophones resented being singled out as disloyal or, even worse, cowardly. New immigrants, who had been encouraged to come to Canada in the first place, were angry that the government came to consider them traitors and "un-Canadian." Voters were appalled at the way Prime Minister Borden had manipulated the vote to get himself re-elected. Democracy itself seemed to have been corrupted.

All of these issues fuelled the unrest that spread across Canada in the months following the war. It represented an unprecedented challenge to the way things had always been done. And it sparked an unprecedented reaction from government and economic decision-makers who tried to discredit the demands for change by labelling them "Red," a word that came to stand for everything that was foreign, untrustworthy, revolutionary, and anti-Canadian.

FIGURE 9 Toronto's *Maclean's* magazine considered Santeri Nuorteva (L) and Ludwig Martens, two officials at the Russian Soviet Government Bureau in New York, to be the leading Bolshevik conspirators in North America. According to Red scaremongers, the Bureau was the command post of the conspiracy, sending money and agents north to Canada.

CHAPTER TWO

A Quite Widespread and Dangerous Propaganda

"Here is grave danger to the peace and security of the country."
—*Commissioner A. Bowen Perry, RNWMP*

As the world war drew to a close, the government of Prime Minister Robert Borden grew alarmed at reports that radical political activity was increasing around the country. In response, it launched a campaign to oppose what it took to be the growing Red menace. Publicly it passed a set of draconian laws to smash radical organizations, discredit their leaders, and repress dissent. Surreptitiously it requested police and military authorities to create a network of spies and secret agents to infiltrate labour unions and political groups to gather evidence of revolutionary activities. Although he was not his government's most enthusiastic anti-radical, the prime minister was unapologetic about his war on Canada's Reds. "In some cities there was a deliberate attempt to overthrow the existing organization of the Government," he later recalled, "and to supersede it by crude, fantastic methods founded upon absurd conceptions of what had been accomplished in Russia. It became necessary [...] to repress revolutionary methods with a stern hand and from this I did not shrink."[1]

The government campaign against the Reds originated as part of the war effort. With fighting in the trenches of Europe going badly, steps had to be taken on the home front to ensure that the determination of Canadians to keep up the sacrifice did not falter. As far as the government was concerned, any activity that hampered the war effort smacked of sedition and could not be tolerated. That included workers who opposed conscription and fellow-travellers who wanted a radical restructuring of the social order. Mobilization for war had to be total.

As the war entered its final year, however, the government shifted its attention from "enemy aliens" to political radicals and labour organizers—so-called Bolshevik revolutionaries—whose activities seemed to threaten the country in a more profound way. Not just the war effort but the very fabric of Canadian society seemed to be at risk. This could not be tolerated, and the government was willing to seize whatever authority and take whatever steps it thought necessary to thwart the looming possibility of revolution. What in fact took place was a conspiracy by the government of Canada against its own people.

+ + +

Since before the outbreak of war, security agencies had identified the Wobblies as the most dangerous radical group in the country. This notoriety continued during the war. Early in 1918 the minister of labour, Senator Gideon Robertson, recommended to his cabinet colleagues that "inasmuch as the policies and purposes of the IWW was [*sic*] vicious in their character and intent [...] the Department of Justice and Department of Labour ought to have a few men on the ground to collect evidence and prosecute agents of the IWW who are attempting to spread sedition and foment industrial unrest in British Columbia." Robertson, a former railway telegrapher whom Borden had appointed to the Cabinet as a sop to organized labour, wanted the post office to intercept IWW material in the mails and suggested that if a few Wobbly leaders were intimidated with legal action, it would stop others from arriving from south of the border to foment unrest.[2]

Borden followed up Robertson's suggestion by asking A.J. Cawdron, chief commissioner of the Dominion Police, to investigate the activities of the IWW. Cawdron was already alert to the Wobblies, of course. "I consider them a very dangerous, socialistic and perhaps murderous lot," he wrote to the minister of justice on March 5, 1918, recommending that if the IWW had a Canadian headquarters it should be raided, all the literature seized, and "the principals sent to Penitentiary." Later in the month, with his preliminary investigation complete, Cawdron reported that he was installing two undercover agents to spy on the IWW leadership. He advised the government to pass orders-in-council banning foreign-language meetings and the distribution of all socialist literature. These measures would allow the courts to prosecute the IWW for holding meetings and, in Cawdron's opinion, be sufficient to "crimp their operations."[3]

Borden took his top cop's report seriously. Rumours swirled that the activities of radical organizations were funded by Germany and calculated to disrupt the war effort. In May the prime minister appointed a special inquiry into the extent of radicalism in Canada, headed by Charles Cahan, a Montreal lawyer.[4] Cahan and Borden knew each other well. As young men, both had been prominent lawyers in Halifax, and in 1896 they had competed for the right to carry the Conservative Party standard in the federal election for a city riding. Cahan believed that he deserved the nomination by virtue of the loyal service he had given to the party as leader of the opposition in the provincial legislature, and as editor of the Halifax *Herald*, a Tory mouthpiece. Privately he accused Borden, a former Liberal who had once supported the Fielding government in Nova Scotia, of blatant opportunism. The charge was true enough, but could not overcome the advantages the young Borden enjoyed as a partner in the law firm of Weatherbe and Graham, the leading Tory firm in Halifax. Two prime ministers, John Thompson and Charles Tupper, belonged to the ranks of the firm's former partners, and it was Tupper who recruited Borden for the nomination. A furious Cahan was asked to step aside and settle for a less safe riding, which he lost in the subsequent election. Meanwhile, Borden sailed to victory, a parliamentary seat in Ottawa, and a successful career on the national stage.[5]

In 1918 Cahan, who was then fifty-eight years old and practising law in Montreal, subdued whatever lingering resentment he might have felt toward his former rival and agreed to undertake the inquiry into radical activity. Conservative though he was, Cahan initially did not share the anxiety of police officials. In mid-July he made an interim report that minimized the threat of pro-German feeling in the country and suggested that existing police forces were quite adequate to the job of handling what little there was. On the other hand, he did acknowledge that "widespread unrest and discontent" were prevalent. The war was taking its toll, Cahan warned, and the willingness of the people to continue to sacrifice was eroding. "Canada has more need of a great moral and intellectual propaganda in favour of successful prosecution of the war to a better end," he told the minister of justice, "than of an organized crusade against local German propaganda."[6]

But that summer, events were occurring that changed the opinions of Cahan and a lot of others who were not yet fully converted to the crusade against the Reds. A series of strikes indicated that working people across the country, and especially in the West, were no longer willing to accept the war as an excuse for delaying the wage increases they thought were long overdue. Early in May civic employees in Winnipeg began walking off the job, unhappy with a wage offer they had received from the city. The City Council abruptly laid off the workers, and the issue escalated from wages to the right to strike. Other unions joined the stoppage in support of the civic workers; Council was soon facing a broad general strike. When negotiations at the local level failed, Prime Minister Borden, fearing that the strike might disrupt railway traffic and threaten other war-sensitive industries, sent Gideon Robertson to Winnipeg as his special envoy to find a solution to the impasse. Robertson convinced the city to settle on terms favourable to the unions, and on May 25 all the strikers went back to work. Labour declared victory and warned that it would not hesitate to use the general strike strategy again. It was an ominous warning.

Robertson was back on the firing line in June, this time in Vancouver where 5,000 shipyard workers struck for higher wages and union recognition. For a second time, he managed to coax a settlement that satisfied the workers. Then, on July 22, the country's first national postal strike began. Again the main issue was the failure of wages to keep pace with the rising cost of living, and again labour won concessions from the employer. In the case of the postal

FIGURE 10 Gideon Robertson, a conservative labour unionist, served as Borden's minister of labour and played a key role in negotiating settlements for several industrial disputes in the post-war period. *Photo: National Archives of Canada, PA-033996*

workers, it was a victory for the rank and file over the more cautious approach of their leadership.

While the postal strike was still going on, Vancouver was convulsed by its own general strike, which seemed to focus much of the anger and resentment present in the country that summer. On July 27, 1918, a police special constable shot a draft resister named Albert "Ginger" Goodwin in the wooded hill country near Comox Lake on Vancouver Island. Goodwin was a coal miner, an organizer for the Socialist Party of Canada, and a prominent activist in the United Mineworkers union.[7] A thin, frail man, suffering from an ulcer and debilitating lung disease, he was initially considered unfit for service under the new conscription laws. But shortly after he led a strike for the eight-hour day at the smelter in Trail, he was reclassified fit for combat. Most of his friends thought the authorities were out to railroad him into the army in order to rid themselves of a troublesome agitator. Instead of reporting for duty, Goodwin, who had moved out to the coast, took to the hills around Cumberland with several other draft evaders, hiding out in abandoned hunting shacks and surviving on wild game and food slipped to them by local sympathizers. The police "special," Dan Campbell, was out looking for resisters when he came upon Goodwin walking across a wooded slope and shot him through the neck, killing him instantly. Campbell claimed that Goodwin had pointed a rifle at him and that he had fired in self-defence, a claim that seems to have been believed by the grand jury, which later exonerated him without trial. Goodwin's comrades nonetheless believed it was a case of cold-blooded murder; that a rifle found by the corpse was planted by Campbell; that the policeman was a "government torpedo man," in the words of one old-timer, whose intention all along was to hunt Goodwin down and kill him.

The labour movement reacted to the shooting immediately. The Trades and Labour Council in Vancouver, supported by the Metal Trades Council, called a protest strike to begin at noon on August 2, the same day Goodwin was buried in Cumberland. Streetcar drivers, stevedores, shipyard workers, garment workers, and the building trades all walked off the job, bringing the city to a halt. It was British Columbia's first general strike. Returned veterans, who considered draft resisters like Goodwin to be traitors—the war was still on, of course—turned out in force to oppose the strike. A mob bulled its way into the downtown Labor Temple on Dunsmuir Street and ransacked it, breaking windows and heaving furniture and files into the street. After attempting to toss Victor Midgley, the Vancouver Trades and Labour Council secretary, out of a second-storey window, the veterans were getting ready to make a second attempt when Frances Foxcroft, a secretary in the office, threw herself in front of the window and began wrestling with the interlopers. Midgley was saved, though the frustrated veterans beat him up instead and forced him to kiss the British flag. At streetcorner rallies, speakers denounced the strike leaders as Bolsheviks and Hun sympathizers. Mayor Harry Gale and the local Chamber of Commerce supported the veterans. Together they drew up a blacklist of names of prominent labour leaders who they said must leave the city. The following day soldiers and workers brawled at the Longshoreman's Hall, and once again the veterans demanded that strike leaders clear out of the city. Eventually, the combatants ran out of steam and such confrontations died away.[8]

Police and politicians watched as all across the West that summer, labour seemed to be radicalized. In Calgary, Vancouver, Winnipeg, and Edmonton, known radicals moved into positions of influence in the labour movement. Many of them were inspired by the revolution in Russia and were not reluctant to say so. Members of the Socialist Party signed their letters to one another, "Yours in Revolt." There was a strong feeling of dramatic change in the air. Suddenly the threat of marginal pro-German agitation by a few Wobblies was overshadowed by the possibility of actual Red revolt.

Charles Cahan was keeping his eye on these developments as he prepared his final, secret report for the government, and they must have played some part in transforming him into a zealous anti-Bolshevik crusader, because by the time he submitted the report in the middle of September, that is what he had become. "Since the outbreak of the present war," he wrote, "revolutionary groups of Russians, Ukrainians and Finns have been organized throughout Canada, and are known as the Social Democratic Party of Canada, the Ukrainian Revolutionary Group, the Russian Revolutionary Groups and others." Members of these groups, warned Cahan, were "carrying on in Canada a most pernicious propaganda." He continued: "The Bolsheviki Associations in Canada have gone so far as to form their own Soviets in certain industrial communities, issue their own passports, provide punishments for infractions of their own regulations, to incite industrial strikes, and, generally, to terrorize those of their own nationality who desire to follow their peaceful pursuits."

Cahan concluded that propaganda issued by these "Bolsheviki" organizations was a root cause of much of the labour unrest in the country. They were, after all, "advocating the destruction of all state authority, the subversion of religion and the obliteration of all property rights." Urging Borden to take strong measures to quash the dissenters, he listed a number of political groups which he suggested the government should declare illegal by order-in-council. Membership in these groups, or advocacy of the "pernicious" doctrines they espoused, should be illegal and punishable by imprisonment. The police should receive wide powers to search premises and destroy printed materials. All foreign-language publications should have to obtain a government licence. Fearing that law enforcement was divided among too many different agencies, he proposed the creation of a Public Safety Branch for "securing the efficient enforcement of the federal laws and regulations" and "to preserve public order and safety ..."[9]

Cahan's was not the only voice urging the government to suppress radical dissent—especially on the part of "aliens"—in the country. Since January the chief press censor, Ernest Chambers, had been recommending a complete ban on all foreign-language publications. His recommendation was motivated by the contents of the publications and also by the threat of violence directed against them by returned soldiers. Twice during the previous year, rioters in Regina had smashed up the offices of a German-language publisher; the censor feared an increase in civil unrest if the newspapers were not closed. As well, the Great War Veterans Association (GWVA), founded in Winnipeg the previous year, was pressuring Prime Minister Borden to suppress enemy alien newspapers. Members of the GWVA were very antagonistic to enemy aliens, believing that they occupied jobs and houses that rightfully belonged to loyal Canadians who had served in the war. On occasion the veterans even volunteered themselves as the shock troops in the struggle to cleanse the country of foreigners. At the GWVA convention in Toronto in early August, delegates roamed through downtown streets ransacking foreign-owned cafés in response to a rumour that a Greek waiter had attacked a disabled veteran. When police intervened, it only made the mob angrier. Led by returned soldiers with crutches and missing limbs, members of the crowd dragged non-British café owners onto the sidewalk and forced them to salute the Union Jack. By the time police got matters under control, fifteen restaurants had been trashed and many people injured. Disturbances continued for several days, fuelled by resentment against aliens. Finally, after Toronto Mayor Tommy Church banned all public meetings and a force of 500 soldiers arrived in the city to intimidate the protestors, order was restored. Then, in September, the minister of immigration, James A. Calder, wired Borden from Saskatchewan, warning him that if the government did not immediately silence the foreign-language press, returned veterans would take matters into their own hands there as well: Western cities, already war weary and moody with labour unrest, might erupt into street violence aimed at the alien population.[10]

Spooked by these reports, and by the violence in the streets of Toronto, Borden and his cabinet did not hesitate. On September 25 they passed an order-in-council (PC 2381) prohibiting publications in an "enemy language": German, Hungarian, Bulgarian, Romanian, Turkish, Ukrainian, Russian, Finnish, Croatian, Austrian, Estonian, Ruthenian (a term applied to Ukrainians), Syrian, and Livonian (Livonia is now Latvia and Estonia). Overnight, thousands of residents of Canada faced stiff fines and jail sentences for reading or writing their own language.

Three days later, the cabinet passed another order-in-council (PC 2384), this one banning fourteen political and labour organizations targeted by Cahan in his report. "All enemy tongue newspapers are to be cut out during the war and revolutionary and industrial associations of the IWW stripe to be prohibited," Sir George Foster, the minister of trade and commerce, noted with satisfaction in his diary. "Cahan's investigations and the information gathered by the Dominion Police show a quite widespread and dangerous propaganda ..."[11] The prohibited groups included the IWW, the Russian Social Democratic Party, the Russian Revolutionary Group, the Russian Social Revolutionists, the Russian Workers' Union, the Ukrainian Revolutionary Group, the Ukrainian Social Labour Party, the Group of Social Democrats of Bolsheviki, the Group of Social Democrats of Anarchists, the Workers International Industrial Union, the Chinese Nationalist League, the Chinese Labour Association, and the Social Democratic Party. Membership in these groups, as well as in any organization advocating violent social change, was illegal now, and retroactively. Anyone convicted under the new ban was subject to fines up to $5,000 or a maximum five-year prison sentence.

In addition to enacting the orders-in-council, Borden took Cahan's advice and, on October 2, created the Orwellian-sounding Public Safety Branch. Not surprisingly, Cahan became the first Director of Public Safety, with responsibility, as he wrote the prime minister, for "perfecting an organization that would enable your government to control, if not to extirpate, the enemy and revolutionary propaganda now being carried on throughout Canada."[12] Increasingly, those in authority were blurring the line between legitimate political dissent and treason. So long as the war continued, however, it was still possible to stifle radical dissent in the name of national unity and patriotism. (On October 11, 1918, the government introduced yet another order-in-council, PC 2525, banning strikes for the duration of the war and imposing fines and prison terms on anyone who violated the ban; the order was repealed at the end of the war just one month later.)

Not everyone shared Cahan's zealous dedication to stamping out anti-war activities at the expense of civil liberties. Most of the groups and publications banned by the September orders-in-council belonged to immigrant communities in Canada. Their suppression attracted little notice from mainstream opinion-makers. However, the Social Democratic Party (SDP) turned out to be an exception. The SDP had been founded in 1910 by disaffected members of the Socialist Party of Canada (SPC). The SPC originated six years earlier with a group of British Columbia socialists known for their uncompromising adherence to the class struggle. Many of these militants believed that reform of capitalism was impossible, hence they were known as "impossibilists." What was needed was a complete overthrow of the system, they argued, not slow, step-by-step improvement. They were willing to engage in short-term alliances with trade unions, but ultimately they believed that political action, not labour action, was the way to make fundamental change. Leadership of the SPC was drawn from British working-class immigrants, and the party, which never had more than 5,500 members, enjoyed mixed success among foreign-language workers. Nonetheless, it played a significant role in the "labour revolt" and specifically in the organization of the One Big Union (OBU) in the spring of 1919. Eventually though, its antipathy to reformism and to unions led to a split, resulting in the formation of the more moderate Social Democratic Party. Social Democrats sought a less doctrinaire, more pragmatic road to the socialist utopia. The SDP was certainly anti-war and anti-capitalist, but its members believed in working democratically and in cooperation with trade unions for limited reforms such as the eight-hour day. Historian Ian McKay points out that, of all the various radical parties and factions, the SDP was notable for its willingness to work with allies of any national or ethnic background.[13] It was in part this openness to the "foreign-born" that made the SDP a special target of the scare-mongers. Yet because the SPC was the more radical party, it is hard to understand why it was not included in the government's ban on political organization, even though PC 2381 did ban its newspaper, *The Western Clarion*.

Newton Rowell, the minister in charge of the RNWMP, was not present when the cabinet passed the repressive orders-in-council, and when he found out about it he was unhappy with the inclusion of the SDP. It was, he wrote Minister of Justice Charles Doherty, "an organized labour party to which many of the leading members of labour belong and they should have the same right of meeting, association and of propaganda as any other political party in Canada possesses."[14] Another member of the cabinet, Minister of Agriculture T.A. Crerar, agreed. (Both Crerar and Rowell were Liberals who had joined Borden's Unionist Government to support conscription; their misgivings about how far to take the banning of left-wing political organizations indicates that at least some members of the Liberal faction in the federal cabinet did not endorse the Conservative's Red Scare tactics.) In a memo to the prime minister, Crerar argued that the SDP was "a definite political party," no different from the Labour Party in Britain. He complained that Cahan seemed to have singled out the SDP "as the particular object of his attention," but in the name of free speech he urged Borden to overrule the ban.[15]

The concerns which Rowell and Crerar presented behind the scenes were aired publicly in the press. The banning of the SDP was "An Infringement of Liberty" according to the Toronto *Globe*, which argued that the party advocated non-violent social revolution and that, however "fantastic, utopian or unjust" its ideas appeared to be, the party should not be banned from expressing them.[16] The

FIGURE 11 Charles Doherty, the minister of justice in Ottawa, was one of the hard-line anti-Reds in the Borden government. *Source: National Archives of Canada, PA-005580*

Ottawa Citizen agreed. The social democratic movement was hurt more by its own pacifism and anti-war propagandizing than by government suppression, the paper argued. "Canada, of all countries, has need to be alert when the government assumes power to extirpate what might be called socialist propaganda. Forces of reaction have been allowed almost unlimited scope in this country."[17]

Charles Cahan, newly ensconced in Ottawa in his position as director of public safety, was dismayed that not everyone shared his appreciation of the Bolshevik threat. If the government lifted the ban on the SDP, he warned the minister of justice, radical elements would take it as a sign that "they are at liberty in Canada to undermine [...] the very foundation of our social, industrial and political system." The SDP, he argued, was an agent of German propaganda, spouting seditious, anti-war, Bolshevik doctrines that were creating unrest among the working population. "It cannot justly be contended that the Social Democratic Party is a political party in the ordinary meaning of those words," he thundered. "It is a party of Red Revolution, advocating submission to German might, subversion of all constitutional government, robbery of personal property, and the accomplishment of its avowed aims by sabotage and general strikes."[18] Cahan's vehemence was not enough to counter the misgivings of Rowell and Crerar, however, and the SDP was removed from the list of banned organizations.

+ + +

The government introduced its wide-ranging measures to stifle Red propaganda at the same time as Canada was experiencing its worst public health emergency of the twentieth century. The two events were unrelated, but both contributed to the sense of uncertainty, even crisis, that gripped the country during the final days of the war.

The first signs of influenza appeared in eastern Canada in the summer of 1918, brought from Europe aboard ships by returning soldiers. (A global pandemic, it was dubbed the Spanish flu because the first outbreaks to be publicized occurred in Spain, but it seems actually to have originated in Asia.) The first large civilian outbreak occurred in early September at a college in Victoriaville, Quebec, where 400 students fell ill. Troop trains carrying veterans westward to their homes helped to spread the disease across the country like a runaway grass fire. It struck suddenly, with devastating consequences. A victim who was perfectly healthy in the afternoon might be dead by the next morning. By mid-October, fifty people a day were dying in Toronto, 200 a day in Montreal. And it was not just residents of the big cities that suffered; one-third of the population of the coast of Labrador was wiped out, while at the fur trade community of Norway House in northern Manitoba, almost one-fifth of the population died within six weeks.[19] The Aboriginal population was especially hard hit. In British Columbia, for example, the death rate from the flu in the general population was 6.21 per 1,000 people; among Aboriginals the rate was forty-six per 1,000 people.[20]

The Spanish flu was characterized at the onset by cold-like symptoms: sore throat, a cough, stuffy nose, a mild fever. For the lucky ones, this was as far as it progressed. For others the fever worsened, accompanied by general achiness, extreme lassitude, head pains, and perhaps even delirium. In the worst cases, pneumonia set in, leaving the patient with only a fifty-percent chance of recovery. Often, as death approached, the body turned blue, and the victim began to cough up blood.

The medical community was powerless to treat the flu. There

was no drug, no pill, no vaccine. Antibiotics had not yet been invented. Isolation was considered the best prevention. Public health officials urged people to avoid contact, not to kiss anyone or shake hands, to keep indoors and away from crowds. Schools closed; churches, pool halls, and theatres emptied; shops shut early and authorities imposed a ban on all public meetings and sporting events. In Toronto, it became against the law to cough or sneeze in public or to spit in the street. People were told to walk to work instead of taking a crowded streetcar. Vancouver was declared a "closed town," which meant, according to a public notice: "Every place of assembly closed, every meeting stopped, all public amusement curtailed."[21] An eerie silence descended on most communities, broken by the tolling of the funeral bells or the clip-clop of the horse-drawn hearse. "It was as if a black, sombre cloud fell over all," recalled one Toronto resident. "People closed their doors and stayed within to keep their lives. When we did go out we saw black crepe sashes on front doors, and when we heard the church bells ring at St. Alban's we knew another one had died." There were so many funerals during the peak period of October and November that it was hard to find a casket or fresh flowers with which to bury a relative.

Infected homes were quarantined and placarded with signs that read "Spanish Influenza." Deaths were sometimes marked by coloured ribbons: white for a child, purple for the elderly, grey for everyone in between. On the advice of doctors, people went about wearing cheesecloth masks over their mouths and small bags of camphor around their necks (the fumes were said to be healthful). While all manner of home remedies were invoked, from snuffing salt water up the nose to applying chest poultices of lard and oil, nothing had much effect. The hospitals filled to overflowing, often

FIGURE 12 During the deadly epidemic of influenza that followed the war, Canadians were encouraged to wear masks to ward off infection—but the masks offered little protection. About 50,000 Canadians died in the epidemic. *Photo: National Archives of Canada, PA-025025*

relying on volunteer staff because so many doctors and nurses were either overseas at the war or sick themselves.

A total of two million Canadians out of a population of about eight million came down with the flu. Of those afflicted, about 50,000, perhaps more, died, part of a global death toll that exceeded thirty million before the disease petered out in the spring of 1919. For some reason the epidemic struck hardest at young adults, normally the hardiest segment of the population and the same cohort that had been asked to sacrifice so much for the war effort. It was a tragic, ironic end to a conflict that had already claimed so many lives.

Terrible as it was, the epidemic did not dampen the victory celebrations that erupted when news of the armistice arrived in the early hours of November 11. But it was a traumatized population that came out into the streets to celebrate.

+ + +

Immediately after the passage of the September orders-in-council, the police began using their new authority in a series of raids aimed at getting the Reds off the streets. In Winnipeg in early October, Michael Charitinoff, a Russian Jew and former editor of the Russian-language weekly *Robotchny Narod* (Working People), was arrested for possession of illegal literature. Security forces had targeted Charitinoff as Lenin's "ambassador to Western Canada," supposedly sent to Canada with a $7,000 bankroll to foment revolution. Police magistrate Hugh John Macdonald, the sixty-eight-year-old son of Sir John A., the former prime minister, and a former Manitoba premier himself, sentenced Charitinoff to three years in prison and a $1,000 fine, though the editor won release on a technicality. Charitinoff was one of more than 200 people convicted of political offences—possessing banned literature, belonging to an illegal group, or attending illegal meetings—across the country between October 1918 and June 1919. Fines ranged up to $4,000, though most were much lower, and prison terms ran anywhere from a month to five years.[22]

In Ontario, police stormed the offices of several of the banned organizations, seizing correspondence, books, and pamphlets, and arresting dozens of people in Toronto and other, smaller communities. Eighteen Finnish-Canadian militants were arrested in Sudbury and Sault Ste. Marie. In Brantford, the local police chief, testifying at the trial of Andra Tretjak, a young Russian immigrant found guilty of conspiracy, claimed that the town was "the headquarters of Bolshevik advocates in Canada," the centre of a vast distribution network of seditious literature.[23] (The police enjoyed fearmongering about alleged conspiracies; the previous summer they had uncovered a nest of Russian conspirators in Windsor, Ontario, who, they told the newspapers, were at the centre of "a continent-wide plot to overthrow lawful authority and establish a similar regime to that instituted in Russia by Trotzky and Lenine."[24])

In Toronto, police descended on the offices of political and ethnic organizations across the city, arresting dozens of people, all of whom were alleged to be "active Socialists and Bolsheviks." They carted away stacks of mail, flyers, pamphlets, books, and magazines. Among the twenty-two arrestees at the headquarters of the Social Democratic Party on Queen Street West were Isaac Bainbridge, secretary of the SDP, and Alfred Manse, the circulation manager of both the *Industrial Banner* and the *Canadian Forward*, the party newspaper. Bainbridge, who was a thirty-eight-year-old stonemason and the editor of the *Forward*, was all too familiar with this kind of harassment. During the previous year and a half, he had been arrested three times on charges of sedition and spent a total of four months in jail for promoting ideas that were considered anti-conscription.[25]

Detainees appeared before magistrates, several of whom took very seriously their self-appointed role as the last bastions against Bolshevism. In Stratford, Ontario, where police arrested twenty-two militants, the case of Arthur Skidmore, a machinist and a member of the local trades council, attracted the most notoriety. He was sentenced to thirty days in jail and a fine of $500 for having in his possession a copy of the *Forward*. Following appeals to the government from his fellow union members, he was released after twelve days. Magistrate Makins, who had sent Skidmore to jail, chided the government for overruling his decision. "Skidmore's release is having the effect of making these men very bold and defiant," Makins told the *Toronto Daily Star*. "I feel that a stand will have to be taken in the near future against just such men."[26] And in Toronto, Magistrate Kingsford handed out a three-year prison term in the Kingston Penitentiary to Charles Watson for distributing a variety of books and leaflets that three months before had been perfectly legal. As a large deputation from the Carpenters' Union massed in the street outside the court in protest, Kingsford declaimed from the bench: "Free speech has always been and is the birthright of every British subject; but free speech is not license [...] Sedition will not be tolerated [...] Persons of British birth or descent above all should not forget the orderly traditions of their race. It would be a disgrace if they associated themselves with the propaganda of foreign cut-throats." Kingsford went on in his condescending manner: "Theoretical discussions about Socialism may do no harm even if, in the hands of uneducated men, they lead to erroneous ideas of political economy. But when they are publications which advocate in so many terms, robbery, plunder, and other crimes against public order and safety, they become a menace and must be dealt with accordingly." [27]

Compared to other publications, the *Toronto Daily Star* took a moderate position on the crackdown. In 1918, Toronto readers could choose from a diverse selection of six daily newspapers, but the diversity of opinion was more apparent than real. Four of the papers supported the Conservative Party. Of the other two, the *Globe* traditionally backed the Liberals. However, since the Liberals were now part of the Unionist coalition, the Borden government could pretty much count on the *Globe*'s support. That left the *Star*. Ironically, the *Star* in its early years under the ownership of F.T. Nicholls, one of the city's leading manufacturers, was a mouthpiece for the Canadian Manufacturers' Association. But Nicholls sold the paper in 1899 to a group of wealthy Liberal businessmen who wished to make it a party organ. The new owners asked a thirty-four-year-old reporter named Joseph Atkinson to come on board as editor. Atkinson agreed to take the job on the condition that he received full independence and, remarkably, the owners allowed it. From the beginning of Atkinson's tenure—he eventually took complete control of the paper in 1913—the *Daily Star* reflected his impoverished family background, his support for social causes, his preference for lively writing, and his nose for a good story. He was known as "Holy Joe" for his austere Methodist beliefs, but there was nothing austere about his newspaper. During the war years, the *Star* began to challenge the *Telegram* as Toronto's most-read paper, especially among the city's working people, mainly because it was the most entertaining. George Fetherling described the *Star*'s technique in his history of Canadian newspapers: "A flying squad of as many as forty reporters and photographers would descend on a single story like wolves and pick its bones of the last bit of sensationalist flesh."[28] As for the government's campaign against the Reds, the *Star* was skeptical, editorializing in favour of free speech and assembly. Most importantly, it reported on the arrests and trials of the so-called Reds in an even-handed manner without inflammatory comments about the Bolshevik menace.

But the *Star* was unique. Most mainstream newspapers and magazines endorsed the government's heavy hand. Toronto's *Saturday Night* magazine was at the opposite end of the spectrum of opinion to the *Star*. Founded in 1887 as a high-society magazine, *Saturday Night* had democratized its content over the years, but it remained a resolute defender of the status quo. "It has been made apparent that the Bolshevik conspiracy, of which the Federal Government warned the public two months ago, was no false alarm," stated the magazine's lead article of December 7, 1918. "The advocates of Workmen's and Soldiers' Councils and of the wholesale massacre of all property holders are at work right here in our midst. Apparently the authors of this campaign in Canada, whoever they are, have hopes of inducing the returned soldier to join in their movement and make the streets of industrial centres like Montreal, Toronto, Winnipeg, Calgary and Vancouver run red with blood after the approved Bolshevik manner." Later in the month, *Saturday Night* warned its readers: "Beware the Bolshevik [...] In proportion to our population we have probably as many Bolshevists as the United States, perhaps more. If these men but talk their crazy prattle, all well and good, but we have unquestioned evidence of late that it is not all talk. Force of this sort must be met by force; there is no other way out."[29]

+ + +

As 1918 drew to a close, the Red Scare was taking root at all levels of government and in the press, fuelled by a mistrust of foreign agitators and an exaggerated fear of the new ideas gaining currency on the left wing of the labour movement. While his government was encouraging a clampdown on political protest at home, Prime Minister Borden was in England, where he had gone in November to prepare for the upcoming peace conference in Paris. (Remarkably, Borden would remain in Europe with his delegation of advisors until mid-May; it is impossible to imagine a modern political leader in the middle of his term of office absenting himself from the country for five months, but given the slow speed of travel and communications and the importance of the peace conference, no one thought twice about it at the time.) Every western leader shared the anxiety about the spread of Bolshevism, and while he was in London Borden received intelligence from British sources that Lenin's regime in Russia was smuggling large sums of money abroad to support a massive propaganda effort in support of its ideology. Borden cabled this information to his acting prime minister, Thomas White, and warned that this subversive propaganda campaign would be spreading to North America early in the new year.[30] Repressive measures inaugurated in wartime to maintain support for the war effort at home were, in the nervous aftermath of war, justified as essential weapons against this new enemy, the radical union activists and Bolsheviks who desired the overthrow of democracy and the Canadian way of life.

"The conditions existing in Canada are entirely novel," wrote Charles Cahan at the beginning of 1919, "for never before in our political history has the Government of one country [i.e., Russia] inaugurated so widespread and persistent a propaganda to bring about internal revolution in an enemy country, as that which is now being carried on in the United States and Canada." (Cahan was conveniently forgetting that western countries, including Canada, were actively intervening in Russia to support attempts by counter-revolutionary forces to topple the Soviet regime.) In a letter to the minister of justice, Cahan warned of "incipient revolution raising its head, with accompanying civil disorder and bloodshed."[31]

Cahan's apocalyptic language was echoed by A.P. Sherwood, who marked his retirement as chief commissioner of the Dominion Police with a dire analysis of the challenge facing the country. Sherwood had been head of the Dominion force for thirty-six years. During the war, he had been in charge of Canada's domestic security, the "Canadian spymaster" as one historian calls him.[32] In theory, no one was better situated to assess the terrorist threat facing the country. "During the past year or so," Sherwood wrote, "an old type of criminal with a new name and new methods has been very active not only in Canada but in almost all parts of the world. The old name was just plain 'Anarchist'; the new one is 'Bolsheviki', which stands for a distorted form of Socialism and is being developed for the most part in our uneducated foreign population. The method of development is by agents through direct contact and propaganda which is circulated by means of every cunning device that can be employed." Sherwood called for the continuance of repressive measures "until the Anarchists whether known by the designation Industrial Workers of the World, Bolsheviki, or other specious terms, and their teachings, shall be either stamped out or driven back to the home that gave birth to this dangerous form of madness." The retiring spymaster concluded defiantly: "Canada is no safe place for Bolsheviki agents or any other kind of trouble breeder ..."[33]

The end of the war had not brought peace. Canadians had to remain on guard against secret forces of evil working surreptitiously to undermine the foundations of the social and economic order. This was the message of the Red Scare, a message used by authorities to wage their own secret war against the enemy within.

+ + +

During the winter of 1918–19, Ottawa was rattled by the extreme rhetoric it was hearing from some of the country's labour leaders. Police spies were sending in alarmist reports that unions were seething with revolutionary discontent. In response, the government set in motion a campaign of counter-propaganda to discredit the Reds. Chief press censor Ernest Chambers routinely fed information gleaned from police reports to members of the print media. Chambers kept his eyes peeled for anti-Red articles in the daily press so that he could dash off a letter offering the author more inflammatory information about the present danger. He did his best to orchestrate a comprehensive propaganda campaign, involving the press, university professors, service clubs, churches, even movies, all fuelled by information of the right type provided by his department. In January he wrote to the presidents of several major universities asking that they makes speeches or write articles exposing the fallacies of "extreme red Socialism and Bolshevism." At the same time, he warned against revealing the existence of this anti-Red campaign. "Were the agitators conducting this propaganda able to plead that they are being made the subject of organized attack," he wrote the president of the University of Toronto, Sir Robert Falconer, "it would aid them tremendously in their campaign with the disaffected." (Falconer wrote back declining the invitation to take part in Chambers' campaign: "If prices could be kept down and employment could be assured," he told the censor, "I think many of our immediate troubles could be quickly surmounted.")[34]

The kind of information Chambers wanted to disseminate could be found in the *Canadian Annual Review of Public Affairs*, published by J. Castell Hopkins, a prolific author of popular biographies and encyclopedias. Hopkins' portrait of the Soviet Union under Bolshevik rule exemplified the mixture of misinformation, fear, and smug middle-class superiority which fuelled anti-Red hysteria in Canada. "In Russia," he told his readers, "disorganization, starvation, individual license, robbery, brutal crime, the over-throw of social laws and religious influence and ordered government, whole-sale immorality, were natural products of the rule of men who were ignorant of all but wild theories nursed in malignant or disordered minds." For Hopkins, Bolshevism simply meant "wholesale pillage and the murder of the classes owning money or property." Things were better under the tsars, he said; at least the Romanovs were honest and meant well. The Bolsheviks were terrorists who roused the basest instincts in the Russian masses and rode them to power. Life in Russia, he told his readers, had become a living hell. There was no free speech, no democracy, no private property, only terror, mass executions, and torture, "including mutilations of all kinds, slow starvation, burning alive, piercing with bayonets [...], deliber-ate breaking of arms and legs, stamping on wounded living bodies with hob-nailed boots, nailing officers' shoulder straps to their bod-ies, thrusting of gramophone needles through finger nails, blinding in most brutal forms." Hopkins' list of bizarre atrocities was rem-iniscent of the most extreme anti-German propaganda during the war, now turned against a new enemy, the Bolshevik.[35]

Implicit in Hopkins' overheated prose was a warning to his Can-adian readers: This could happen here. The IWW and other social-ists preached a form of class warfare every bit as frightening as their Russian counterparts, he said. Working under the cover of the One Big Union and organizations such as the Social Democratic Party, they intended to destabilize the economic situation with general strikes and exploit the chaos to seize power from the government. According to Hopkins, this was no theoretical danger. "At the end of 1918 there were 21 Soviets established in the country awaiting for action," he announced, without any evidence whatsoever.[36]

One powerful institution that shared the concern about the in-sidious threat of Bolshevism was the Canadian Pacific Railway. In the fall of 1918, John Murray Gibbon, CPR publicist, broached the subject with filmmaker George Brownridge. Gibbon was one of the country's leading intellectuals. A graduate of Oxford University and an experienced journalist, he had joined the CPR's London operations in 1907 and had moved to the company's Montreal head office just before the war. He was not only an ambassador for the railway but, as author and festival impresario, he was an energetic promoter of Canadian culture as well. The CPR had a problem with Bolsheviks stirring up its workers, Gibbon told Brownridge, and he thought that the film industry could do something about it. During the war Brownridge had established a studio, Canadian National Features, in Trenton, Ontario, where he managed to make two feature films before going broke. Neither of those films was ever released, but the indefatigable Brownridge was back in business at Trenton two years later as the Adanac Producing Company (the name is Canada spelled backwards) and eager to attract corporate support from the likes of the CPR.

After talking to Gibbon, Brownridge, armed with a suitable script about a Red plot to take over a trade union, came back to the railway for financial help. Eventually the CPR and several other large employers did put up the money. CPR president Edward Beatty made his position clear in a letter that he wrote to journalist and president of the Canadian Reconstruction Association, John Willison. "Of course there can be no doubt that from one end of the country to the other an effort must be made to stamp out this extreme socialism which practically amounts to disloyalty..."[37] Brownridge began work on his film, called *The Great Shadow* and starring Tyrone Power Sr. The film was directed by Harley Knoles, who had just completed another anti-Red feature in the United States called *Bolshevism on Trial* co-starring his Canadian-born wife

Pinna Nesbitt. The final script of the new film included most of the elements of Red Scare melodrama: vicious Bolsheviks determined to destroy society by setting one class against another; a handsome secret service agent to provide love interest; a fair-minded employer who only wants what is best for his workers; and a "responsible" labour leader who must wage a life-and-death struggle to keep his union free of extremism. *The Great Shadow* was one of several Red Scare features to appear at this time in Canada and the US. The newest forms of popular entertainment were not ignored when it came to combatting the threat of Bolshevism. The film was finished too late to influence opinion during the crucial spring of 1919, but when it did reach the screen in the late fall it met with widespread critical praise. Unfortunately, no copy has survived.

Another busy scaremonger was Charles Cahan. In January Cahan, whose extreme views had managed to alienate most of his support in the federal Cabinet, resigned from his job as director of public safety. He had failed to convince the government to create a secret service modelled on the American Bureau of Investigation, and with his departure the entire Public Safety Branch was abolished after just three months in operation. In a letter to Prime Minister Borden, Cahan explained that, "I tried in vain, after your departure [for Europe], to obtain a hearing from your colleagues; but they treated my representations with such contemptuous indifference, that there was for me no alternative but to retire quietly and await events." In Cahan's view, the ultimate aim of the "Reds" was to "kick the Government off Parliament Hill."[38]

Cahan had no intention of retiring quietly; far from it. He continued to speak out at every opportunity about the Bolshevik threat, and one of his speeches, "Socialistic Propaganda in Canada," was printed as a pamphlet and had wide distribution. In it, he summarized the four main doctrines of "International Socialism" as he understood them. First of all, class warfare between workers and capitalists caused "envy and hatred of all who have acquired property of any kind whatsoever." Second, the state acquired ownership of all means of production and responsibility for all social relationships. Third, only the interests of workers had any importance. And last, the capitalist class was stripped of all possessions. Propaganda in favour of these views was flooding the western world, said Cahan. In Canada it was mainly the IWW that was fomenting class warfare, especially among the large "alien" population. If this was allowed to continue, he warned, there would be "tumults and disorders" that would require the intervention of the army. He suggested denying the right to strike, keeping a watchful eye on labour organizations and the foreign-language press, restricting immigration, and the speedy acculturation of immigrant children in the schools. Cahan's basic message was that anyone who accepted the concept of class differences was contributing to a civil war in Canada that threatened democratic institutions and individual liberties.[39]

Cahan carried his campaign to the pages of *Maclean's* magazine. Under the ownership of Colonel John Bayne Maclean and the editorship of Thomas Costain, this magazine had become a major organ of the Red Scare. Cahan sounded his familiar warning about the IWW and other "Red" elements who were spreading "pacifist, socialistic, revolutionary and seditious literature" and organizing "societies for the insidious propagation of doctrines destructive of our existing political, social and industrial institutions." He revealed that these activities were funded by thousands of dollars provided by agents of the Russian government, and he even hinted that the conspiracy to overthrow the government reached into the corridors of power in Ottawa. In the absence of Borden (in Europe), he wrote, the cabinet had been "utterly lacking in unity of purpose and in courageous action." In case after case, Cahan claimed, federal authorities had intervened to secure the release of agitators who had been arrested for their activities. And, of course, had he not been removed from any position of influence under suspicious circumstances?[40]

Colonel Maclean was an enthusiastic proponent of conspiracy theories. A long-time member of the militia, he had encouraged the government to take a hard-line, anti-Hun, anti-pacifist approach during the war. At the end of 1918, he wrote in his magazine that the Germans, had they won the war, had plans to dismember Canada and distribute parts of it to their leading bankers, nobles, and businessmen. Quite literally, therefore, the Canadian army had saved the country from extinction; it only made sense, wrote Maclean, to put the army in charge of society now that the war was over. He recommended, for instance, that military men take control of the school system. "It makes one dizzy to think of the great things that could be accomplished," he wrote.[41]

The January 1919 edition of *Maclean's* carried an article titled "Is Bolshevism Brewing in Canada?" to which the author, Thomas Fraser, answered with an emphatic "Yes." The magazine had commissioned Fraser to discover if Bolshevism was present in Canada. His conclusion: "There is a bold, systematic and dangerous effort being made to lay the fuse of Bolshevism from one end of the Dominion to the other." The IWW was behind it, he explained. "Their idea is to seize control of all industries and abolish the wage system." Their aims were completely hostile to democracy, Fraser warned, and to the middle class. The "root of the whole matter" was that "much of the good old Anglo-Saxon stock" was gone, slaughtered in the recent war, and Canada was filled up with "workmen of foreign extraction" sympathetic to Bolshevik propaganda.[42]

One appreciative reader of Fraser's article was press censor Ernest Chambers. He wrote Colonel Maclean a congratulatory note in which he warned that "the situation is very much more dangerous, in my opinion, than the public has the least conception of." Encouraging Maclean to continue to raise the alarm, he concluded: "I am firmly convinced that, without the real solid, sensible people of the country taking into their own hand the active combatting of this Bolshevist propaganda, we run the risk of reaching, within measureable time, the conditions which at present prevail in Russia."[43] Among the more extreme anti-Red fanatics, a rationale seemed to be emerging that justified taking the law into their own hands to preserve the nation from revolution.

In the June 1919 issue of his magazine, Maclean himself took Chambers' advice. In a provocative article titled "Why Did We Let Trotzky Go?" he blamed unnamed "politicians or officials" in Ottawa for allowing Trotsky to leave his Amherst internment camp and return to Russia to lead the revolution there. Trotsky, claimed Maclean, was a German agent paid to take Russia out of the war. If Canada had held onto him, the war would have been shortened by a year. This was a familiar belief at the time, but Maclean went further. He claimed that Trotsky had organized groups of revolutionaries in Toronto and Ottawa who were poised to take over the country. Charles Cahan had revealed some of this threat, wrote Maclean, but then "the Trotzky influences got busy and Mr. Cahan was ordered to cease his inquiries and send in his resignation."[44] (Despite the allegations of Cahan and Maclean, no evidence was ever produced that Leon Trotsky had supporters within the Canadian government who were twisting its policies in his favour.)

By the August issue, Maclean was getting even more alarmist. By then, of course, the Winnipeg General Strike had taken place. Not surprisingly, *Maclean's* saw it as a prelude to revolution. The Bolsheviks were pouring money into the country to cause strikes and encourage social unrest, the Colonel wrote. It was all a conspiracy organized by the Germans and their Russian Bolshevik agents to disrupt western countries so that Germany could rebuild its economy and regain its markets.[45] For Maclean, and for many others, the Hun and the Bolshevik were indistinguishable. In their view, the war was still going on and it was being fought in the streets of Winnipeg and other Canadian cities.

In his August editorial, Maclean introduced readers to Santeri Nuorteva, whom he characterized as the kingpin of the Bolshevik conspiracy in North America. Based at the Soviet government information bureau in New York, Nuorteva had bankrolled the Winnipeg strike, Maclean wrote, and was "preparing Eastern Canada, particularly Quebec and the Maritime Provinces, for the revolution." Nuorteva allegedly had powerful friends in government circles in Ottawa, "where he frequently went." When *Maclean's* readers looked at the photograph of the stocky, bald, bespectacled man that accompanied the article, they were told they were looking into the very face of the revolutionary conspiracy against their way of life.

Nuorteva was not the shadowy figure that Maclean made him out to be. Anyone who had been paying attention to the American press knew him well. In fact, most of the "facts" about the Soviet Bureau that *Maclean's* was recycling came from testimony given to a New York State Senate committee in June. The Lusk Committee, named for its chair, State Senator Clayton Lusk, was investigating radical activity in New York City and had targeted the Soviet Bureau as the command post of the North American

Bolshevik conspiracy. On June 12, 1919, agents of the committee raided the Bureau's offices in the World Tower Building in Manhattan, carting away tons of documents and detaining five of the Bureau's employees, including Nuorteva and his boss, the director of the Bureau, Ludwig Martens. Martens, an engineer by training, was the Bolshevik regime's unofficial ambassador to the United States. While he lobbied unsuccessfully to get official recognition from the Americans—the US would not recognize the Soviets until 1933—Martens went ahead and opened the Soviet Bureau where soon a staff of thirty-five was busily promoting commercial relations between the US and Russia and producing an array of pro-Soviet propaganda. This was all he was doing, claimed Martens. Benjamin Gitlow, the American communist leader, described Martens as "a quiet, mild-tempered man [...] Fair of complexion, with blond hair and mustache, he looked more like a middle-class businessman than what went for the accepted description of a Bolshevik."[46] But American authorities believed that he and his colleagues were in fact conspiring to destabilize western governments using money smuggled in from Moscow. According to Red hunters like Senator Lusk, Martens was "the American Lenin," and he hounded him mercilessly. There is no question that the Soviet Bureau did what it could to counter anti-Bolshevik propaganda in North America. But in the end, no evidence emerged from any investigation to prove that Martens and Nuorteva were fomenting revolution in America—quite the reverse; the Bureau had barely enough money to keep its doors open. After a year and a half of harassment and prosecution, the US government finally deported Martens, who sailed for Russia. As for Nuorteva, he too returned to Russia, where the regime for which he was supposedly a spy threw him in jail for a year then exiled him to a minor job in Siberia.

+ + +

By early in 1919, the government had deployed all its weapons in the war against the Reds. Secret police agents had infiltrated labour unions and socialist political groups.

They were filing reports that confirmed that a dangerous conspiracy existed and was fomenting unrest across the country. The federal government had enacted laws that gave it the power to come down hard on dissenters. Local, provincial, and national police forces were raiding the offices of targeted organizations, seizing incriminating literature, and jailing hundreds of left-wing activists in an attempt to shatter the conspiracy. The chief press censor was orchestrating a national propaganda campaign to discredit anyone who showed sympathy for socialist ideas. The press had hopped on the bandwagon. Newspapers and magazines were publishing articles that whipped up public concern about the Red threat. The most extreme voices were urging the government to be ruthless and uncompromising in squashing any challenge to the status quo. The situation in most of the large cities was volatile, with militant workers, socialist activists, and ethnic leaders refusing to accept the heavy hand of repression. The stage seemed to be set for a violent clash.

FIGURE 13 Roger Bray, a leader of the returned soldiers, speaking to a rally in Victoria Park, Winnipeg, June 1919. Many of the Reds were accomplished orators who could hold an audience's attention for hours at a time. A police spy called Bray the most dangerous man in the city because of his influence with the returned soldiers, a volatile group. *Photo: Manitoba Archives, Foote Collection, SIS N2742*

CHAPTER THREE

Fighting Back

"I am a Socialist and proud of it. You can call me a Bolsheviki if you want to."
—*Dick Johns, Winnipeg strike leader*

The so-called Reds did not apologize for their radical views; neither did they accept the government's right to suppress them. "I am a Bolshevist," declared the Nova Scotia labour organizer Clifford Dane, "and I will warn these two governments that trouble is coming and the men will have what belongs to them."[1] The Reds fought back, with results that at times resembled a civil war. From their point of view, they were resisting an oppressive government that had taken away basic democratic rights of free speech and assembly. Indeed, the government helped to create a confrontational situation by providing in its repressive policies a rallying point that united factions on the left. The Reds felt themselves to be riding a wave, part of a worldwide movement for change. "To be a leftist in the atmosphere of 1917–1920," writes historian Ian McKay, "was to breath a very special atmosphere, one in which a top to bottom reconstruction of society had seemingly gone from being a utopian dream to a real possibility."[2] Confident that history was on their side, radicals relished thumbing their noses at the authorities. Meetings invariably ended, as one in Toronto did in January 1919, with three cheers for "Bolshevism, Karl Liebknecht, the Social Revolution and Leon Trotsky." (Liebknecht was a soon-to-be martyred German revolutionary.) No wonder a nervous government thought they were plotting revolution.

+ + +

On a Sunday afternoon in December, three days before Christmas 1918, the Winnipeg Trades and Labor Council and the Socialist Party of Canada convened a public meeting at the Walker Theatre, one of the city's largest live performance venues, on Smith Street near Portage Avenue. (The Walker, which opened in 1907 with a performance of *Madama Butterfly*, continues in operation as the Burton Cummings Theatre.) The 1,700 people who crammed into the theatre's main floor and two balconies were in a boisterous, combative mood. "The remarks of the various speakers were frequently punctuated with deafening applause," reported the *Free Press*, "particularly the references to 'the coming revolution in this country'."[3] Perhaps the only person not shouting and clapping was Sgt-Major Francis Langdale, undercover officer with military intelligence, who was too busy at the back of the meeting furtively scribbling down notes of what was being said.

The official business of the afternoon was to pass three resolutions. The first, moved from the stage by Bill Hoop and seconded by George Armstrong, both well-known members of the Socialist Party in the city, protested the federal orders-in-council imposed in September: "Whereas, we, in Canada, have the form of Representative Government; and, whereas, Government by Order-in-Council takes away the prerogative of the people's representatives, and is a distinct violation of the principles of democracy, therefore, we, citizens of Winnipeg, in mass meeting assembled, protest against Government by Orders-in-Council, and demand the repeal of all such orders, and a return to a democratic form of Government." Hoop insisted, "The Order-in-Council is a negation of all that we have fought for and obtained for centuries. We do not propose for one moment to sacrifice those liberties—not for one moment."[4]

The second resolution accused the government of jailing activists "for offences purely political" and demanded the release of all political prisoners, meaning especially the many men who had been swept up in police raids since the passage of the orders-in-council. It was moved by the Reverend William Ivens, the forty-one-year-old editor of the *Western Labor News*. During the war, the hierarchy in the Methodist Church had expelled Ivens because of his outspoken pacifism and anti-war activism. In response he founded the Labour Church, a non-denominational debating club that held meetings in halls and theatres around Winnipeg and was a focus for much of the left-wing intellectual ferment in the city. Fred Dixon, a labour member of the Manitoba legislature, seconded the resolution. Unlike most of the other activists with whom he shared the stage, Dixon rejected hard-line socialism. He was a liberal who was as suspicious of collectivism as he was of capitalism. Most socialists viewed him as a moderate, bourgeois reformer, yet his passionate opposition to the war and support for free speech placed him in the same camp with the Reds.

Third, the meeting endorsed a motion demanding that Allied intervention in the Russian Civil War end immediately. When the Bolsheviks came to power in Russia, they negotiated a separate peace with Germany to end the fighting on the eastern front, a peace that was formalized in the Treaty of Brest-Litovsk in March 1918, leaving the Allied powers affronted at what they considered to be the Bolsheviks' betrayal of the war effort. With the outbreak of civil war in Russia, the Allies committed their own troops to help the White Army topple Lenin's regime and, optimistically, to get the Russians back into the war. Canada had a few soldiers involved in the Caucasus and a few more attached to an expeditionary force sent to Murmansk, ostensibly to secure Allied provisions there. But the most significant Canadian involvement was in Siberia, where the Borden government promised several thousand soldiers.

The Canadian Siberian Expeditionary Force, announced in August 1918, was not popular with the public, but so long as the war continued Borden felt it was justified. However, by the time the bulk of the men were assembled at a camp near Victoria, BC, to prepare for embarkation to Russia it was December, the war was over, and it was harder to explain why Canadian soldiers should be involved in a dubious foreign adventure that seemed to serve no national interest. Still, Borden was adamant the men should go. About a third of the soldiers were conscripts from Quebec. Resentful at having to serve in the army in the first place, they were a receptive audience for local leftists who propagandized against the expedition. By December 4, the British Columbia lieutenant governor, Frank Barnard, was so afraid of an outbreak of violence in the military camp over the issue that he petitioned Ottawa to ask Great Britain to send warships to the Pacific Coast to keep the peace.[5] Finally, on December 21, the day before the Walker Theatre meeting in Winnipeg, about 900 members of the force began to move through the streets of Victoria to the docks to embark for Vladivostok. During the march some of the men mutinied, refusing to proceed to the troopship. Officers ordered other soldiers to remove their belts and whip the recalcitrants back into line. Urged along at gunpoint, the mutineers eventually boarded the ship and the expeditionary force sailed for Siberia.

At the Walker Theatre the next day, the crowd would not have known about these recent events on the Pacific Coast. Nonetheless, it had been public knowledge since the summer that Canada intended to send soldiers to Siberia, and it was the will of the Winnipeg meeting that Canada not intervene. Russia should be left alone "to work out her own political freedom without outside intervention," read the motion, which was introduced by Bob Russell, a Scottish-born machinist who had been in Canada less than eight years but already was on the national executive of his union and a leading member of the Socialist Party. (Capitalism was "defunct and must disappear," he told the audience.) The seconder was Sam Blumenberg, resplendent in a red tie and matching handkerchief. Blumenberg, a thirty-three-year-old Jew from Romania, reportedly told the meeting that Russians under Bolshevism enjoyed better living conditions than Canadian workers.[6] He would soon have cause to regret his remarks.

The meeting ended with the chairman, John Queen, a city alderman and member of the Social Democratic Party, calling for three cheers for the Russian Revolution, after which the crowd spilled out into the fading light of the afternoon with shouts of "Long Live the Russian Soviet Republic! Long live Karl Liebknecht! Long live the working class!" An excited Bob Russell wrote to his friend Joe Knight, a Socialist Party activist in Edmonton, that the meeting "has put new life into the movement. We are arranging meetings now for all Winter."[7]

In Toronto as well, organized labour was fighting back against
the mass arrests that had taken place under the auspices of the federal orders-in-council. Various activists had been jailed for possessing
and distributing banned literature and belonging to illegal organizations, and supporters had formed the Political Defence League of
Ontario to demand their release. On January 12, a Sunday evening,
1,200 men and women jammed into the Broadway Hall to listen
to a roster of speakers denounce government-by-order-in-council.
The audience overflowed into a second meeting room upstairs
where another 300 people waited to hear the speakers when they
had finished below. Donations were collected to pay the fines of the
detainees and a petition circulated demanding repeal of the orders-
in-council and release of the "political prisoners." As the meeting
dispersed onto Spadina Avenue, people were singing the socialist
anthem "Red Flag."[8]

> Then raise the scarlet standard high,
> Within its shade we'll live and die,
> Though cowards flinch and traitors sneer,
> We'll keep the red flag flying here.

Further assemblies in the city that week maintained the drum-
beat of protest. It appeared that the government had misjudged the
passivity of organized labour, but now Ottawa got the message.
Moderate members of the Cabinet were able to convince their colleagues that the anti-Red hard line was alienating important labour
support. As a result, the government took a step back and sentences
for some high-profile militants were reduced. Charles Watson, for
example, who had received a three-year term, had his sentence re-

duced to thirty days. The labour strategy of vociferous public protest had paid off.

By this time the focus of radical protest had shifted back to Winnipeg. Elated at the success of the Walker Theatre event, the Socialist Party of Canada decided to stage another meeting in the Prairie capital, this time at the Majestic Theatre on Portage Avenue on January 10. At this meeting the rhetoric was a little bolder, the challenge to the government a little more flagrant. Speakers George Armstrong, Dick Johns, Bob Russell, and Sam Blumenberg gave what amounted to tutorials on socialist economics. Armstrong, who traced his family ancestry back to the United Empire Loyalists in Ontario, explained the theory of surplus value and warned his listeners that, in the name of post-war reconstruction, they would be asked to support all kinds of policies that were not in their interest. "We ask you to support only such schemes as will abolish all exploitation of the working class," he said, "which means the destruction of all property rights in the wealth of society." Bob Russell argued that any attempt to remodel the old economy was doomed to failure. What was needed was a thorough overhaul of the system, putting the working class, "the only useful class," in control. Sam Blumenberg continued this attack on the "reconstruction gang." Disparaging all politicians in the mainstream political parties as "tricksters and pirates," Blumenberg shouted: "They tell you that we are going to have prosperity, but let me tell you that capitalist prosperity means poverty for the working class."[9]

Sgt-Major Langdale was in the crowd again, along with another undercover spy, Detective Sergeant Albert Reames of the Mounted Police. Testifying in court some months later, Reames described the series of inflammatory speeches warning workers to prepare themselves for the outbreak of imminent social revolution in Canada.

The speeches, Reames said, "had a very bad effect" on the many returned veterans in the city. Authorities would use his report to make a direct connection between the Majestic Theatre meeting and the events which followed, claiming, in effect, that the citizens of Winnipeg had no alternative but to take the law into their own hands to preserve their community from Red revolution.

A follow-up meeting was scheduled, again for the Majestic, but tension in the city had become so palpable that the owner of the theatre convinced the organizers to cancel. Instead people gathered outside in Market Square next to City Hall on Sunday, January 26, to listen to more speakers. According to the *Manitoba Free Press* it was "a revolutionary socialist meeting" with a heavy component of "aliens."[10] Resentment at German and Slavic immigrants—still called "enemy aliens" even though the war had been over since the previous November—had been building for months. This, combined with the high level of unemployment in the city and general antipathy toward socialist ideas, was enough to touch off an ugly explosion.

A mob consisting principally of several hundred returned soldiers appeared in the Square and began to rough up some of the "aliens." The veterans decided to march to the headquarters of the Socialist Party, above Jimmy's Restaurant on Smith Street. They barged up the stairs and into the office where they tossed furniture, books, and bundles of literature into the street and set them afire, along with a large red flag. Detective Reames followed along taking notes as the veterans headed off toward the North End. "The crowd then went up into Main Street," he reported, where it "beat up several foreigners, or apparent foreigners" before attacking the German Club. "The windows were smashed at this place," continued Reames, "and a piano came out of the second-floor window which was promptly jumped upon and smashed up and pieces taken away as souvenirs by the crowd."[11] Looting and rioting continued into the evening with the police observing the vandalism but not making any attempt to stop it. At ten o'clock, about 2,500 veterans gathered outside the police station demanding to know if any of their number had been arrested. When police Chief Donald Mac-Pherson assured them that they had not, the veterans moved off and gradually dispersed.

The next day anti-alien demonstrations flared up again. A group of what the *Free Press* called "returned men and sympathizers" appeared at the gates of the Swift Canadian meat-packing plant demanding that all foreign workers be fired and replaced by "white labor." The men were in an ugly mood, and they were threatening to break into the plant to remove the "aliens" when Mayor Charles Gray drove up in the company of the senior military commander in the district, General H.D.B. Ketchen. Instead of arresting the veterans, who were, after all, threatening to destroy private property and assault innocent citizens, Ketchen and Gray promised to give them everything they wanted if they would only disperse quietly. "I am an Englishman," Gray told the crowd, "and I want you men to give British fair play. We want to get the aliens out and I am with you in that, but let us do it constitutionally. Go back to the city and show them [the employer] that you will give them a chance to get rid of the aliens and if they don't do it then is the time for reckoning. [...] You know I am with you boys."[12] Having forced the army to capitulate, the mob was feeling its oats. It moved leisurely through the city, smashing windows, looting bars and restaurants, and beating up supposed "aliens" and forcing them to kiss the Union Jack. The police followed along in a paddy wagon but did not intervene.

Through all of this, known radicals kept a low profile—wisely so, if the case of Sam Blumenberg was an example. About 100 of the protestors showed up at his dry-cleaning business on Portage Avenue. Frustrated at not finding him there, they broke his windows and went on their way. Later in the evening, they returned and completely smashed up the premises.

Official response to these two days of unprecedented mob violence was muted, to say the least. No charges were laid; it was almost as if the victims were felt to be at fault. The riots were seen by some as a necessary pre-emptive strike against the forces of Red revolution. Editorializing against unrestricted free speech, the Winnipeg *Telegram* warned that "with such a creed, treason becomes a mere name; loyalty a meaningless word. Anarchy may run riot. Bloodshed, theft, incendiarism and every form of vice may openly be advocated."[13] Defenders of chaos should not have free speech, declared the *Telegram*. It was to teach this lesson that the riots began. Other observers chuckled at the "hijinks" in Winnipeg. "The Bolshevist in that city overreached himself, didn't he?" wrote the editor of the Ottawa *Journal*, E. Norman Smith, in a letter to Ernest Chambers. "By shooting off his mouth he called attention to the fact that he existed in the city. Hereafter, perhaps some of these foreigners will learn to lie low and keep their mouths shut."[14] For its part, the government of Manitoba responded by establishing an Alien Investigation Board that made it more difficult for immigrant workers to get, or keep, a job.

It is difficult to tell to what degree anti-Semitism may have played a role in the street disturbances in Winnipeg, or in the Red Scare generally. Sam Blumenberg was Jewish, and other targets of mob violence may have been as well. There is no question that anti-Semitism was present in Canada at the time.[15] During the prewar immigration boom, the government did not encourage Jewish immigrants. Settling the agricultural West was the priority, and Jews were considered to be urban dwellers unsuited to agricultural pursuits. At the same time, immigration officials did not actively discriminate against Jews, as was the case with Asian newcomers or African-Americans. Jews entered the country without much trouble; the 1911 census revealed that there were almost 75,000 living in Canada, principally in large urban centres such as Montreal and Toronto. Once in the country, however, Jews experienced discrimination. Access to certain schools and to job opportunities was limited. Resorts, hotels, recreational facilities, and clubs routinely, if covertly, barred Jews. The hostility was especially strong in Quebec where Jews were seen as a threat to the hegemony of the dominant Catholic Church. Henri Bourassa, for example, a leading nationalist politician and founder of the prestigious *Le Devoir* newspaper, was a virulent anti-Semite.

During the Red Scare, however, anti-Semitism seems to have been subsumed under the broader fear of, and hostility toward, foreigners in general. Sam Blumenberg, for instance, was singled out for being an "alien" and a Bolshevik, not for being a Jew. Police reports mentioned that certain Jewish organizations seemed sympathetic to Red ideas, but no more so than other suspect foreign communities such as Finns or Ukrainians. As Gerald Tulchinsky concludes in his study of Jews in Canada, "during this period, anti-Semitism was part and parcel of the antipathy for foreigners."[16]

+ + +

On Monday, February 17, 1919, Canada's winter of discontent was interrupted by the sudden death of the former prime minister, Wilfrid Laurier. He had been working alone in his Parliament Hill office the previous Saturday afternoon when he had fallen onto the carpet in a dead faint. Rousing himself, he made his way home by streetcar and seemed to have recovered, but the next morning a second stroke left him bedridden and moving in and out of consciousness. "C'est fini," he told his wife Zoé. He lingered through the night, growing weaker. A priest arrived to administer the last rites. Just before three o'clock in the afternoon a final, fatal stroke stirred him from a restless slumber, and he died.

"Canada Mourns Her Most Distinguished Son," ran the *Globe*'s banner headline. At age seventy-seven, Laurier was the Grand Old Man of Canadian politics. He had entered the House of Commons in 1874, when the country was in its infancy. During the next forty-five years, he lost just once at the polls. Hardly a voter in the country could remember a time when Laurier had not been captain of the Liberal team. As a young man he had opposed Confederation, fearing it would annihilate the Quebeçois as a distinct people, but once it was accomplished he reconciled himself to it and devoted the rest of his career to protecting and strengthening the French fact in Canada. He became leader of the Liberal Party in 1887 and nine years later became the country's first Francophone prime minister. Most of the major challenges faced by his government involved mediating the often opposed interests of French and English, whether it was Canada's role in the British Empire or the place of the French language in the rest of the country. "He has always stood for moderation and conciliation, and for a good understanding between Canadians of his own and other races," the *Toronto Star* editorialized.[17] By temperament a moderate, Laurier was adept at finding the middle path of compromise. "My object is to consolidate Confederation," he once wrote a friend, "and to bring our people long estranged from one another, gradually to become a nation."[18] He had the appearance of a patrician, yet colleagues admired his open personality and charm, his famous "sunny ways." At the same time he was a tenacious competitor who enjoyed politics as a blood sport. "He told me once," revealed his first biographer, the journalist Sir John Willison, "that he was in politics for one reason only—to beat the other man."[19]

It was Laurier's good fortune to serve as prime minister during a period of tremendous economic expansion. Not surprisingly, Canadians looked back at those pre-war years of Liberal government as a sort of golden age. "The fifteen years of his Premiership form one of the brightest periods in the history of Canada," pronounced the *Star*.[20] Laurier was famous for declaring that "the twentieth century shall be the century of Canada." And why not? The population soared, thanks to an aggressive immigration policy aimed at populating the Prairie West with newcomers from Europe. The grain economy was established. A second transcontinental railway was pushed across the country. Two new provinces, Alberta and Saskatchewan, joined the federation. In Central Canada, manufacturing output from the mills, smelters, and factories skyrocketed. The country even acquired the beginnings of its own navy. The *Globe* had a point when it said that "a new Canada came into being" during Laurier's tenure.[21]

On the Thursday following Laurier's death, Parliament convened in the Victoria Museum, its temporary location since the Centre Block on Parliament Hill was damaged by fire in 1916. The Governor General, the Duke of Devonshire, read the Speech from the Throne after which the session immediately adjourned. Laurier's body was carried to the Senate chamber where it lay in state for two days. Tens of thousands of people filed past the open bronze casket from early in the morning until late at night to pay their respects. Even when a snowstorm blew up in the afternoon, it did not discourage the mourners, some of whom waited for hours, choking the streets around the museum. On Saturday the capital overflowed with new arrivals, transported to the city by the thousands on special trains to mass outside the funeral at the Sacred Heart Church. As the leaden skies of morning gave way to an afternoon of bright winter sunshine, they jostled together, bareheaded, for a better look at the cortege as it wound through the city streets. "Daring folk climbed telegraph poles and trees to get a better look," described a reporter for the *Globe*. "Every window had its quota and large crowds were upon the roofs." The coffin, preceded by seven horse-drawn sleighs spilling over with flowers and followed by hundreds of political heavyweights from all parts of the country, made its way down into the suburban enclave of Eastview and the cemetery of Notre Dame where the body was laid to rest.

Given Laurier's stature and longevity, it was inevitable that commentators would describe his death as the passing of an era. But there was truth to the cliché. Laurier was an old-fashioned nineteenth-century liberal. His government had unleashed many of the forces that were transforming Canadian society, but he was not ready to respond to them. He had little inclination to interfere in the business of business or to think about ways that the county's expanding wealth might be distributed more equitably among all its citizens. And he had little to contribute to the emerging debates about worker control and industrial unionism that were rocking the country. "We are now faced with problems of a different kind from those which it was his part to study," wrote the *Star*'s editorialist. "The death of Laurier in 1919 was symbolic of the end of an old era," social gospeller and Labour MLA A.E. Smith wrote in his memoirs. "Monopoly large-scale capitalism was arriving. Labour was stirring in its new strength."[22]

But Laurier was not the leader to cope with these new challenges. For that the Liberal Party at its August leadership convention turned to a younger generation. This event was the first time in Canadian history that members of a political party came together to choose a leader; previously it had been the job of the party's parliamentary caucus. Heading into the Ottawa convention, the two front-runners were W.S. Fielding, the seventy-year-old former premier of Nova Scotia, and William Lyon Mackenzie King, who had spent much of the war in the United States working as a labour consultant for the Rockefeller Foundation. Earlier in his career Fielding had been a secessionist, supporting independence for Nova Scotia from the Dominion of Canada. That enthusiasm had long faded and during the Laurier years (1896–1911) he had served ably as minister of finance and was seen by many as the natural heir apparent. Fielding had a serious deficiency, however; during the war, he broke with Laurier over the issue of conscription. Fielding supported it, and though he did not go so far as to join the Borden government, as many of his Liberal colleagues did, it was a liability at a convention where loyalty to the memory of the Old Man was paramount. At forty-five years of age, King was much younger and more vigorous than his opponent, but his main advantage was that he had stuck with Laurier over conscription, opposing it and even going down to defeat in the 1917 election because of it. As a result, he enjoyed the support of the Quebec wing of the party, support that Fielding in the end could not overcome. The convention went with King on a third ballot by a narrow margin.

Posterity thinks of Mackenzie King as a stodgy mama's boy who, in the words of the poet F.R. Scott, "will be remembered wherever

FIGURE 14 When he was prime minister, Wilfrid Laurier (L) invited young William Lyon Mackenzie King (R) to join his cabinet as minister of labour in 1909. King remained loyal to Laurier through the conscription crisis and it was this loyalty, and his knowledge of industrial relations, that won him the leadership of the Liberal Party at Laurier's death in 1919. *Photo: National Archives of Canada, C-031020*

men honour ingenuity, ambiguity, inactivity, and political longevity." But in 1919 King was on the progressive wing of Canadian politics. Where Laurier had been a small-town Quebec lawyer, King
had studied economics at Chicago and Harvard. He had experience
as an industrial mediator, had served as deputy minister of labour,
and had written a book, *Industry and Humanity* (1918), which while
generally acknowledged to be unreadable, nevertheless established
his credentials as an innovative thinker. A large part of his appeal to
his fellow Liberals was the belief that he knew the secret to securing labour peace. The transition from Laurier to King did indeed
suggest that Ottawa, or at least the Liberal Party, was responding
to the tempest of unrest swirling across the country.

+ + +

On the afternoon of Thursday March 13, 1919, the 237 delegates
attending an historic assembly of labour representatives from Western Canada at Calgary's Paget Hall were preparing to begin their
meeting when David Rees, a coal miner from Nanaimo, rose from
his seat to make an announcement. There was a police spy in the
auditorium. As delegates craned their necks to get a better look,
Rees pointed dramatically into the visitors' gallery. "I want to warn
my friends there is a man masquerading here under the name of
Smith," he shouted. "The real name of this man is Bob Gosden, and
who, in my opinion, is a police spy and stool-pigeon. I would warn
the delegates to be guarded as to their statements."[23]

As delegates called for his ejection, the man Rees had identified asked if he could address the meeting to defend himself. This
request was denied, but after much debate the motion to toss him
out was also defeated. "We need not be afraid of any Secret Service

men," declared Jack Kavanaugh, the socialist leader from Vancouver. It was a public meeting; delegates had nothing to hide. Gosden was allowed to stay, to take his notes, and make his report.

Gosden, whose police code name was "Agent 10," was not a typical undercover police agent. Well-known within labour circles for his activities on behalf of striking workers in BC before and during the war, he would not have expected to go unnoticed at the convention. Following his arrival in North America from his native England, Gosden joined the ranks of the blanketstiffs. A supporter of the Wobblies, he served time in jail for his activism and was known for his aggressive rhetoric and his support for direct action. (He once gave a speech in Vancouver threatening the lives of the premier and his attorney general.[24]) During the war, Gosden's politics moderated, and by 1916 he was an organizer for the provincial Liberals, helping them woo the labour vote in Vancouver. But following a spring by-election in Vancouver, he was drawn into a nasty political scandal. The Conservatives accused the Liberals of buying votes during the election and set up a commission to investigate. Gosden's testimony was crucial. He revealed the extent of the vote buying and dirty tricks engaged in by the Liberal machine. Naturally the Liberals fought back, charging Gosden with perjury. Twice he defended himself in court, and twice he got off, but the whole affair left him with few friends in any of the political parties and no money.

At this point Gosden travelled to Alberta, where he seemed to revert to his radical views (or perhaps he had never really abandoned them in the first place). After he attempted to organize a labourers' union in Calgary, the local police ran him out of town, and not long after that, the RCMP opened a file on him. But as labour historian Mark Leier reveals in his book on Gosden, by early in 1919 the one-time Wobbly had turned RCMP informant.[25] He was one of thirty-five secret agents recruited by the force in the first six months of 1919, allowing Commissioner Perry to boast that "we have operatives who are members of practically every known organization in the west, which has been in any way connected with or influenced by the present wave of Bolshevik and socialistic propaganda."[26] For five dollars a day, a significant sum at the time, these men were expected to cultivate contacts in the labour movement and pass on any information they collected about radical activity. Their identities were often not known even to their controlling officers, though in the case of Gosden, the truth came out on the floor of the Calgary convention.

The Western Labor Conference was a meeting of union representatives from across Western Canada. It was called in response to what delegates perceived to be the conservative policies of the national trade union body, the Trades and Labor Congress of Canada (TLC). Union militancy had been increasing, especially in western Canada, where many leaders rejected the Congress's conciliatory attitude towards the government on conscription and other issues. At the TLC's national meeting in Quebec City the previous autumn, western delegates, outnumbered by easterners ten-to-one, were frustrated when their views failed to gain any traction with the conservative national leadership. With the support of some eastern radicals, they criticized the executive for accepting conscription and put forward motions in support of industrial unions and liberating jailed anti-war activists. But they lost every vote. In the end, the Congress chose Tom Moore as its new president. Moore was an Ontario carpenter, a supporter of conscription, and a dyed-in-the-wool craft unionist; in other words, an enemy of change. (Moore was so unpopular on the left that a couple of months later when he spoke in Toronto at a meeting to protest the arrests of union activists, his remarks were repeatedly interrupted by jeers, booing, and demands that he "sit down" and "shut up."[27]) A direct result of the Quebec convention was that a number of westerners decided to call their own, regional meeting to promote a more radical agenda.

The Calgary conference spooked the government more than any of the other meetings that took place that protest-filled winter. It seemed to be the true beginning of Red revolution. With the usual rhetorical flourishes in solidarity with Bolshevism, delegates passed resolutions condemning capitalism and old-style unionism in favour of One Big Union and the "Proletarian Dictatorship." Queen's University professor of politics O.D. Skelton called it "the most radical social platform ever put forward in Canada."[28] The OBU, a plan to unite all workers in a single industrial union, was a rejection of the traditional union organization, embodied by the TLC with its division of workers into separate organizations based on craft, and it seemed to commit the labour movement to direct political action, a step the government viewed with alarm.

Delegates left Calgary having voted to organize a referendum asking workers whether they endorsed the One Big Union idea. To mainstream unionists, governments, and the public, it was nothing short of a Bolshevik uprising. "Soviet Plotters Busy in Canada," the Montreal *Daily Star* told its readers. "The Bolshevistic spirit in its worst form lies back of the 'Red' activities of last week's convention," wrote an editorialist in the Calgary *Daily Herald*. "There is no place, no room for it in Canada." Veterans' organizations in BC and Alberta called on the government to arrest or deport "the leading apostles of anarchy, sedition and disloyalty."[29]

The OBU referendum was set for June. Meanwhile, Gosden, "Agent 10," made his report. In his opinion the OBU was nothing more than a ruse to solidify the position of radical socialists at the head of the labour movement. Their aim, reported Gosden, was to foment "a social revolution of the Bolsheviki type." They were "intelligent opportunists," he wrote, who were plotting to dupe the rank and file into carrying them to power. By now this analysis was familiar enough, but Gosden proposed a uniquely draconian response. He suggested that the police secretly apprehend several members of the "Red element" and imprison them without trial or publicity in an attempt to terrorize their followers into submission. "After one or two of these leaders had been picked up at various points in a mysterious manner, and disappeared just as mysteriously, the unseen hand would so intimidate the weaker and lesser lights that the agitation would automatically die down." Gosden admitted that "this may not be in strict accordance with the technical law," but desperate times called for desperate measures.[30]

Delegates to the Western Labor Conference may have tolerated Gosden's presence at their meeting. They would have been less sanguine had they realized that the RNWMP had a second undercover agent in attendance. This was Frank Zaneth, known in Calgary labour circles as Harry Blask. Unlike Gosden, who was a paid snitch, Zaneth was a full-fledged member of the force. Born Franco Zanetti, he had emigrated to the US from his native Italy while still a child and had come to Canada in 1911 to take up a homestead near Moose Jaw.[31] He applied to join the Mounted Police in 1917 when he was twenty-seven years old. A short, slight man of undistinguished appearance, able to speak French and Italian, he was perfectly suited to undercover work. In the spring of 1918, police commissioner A. Bowen Perry named him the first member of the force's new secret service, Operative No. 1.

Zaneth's first assignment was to identify draft resisters in Quebec, but once the war was over Perry dispatched him to Drumheller, Alberta, to gather information about agitators in the coal mines. Zaneth took the name "Harry Blask" and pretended to be a Wobbly organizer. He managed to infiltrate one of the unions by getting a job as secretary to one of its leaders. At the same time, he attended secret meetings of the Socialist Party, conferred with its members, sold its banned literature on the streets—and reported everything to his police superiors. At the Western Labor Conference, Zaneth was in the hall, handing out pamphlets and trying his best to remember who said what to whom for the report that he submitted after it was over. His comrades had no idea that he was a spy. In fact, to solidify his false identity, Zaneth went to Regina where Commissioner Perry had him arrested and fined as an alien travelling without a permit.[32] With his bona fides intact, Zaneth was able to continue spying for the police. The first inkling radical leaders had that their friend "Harry Blask" was not who he said he was would not come until December, when he appeared dramatically in a Winnipeg courtroom in full RNWMP uniform to testify against them.

The information supplied by undercover agents was influenced by the political beliefs of the individual spies and it was carefully evaluated by their controlling officers. In the case of Gosden, his alarmist views were received with scepticism, though his report on the Calgary meeting was considered important enough to forward all the way to the prime minister's office. Gosden's controllers in the RNWMP characterized it as "over drawn" and preferred to maintain a watching brief rather than implement any drastic measures, such as "disappearing" the OBU leadership.

Police commissioner Perry decided to invite three of the "Revolutionary Socialists" to a secret meeting to get a sense of their intentions. Victor Midgley, Bill Pritchard, and Jack Kavanagh were all stalwarts of the Socialist Party of Canada from British Columbia. Midgley was the union official beaten by veterans during the sympathetic strike in Vancouver the previous August. He was one of the main organizers of the Calgary conference, which named him secretary of the OBU central committee. Pritchard joined him on the central committee. With his spectacles and a quiff, he had more the appearance of a mild-mannered school teacher than a longshoreman on the Vancouver waterfront. But

FIGURE 15 William "Bill" Pritchard was one of the three Socialist Party activists invited to a secret meeting with RNWMP Commissioner A. Bowen Perry to discuss their intentions. They were "intelligent, well-read men," Perry reported, and a "grave danger to the peace and security of the country." *Photo: City of Burnaby, BC*

Pritchard was a fire-and-brimstone orator who had played a pivotal role planning the Calgary conference, then guiding its debate. He would later serve a year in prison as one of the convicted leaders of the Winnipeg General Strike. Kavanagh, also a longshoreman and newly installed as the president of the BC Federation of Labour, was in charge of the committee that was meant to proselytize in favour of the OBU in British Columbia.

In the report of the meeting that Perry made to his superiors, he described the trio of Reds as "intelligent, well-read men." "They are tireless in pursuit of their objects," he wrote, "and have all the fervour of fanatics." He did not think they were plotting a violent overthrow of the government, but he feared them nonetheless. "I am not prepared to say that they are aiming at a revolution in the ordinary sense of that word, but I do say that they are influencing a section of labour in the West and unchaining forces which, even if they so desire, some day they will be unable to control. Here is grave danger to the peace and security of the country." Even so, Perry urged caution. He feared that repressive measures would simply radicalize the more moderate members of the labour movement. Returning to the subject of armed revolution, he observed that "it can only succeed if a considerable number of returned soldiers join the movement." The Reds knew this and were doing their best to court the veterans. He urged the government, therefore, to promote full employment and whatever other policies it could to placate the grievances of the soldiers.[33]

Another crucial document influencing government thinking about the labour situation was a "Memo on Revolutionary Tendencies in Western Canada" prepared in early April by C.F. Hamilton. Hamilton was a former journalist (he covered the Boer War for the Toronto *Globe*) and wartime press censor. He had been assistant comptroller of the Mounted Police before the war and rejoined the Mounties afterward as an intelligence officer. He was a highly influential official within the force who reported directly to the commissioner. In his thirteen-page memo, Hamilton argued that there was a small but active band of revolutionaries at work in western Canada attempting to subvert the Canadian government. "Their openly avowed aim is to procure the establishment of a Soviet government, with its concomitants of the disappearance of parliamentary government, the subversion of the rule of the majority, the abolition of private ownership of property, and the destruction of the other institutions upon which society is founded." Hamilton admitted that armed insurrection seemed unlikely in Canada, but he argued that there were circumstances in which it could occur. The key was the troubled labour situation, he said, and he sketched out a plausible scenario for the "would-be revolutionists." "What they aim at is an intense conflict between labour and capital, embittered by riots and bloodshed; they calculate on a general dislocation of the industrial system, passing into an uprising of the working classes, probably reinforced by masses of discontented returned soldiers. The whole project turns upon the propagation of bad temper and mutual hate between classes..." Despite his dire prognosis, Hamilton did not believe that direct repression was the correct response. Instead, he called for a campaign of counter-propaganda highlighting the failure of Bolshevism to bring social peace and prosperity to Russia.[34]

As alarmist reports piled up on the desks of senior ministers in Ottawa, the acting prime minister, Sir William Thomas White, panicked. White, a Montreal financier who had won his seat in Parliament in the 1911 election as an opponent of freer trade with the United States and had been rewarded with the finance portfolio in cabinet, was filling in for Borden who was still away at the peace negotiations in Europe. He cabled the absent prime minister in mid-April with the news that Bolshevism was rampant in Canada among soldiers and workers, especially in British Columbia. There was a revolution brewing, White reported, and he wanted Borden to ask the British government to dispatch one of its warships to Vancouver where "the presence of such ship and crew would have steadying influence."[35] Borden was in Paris hobnobbing with heads of state, making the world safe for democracy. He was impatient at White's bothering him with what no doubt seemed like petty, and exaggerated, domestic problems. "I would very much like to reply, For

Heaven's Sake, let me alone," he peevishly confided to his diary.[36] Instead he advised White to do the best he could with the armed forces at his disposal. There would be no request for British help.

+ + +

On April 26, in a meeting room at the Empress Hotel in Victoria, BC, Chief Justice Thomas Mathers of the Manitoba Supreme Court opened the inaugural meeting of the Royal Commission on Industrial Relations. "The upheaval taking place throughout the world, and the state of men's minds during this critical period, make this the time for drastic changes of the industrial and social systems of Canada," Justice Mathers told his audience. Before hearing any evidence at all, Mathers was serving notice that his Commission wanted to be part of the solution, not part of the problem.

The Commission was the public face of the Unionist government's response to the wave of unrest sweeping the country. At the same time as White was secretly asking for naval support, and the military and police forces were dispatching their undercover agents to spy on and harass the Reds, the Borden cabinet wanted to show that it was at least considering the demands for progressive reform coming from many quarters of society. It also wanted to assess how much of the present discontent was based on legitimate grievances and how much on the infamous "outside agitators" that employers loved to blame. As a result, not many days after the Western Labor Conference in Calgary, Ottawa announced the creation of the Mathers Commission, consisting of the Chief Justice and six other commissioners: three business representatives and three from the world of labour, including Tom Moore, president of the national Trades and Labor Congess.

Many activists dismissed the commission as a ploy to camouflage the government's actual disinterest in reform. After it was all
over, John Bruce, one of the labour representatives on the Commission, said it was "one of the bitterest lessons that ever I learned
about political chicanery."[37] But this was probably unfair. Government ministers certainly wanted to defuse the powder keg, but they
hoped that the Commission might actually do some good, first of
all by identifying the extent of the discontent and second by providing some ideas that would help map out a moderate middle ground
between left and right. Or, in the words of Chairman Mathers,
the commission wanted to find ways "for establishing permanent
improvements in the relations between employers and employees."
Obviously the government hoped that organized labour would buy
into the moderate option, but this is not the same thing as calling
the Commission a cynical ploy designed to drown significant reform in an ocean of talk.

As they set about their business, commissioners could be in no
doubt as to the state of mind of Canadian workers. On the second
day of hearings in Victoria, E.S. Woodward, a member of the Victoria Trades and Labor Council, served notice that "no government
has ever impressed the workers, as a class, with more distrust than
the present Government that is sitting at Ottawa."[38] This defiant
tone of opposition was typical of what commissioners would hear
over the subsequent seven weeks of testimony as they made their
way by train across the country. "I advocate government ownership
of everything," declared machinist Frederick Eldridge in Sudbury,
to loud applause from his audience. "I am a Bolshevist," labour organizer Clifford Dane announced at the Halifax hearing, "and I
will warn these two governments that trouble is coming and the
men will have what belongs to them."[39]

In all, commissioners heard from 486 witnesses in twenty-eight cities from Vancouver Island to Cape Breton. Of course, not every witness was a socialist firebrand. Some were business owners who indulged in the customary Red scaremongering. In Vancouver, for example, N.G. Neill, manager of the British Columbia Employers' Association, warned that the Bolsheviks in the city were being allowed to "undermine our whole system" and warned the commission that "we have to take some steps to stop this intrigue." Neill was supported by J.J. Coughlan, a shipyard manager, who blamed socialist labour leaders for all the unrest.[40]

Labour representatives often agreed that a crisis was impending. "Yes, my opinion is that we are on the top of a volcano that is not in any wise latent," warned Thomas Barnard of the New Westminster Trades and Labour Council. But they rejected the notion that a conspiracy of extremists led the unrest. Instead they blamed worker discontent on more prosaic causes: low wages, long working hours, the high cost of living, and lack of security. Vancouver shipwright J.W. Wilkinson put it passionately: "They [the workers] just feel that they are like a piece of merchandise, and that their chances of life are a gamble consisting in the possibility of someone coming along tomorrow to buy them for a day or hire their labour just for a little while, having no personal interest in them whatever more than if they were a piece of wood or a piece of brick."[41] In Calgary, the commissioners heard from William Irvine, a thirty-four-year-old Unitarian minister whose church had removed him from the pulpit for his anti-war opinions. "I think what the working men generally want today is truly democratic control of industry," he told them. "Some people talk of evolution and some of revolution. In Calgary evolution means doing nothing and revolution means doing something." He reassured the panel that he was not proposing violence but rather "a complete fundamental change in the way we live and do business."[42] (Another of the witnesses appearing in Calgary was the RNWMP secret agent Frank Zaneth, using his undercover identity of Harry Blask. Zaneth/Blask attended in his capacity as secretary to union leader George Sangster. The commissioners would have had no idea they were playing host to a police spy.)

Commissioners seemed keen on the idea of industrial councils, known in Great Britain as Whitley Councils after the politician who had conceived of them. These were committees that brought together workers and employers in formal sessions to discuss working conditions and other issues. Some witnesses agreed the idea was worth exploring, but most thought councils were a non-issue. "I do not recognize your authority to interfere with the management of the plant at all," declared a defiant Blythe Rogers, president of BC Sugar Refineries. While at the other end of the spectrum, "Why should labour confer with capital?" asked Socialist Party of Canada member Charles Lester. "It is an insult for it to do so. [...] We are not going to compromise with the master class at all; not at all; we are going to fight this thing out to a finish; we are going to use our political power to get hold of the reins of government and introduce what measures we think fit, and we shall not show the master class the slightest consideration whatever."[43] Lester's language was extreme, but his rejection of councils was typical of the majority of labour representatives meeting with the Commission. In Regina, Saskatchewan, J. Sanbrook, a bricklayer, opposed the idea of councils because they gave an advisory, not a controlling, role to labour. The Commission was operating on the assumption that cooperation was a good thing, he said. Not so. There was a class war going on and cooperation was simply a way "to make a more patient and contented work animal out of a live human being so that the war fattened profiteers may continue their period of prosperity and profit-making."[44]

The Commission reached Winnipeg on May 10. Most of the city's prominent labour leaders refused to come to City Hall where commissioners were hearing witnesses. One exception was William Ivens, editor of the *Western Labor News* and founder of the Labor Church (an organization that business leader A.J. Andrews later called "a camouflage for the preaching of sedition and for fanning the flames of unrest"). Like William Irvine in Calgary, Ivens was a former Methodist preacher who had been fired by his own church because he refused to tone down his anti-war rhetoric. Three months before the Royal Commission arrived in the city, he had warned employers in an editorial in the *Labor News*: "Your system will fall down about your ears with a suddenness and thoroughness that will surprise you. Such was the process in Russia [...] and no man or set of men can stem the tide."[45] Ivens only attended the Commission's hearing so that he could explain why his comrades were not there. Simply put, the inquiry had been appointed by a federal government "which we feel is entirely hostile to labour," he said. As such, labour expected absolutely nothing from its deliberations. One of the great orators of the labour movement, Ivens finished his presentation by mocking the call from management for increased productivity and greater thrift: "Now, if I understand greater thrift, it means that the workers shall wear their overalls just a little bit longer, that they carry just a little bit less in their dinner pails, that their homes which today are not kept warm enough shall be kept one or two degrees colder."[46] (Meanwhile, as Ivens spoke, a boisterous crowd of veterans and their supporters were meeting around the corner from City Hall in Market Square to call on the provincial government either to deport aliens or resign from office.)

It is indicative of the speed with which events were unfolding in the country that the Winnipeg General Strike began just three days after the commissioners left the city. On the one hand, the strike threatened to make their proceedings redundant. The time for talk was over, thought the more alarmist observers; the revolution had already begun. On the other hand, the troubles in Winnipeg added urgency to the commissioners' desire to hear for themselves what was disturbing labour peace across the country and to propose some solutions.

Once they had finished their hearings—the last was in Ottawa on June 13—the commissioners lost no time in preparing their report. It appeared in July and suggested that they had been paying attention to the labour representatives they had heard. The report rejected the proposition that the "labour revolt" was led by a group of fanatical agitators. Instead it suggested that the causes of unrest were far less sinister: the cost of living, long hours of work, unemployment, poor housing, and the unequal status of worker and employer.[4/] In other words, in the majority opinion of the Commission, bread-and-butter issues were driving the discontent, not world revolution. As a response the report recommended a series of progressive reforms, including a minimum wage for women, girls, and the unskilled, an eight-hour workday, collective bargaining rights, welfare measures for the unemployed, the sick, and the elderly, and the creation of something like the Whitley Councils. As things turned out, the Mathers Report, like so many Royal Commission reports before and since, was fated to gather dust on the back shelf of the Parliamentary Library. But for its time, it was an unexpectedly progressive document.

Given the divided nature of the country, it is not surprising that the Commission's majority report was accompanied by a minority opinion submitted by two of the three business representatives on the panel: Richard Smeaton White, publisher of the Montreal *Gazette*, whom Borden had named to the Senate in 1917, and Frank Pauzé, a Montreal lumberman. These two dissenters argued in their brief that unions had been captured by a radical minority of workers, unemployment was an overrated problem, and social welfare measures were a drain on the federal budget and on personal initiative. These ideas found support with the captains of industry who attended the National Industrial Conference that was convened in Ottawa in mid-September to consider issues raised by the Royal Commission. By this time the summer's wave of general strikes was over, apparently put down by a resolute government, and the Red Scare was ebbing. Perhaps that was why the conference amounted to very little. About 200 representatives from labour, business, the churches, and the public met in the Senate Chamber on Parliament Hill where they agreed to disagree on most matters that arose during the subsequent five days. When it began, the Toronto *Globe* hoped the Conference would usher in "an era of good-will and co-operation" between capital and labour. But in the end, both sides were divided on key issues such as the eight-hour day, industrial councils, and collective bargaining.[48] Like the *Globe*, the Borden government had had high hopes for the conference; instead, delegates had to satisfy themselves with vague commitments to mutual understanding and "friendly feeling."

+ + +

One thing that the Mathers Commission illustrated was the national extent of post-war labour unrest. The labour revolt was not, as historians used to argue, a western Canadian phenomenon. The

Calgary conference and the Winnipeg strike may have made it seem that way, but the unrest was strongly expressed in other parts of the country as well. To take just one significant statistic, almost seventy percent of the strikes which occurred during 1919 were east of the Lakehead region of Ontario.[49]

The particular issues may have differed region to region, but from Cape Breton to Vancouver Island, workers were unhappy with the way things were. In the Maritime provinces, they felt the pinch of post-war inflation and worried about job security and working conditions—issues that were shared across the country. But they were also facing a dramatic loss of jobs, which added particular urgency to their protest. In the face of rising freight rates and a downturn in the demand for coal and steel, the Maritime economy stalled. The region was facing a crisis of de-industrialization as companies were bought up, and in many cases relocated out of the region, by central Canadian capitalists. For workers, this meant wage cuts and unemployment, and they fought back as best they could. In Quebec, conservative Catholic unions, which were pro-nationalist and anti-socialist, undercut the workers' militancy. Still, for all its reputed conservatism, the province witnessed a hundred strikes during the year involving thousands of workers. Benjamin Drolet, a labour journalist, warned that *"la classe ouvrière ne retournera plus aux conditions d'avant guerre: elle veut avoir son mot á dire dans la direction des industries"* (the working class will not return to pre-war conditions; it wants a say in the management of industry).[50] In Ontario, strike activity increased sevenfold between 1918 and 1919. Aside from workplace issues, workers were furious at the arrests of socialist activists under the terms of Ottawa's orders-in-council. An Independent Labour Party, founded in 1917, was attracting more than token support from voters.

In short, workers in eastern Canada were just as restive, and just as militant, as those in the West. The fact that the major events of the Scare period—the conference in Calgary, the protest meetings in Winnipeg, followed by the general strike in that city—took place in the West does not contradict the national scope of the protest. It was an aroused working population right across the country that challenged the power elite that spring.

FIGURE 16 The front page of the *Seattle Union Record* announced the beginning of the Seattle General Strike on Monday, February 13, 1919. The Red Scare was a continent-wide phenomenon. As in Winnipeg, authorities in Seattle interpreted the strike there as the beginning of a revolution.

CHAPTER FOUR

A Seething Time

"But what a seething time it is in the world!"
—*Senator George Foster, May 2, 1919*

In the spring of 1919, most Canadians would have agreed with Senator Foster that it was a seething time in the world. Headlines brought news from abroad of one crisis after another. In Great Britain, Members of Parliament from Ireland were refusing to take their seats in Westminster, instead declaring unilateral Irish independence. In Paris, a young anarchist stepped out from behind a public urinal and emptied his revolver into a passing limousine carrying the French president, Georges Clemenceau. (The president took a bullet in the back but returned to work almost immediately.) Russia was convulsed by civil war. Germany was a bloodbath, the streets of Munich and Berlin swarming with homicidal paramilitaries intent on "cleansing" the country of Communists. In Hungary, Communist Béla Kun, fresh out of prison, led a newly established Soviet Republic, nationalizing all private property, establishing collective farms, and unleashing a reign of terror against his op-ponents. "Bolshevism is gaining ground everywhere," despaired the American diplomat Edward House. "Hungary has just succumbed. We are sitting upon an open powder magazine ..."[1] The president of Portugal was murdered. In the city of Amritsar in India, British troops opened fire on a crowd of unarmed people, slaughtering sev-eral hundred men, women, and children. Everywhere assassination and insurrection was in the news.

What had happened to the brave new world the war had been fought to create? A brooding Senator Foster caught the mood of anxiety from his vantage point in Europe, where he was a member of the Canadian delegation to the peace talks at Versailles. "What is brewing, what will result?" he wrote in his diary. "Certainly the foundations of things are being uprooted in a thousand ways—what will be laid down to take their place?"[2]

The Red Scare in Canada took place in this context of world-wide upheaval. A look at the front page of a major Canadian daily newspaper on almost any day would have revealed headlines trum-peting riots in Germany and war in Russia. Bolshevik terrorists were blamed for unrest in half a dozen different countries. The Scare in Canada would never have reached the intensity that it did had it not been part of the wider panic about the state of the world. During the post-war election campaign in Britain, Liberal leader David Lloyd George had said: "At this moment the air of Europe is quivering with revolution. Two-thirds of Europe has been swept by its devastating deluge; the situation is full of perilous possibilities ..."[3] As they read their papers and heard the news from south of the border and abroad, Canadians naturally believed that similar pos-sibilities were at work in their own country.

FIGURE 17 Senator George Foster (L) leans on his umbrella as he pays a visit to the Front in July 1916. Foster, a former professor of classics, had a long political career starting with a position in one of John A. Macdonald's cabinets. In the Borden government, he was minister of trade and commerce and accompanied the Prime Minister to Europe as a member of Canada's peace delegation. His diary offers insight into the events of 1918–19. *Photo: National Archives of Canada, PA-000217*

+ + +

The most important background event to the Red Scare was the Bolshevik Revolution in Russia. The upheaval of October 1917 unnerved the ruling elites and inspired working people, no less in Canada than in the rest of the world. "It was like a bolt out of the blue, like a blinding light," said Socialist Party member Malcolm Bruce. "There was a great uplift amongst the working class."[4] In his memoirs, the Canadian Methodist minister A.E. Smith recalled the effect of the revolution on his own outlook: "I felt the impact of this mighty movement. I reached out to grasp it. I tried to bring some of its lessons to my people. I tried to help them to see the inspiring vision of the future of the world." For Smith, who later joined the Communist Party, and people like him, people who "felt the electric currents that were striking through society," what had happened in Russia gave hope that tired governments everywhere might be relegated to the scrap heap of history and be replaced by dynamic, progressive regimes that would transform humanity for the better.[5]

At the other end of the political spectrum, the revolution was a warning light, not a beacon of hope. With its fundamental antagonism to private property and its commitment to worldwide agitprop, Bolshevism struck terror into the defenders of the established order. No other regime had the same potential to destroy the present system. Winston Churchill, then Britain's secretary of state for war, opposed Lenin and his comrades with these words: "Of all the tyrannies in history, the Bolshevik tyranny is the worst, the most destructive, the most degrading."[6]

As representatives of the Allies gathered for the opening of peace talks at Versailles in mid-January 1919, the situation within Russia was completely unpredictable and almost impossible to ascertain. Civil war had broken out between the Soviet government and several White Army factions that claimed to speak for the "real" Russia. The country was in chaos; at one point, nineteen different governments claimed authority over bits and pieces of Siberia alone. With the benefit of hindsight, we know that the Bolsheviks would win the war and consolidate their regime, but it would be a long struggle, and at the beginning of 1919 it seemed more probable that the old regime would be able to take back power from Lenin's government, which teetered on the verge of collapse. As

White armies closed in on Moscow from the south and the east, counter-revolutionary forces laid claim to a far greater share of the Russian land mass than the Bolsheviks. These White armies also had the support of several foreign governments, including Canada, which sent troops of their own to assist in the conflict.

The Allies briefly believed that they had found their anti-Bolshevik standard bearer in a forty-six-year-old White Russian naval commander named Aleksandr Kolchak. During the war, Kolchak had commanded Russia's Black Sea fleet. When the Bolsheviks came to power, he theatrically flung his sword into the sea and resigned his commission. He was in Japan on his way home from a visit to the United States in 1918 when he learned that Lenin was making peace with Germany. As a military officer, he was appalled and volunteered his services to the British, who hoped the Admiral might forge an effective anti-Bolshevik force from the ragtag of freelance armies active in eastern Siberia.

As Kolchak headed west on the train across Siberia toward the Urals, he arrived at the city of Omsk just as the political situation there reached a crisis point. An attempted alliance of anti-Bolshevik socialists and hard-line conservatives had shattered, leaving its Provisional All-Russian Government in disarray. Kolchak agreed to step in and take command as the grandiosely titled Supreme Ruler. Suddenly this little-known naval officer with no experience in government found himself, nominally at least, dictator of a huge chunk of Russia.

He turned out to be a disaster. In the military, Kolchak was an effective leader; in the civilian world, he proved aloof and vacillating. Awkward in public, in private he was moody and petulant, liable to explode into fits of rage in crisis situations. He had no taste for political intrigue and, as a result, lost control of his own government to the most ruthless and corrupt of his subordinates. Members of his general staff lined their own pockets with graft and profits from the black market while soldiers went into battle without boots or guns that could shoot straight. Kolchak allowed a purge of left-wing elements that saw hundreds of former allies rounded up and executed without trial. Economically his territory was a mess. Thirty kinds of currency were in circulation; some people were even using the labels off cigarette packs. Inflation was crippling. With railway service disrupted, goods were scarce, and the government had to requisition what it needed at the point of a gun. Kolchak had inherited much of this chaos, but he did nothing to correct it.

Meanwhile the Supreme Ruler prepared a grand military offensive that he hoped would carry him westward all the way to Moscow. As 1919 began, his armies enjoyed enough success to inspire confidence in the outside world. Had the Allies found the anti-Bolshevik champion who would return Russia to the ranks of the "civilized" nations? Winston Churchill, who firmly believed so, pressed his Cabinet colleagues to recognize Kolchak's regime as the legitimate government, and the British began to set the wheels in motion. They pressed Anton Denikin, the only other White commander with pretensions to leadership, to accept Kolchak as Supreme Ruler. Much as they cheered on Kolchak from the sidelines, however, the Allies would not agree to commit more troops to help him. Instead they began to pull their soldiers out. Even with their hatred of Bolshevism, the cost of a foreign adventure so soon after the war was too high. And without more foreign support, Kolchak's fortunes turned. By June the Red Army, skilfully marshalled by Leon Trotsky, had regained the initiative, driving the White Army back eastward. Kolchak's government collapsed, and the Admiral fled, the Bolsheviks chasing close behind. They caught up with him at Irkutsk in the far reaches of Siberia. After a quick trial, his guards executed him one morning before dawn and stuffed his body through a hole in the ice of a nearby river, one more casualty in a civil war that saw millions die.

The Great War had brought terrible suffering to Russia. When it began, the country had a population of 180 million people; when Lenin and the Bolsheviks brought it to an end early in 1918 by making peace with the Germans, about ten million of these people were dead, maimed, sick, or homeless. This was more casualties than in all the other Allied nations combined. Russia was so prostrate that it could not have fought on if it had wanted to. Whether they knew it or not, the Allies' desire for the Russians to maintain the Eastern Front was tantamount to asking them to submit to their own destruction.

And, of course, the suffering did not end with the end of the world war. The civil war flared up to claim its share of victims. Estimates of the military dead alone in this conflict range from 800,000 to more than a million. One-half of these deaths resulted from disease, not bullets. Typhus and typhoid were the greatest killers, claiming almost 180,000 soldiers on both sides. Then there were the civilian deaths, from these same diseases, plus cholera, influenza, famine, and exposure. During the years 1917 to 1922, as many Russians died as there were people living in Canada at the time.

This was the afflicted country that Canada helped to invade at the end of 1918. And this was why so many Canadian workers and activists who identified with the spirit of the Russian revolution objected so strenuously to their troops being a part of that invasion force.

+ + +

On Saturday, January 18, 1919, Canadian newspapers carried news of the sudden deaths in Berlin of the German revolutionaries Rosa Luxemburg and Karl Liebknecht. "No details have as yet been received," reported the Toronto *Globe* on its front page, "but the statement is made that fighting has broken out again, and that troops are being poured into the city to quell the revolt."[7] Luxemburg and Liebknecht were well-known names in Canada, as they were around the world. Protest meetings across the country customarily began or ended with expressions of support for the two German radicals and anyone with any interest in European affairs had been following their exploits for months.

Germany had been shattered by the war. Close to one-fifth of its male population was killed or wounded, the latter often horribly. Food was rationed; heating fuel was in short supply. Unemployment rose dramatically as munitions plants shut down. Civilians were disillusioned with the militaristic regime that had brought defeat and humiliation. Industrial workers looked to radical solutions to fix the system. Millions of demobilized soldiers, many of them still armed, returned to communities that had little to offer them. Social order dissolved into chaos as gangs of freelance militia took to the streets.

The revolution began in the port city of Kiel. Two weeks before the armistice ended the war, sailors refused to obey orders to take their ships to sea to engage the British in a final battle. The sailors did not wish to become sacrificial lambs to the martial honour of their commanders. Instead they mutinied and, with the help of local soldiers and workers, took over the town. From Kiel, the revolt spread. On November 9, the Kaiser abdicated and a coalition of

FIGURE 18 Newspaper readers in Canada followed the events of the German Revolution, fearing that the same thing was happening here at home. Revolutionaries like Rosa Luxemburg (above) and her lover Karl Liebknecht were household names. *Photo: Deutsches Historiches Museum, Berlin, F59/1341*

Social Democrats took control of the new government. But discontent continued to bubble in the form of strikes, demonstrations, and the formation of grassroots councils demanding food, jobs, higher pay, and the creation of a socialist state. Most dangerously, groups of armed paramilitaries and assassins, the *Freikorps*, received carte blanche to put down civil disturbances with force. The Social Democrats sought democracy and stability, but they feared a Bolshevik revolution, so they aligned themselves with the right and endorsed the violence.

Karl Liebknecht and Rosa Luxemburg had come to prominence during the war as founders of the far-left Spartacus Union, named for the Roman gladiator who had led a slave rebellion. The Spartacists preached anti-militarism and revolution. Although small in number, they put enough of a fright into the Kaiser's regime that in 1916 both Luxemburg and Liebknecht were jailed, immediately becoming left-wing martyrs. When Liebknecht was released at the end of the war, a huge parade of workers pulled him through the streets of Berlin in a carriage filled with flowers. Late in that year, the pair took a leading role in the formation of the German Communist Party. Luxemburg, also released from jail, took over as editor of the Spartacist newspaper while Liebknecht negotiated tactics with the other political factions. In the first week of January in Berlin, left-wing leaders, spurred on by a huge demonstration of popular unrest, initiated a general strike and declared a coup. For a few days, the German government wavered; an optimistic Vladimir Lenin sent his congratulations to the revolution's leaders. But then the moment passed. While the revolutionary committee dithered, the government rallied its supporters and unleashed the *Freikorps*. After vicious street fighting, the paramilitaries managed to take control of most of the insurgents' strongholds, and the rebellion was defeated.

Police tracked down and arrested the leaders of the insurrection. On January 15, a squad of soldiers found Liebknecht and Luxemburg hiding together in a city apartment. The pair were held in custody, beaten senseless, then taken away separately and shot in cold blood. Liebknecht was buried in an anonymous grave; Luxemburg's assassins dumped her body in a canal where it was not found for several months.

Shortly after the Berlin uprising, Germans went to the polls to elect a new parliament that would draw up a blueprint for the country's future. The Social Democratic coalition retained power, and a convention set about the business of making a liberal constitution. When it was proclaimed in August, it would usher in the Weimar Republic, the basis of Germany's government for the next fourteen years. But in the meantime the violence in the streets continued. In Munich and other cities, the paramilitaries brutally smashed attempts to establish Soviet-style governments, culminating in a vicious right-wing reign of terror. General strikes, assassinations, violent street fighting, summary execution: anyone watching events in post-war Germany would have been appalled at the anarchy unleashed by the warring political factions. As much as the Russian revolution, the situation in Germany haunted foreign observers who were worried about the potential for revolutionary insurgency in their own countries.

+ + +

It was not just in war-ravaged central and eastern Europe that insurrectionists beat on the doors of the old regimes. Canadians might have shrugged off these unsettling events as just to be expected in countries that were so desolated by the war. Great Britain, however, the Mother Country, was a different matter entirely, and there too the forces of disorder seemed to be loose in the streets. At the end of January 1919, in scenes that were prescient of things to come in Canada, a general strike in support of a shorter work week turned the streets of Glasgow into a bloodbath. Truncheon-wielding police waded into a crowd of demonstrators who responded with showers of bricks and bottles; trolley cars were tipped over; the mayor read the Riot Act, then let loose a troop of officers on horseback into the crowd. Ten thousand soldiers equipped with machine guns, mortars, and tanks occupied the city. The press accused strike leaders of being Bolsheviks who aimed to establish a Soviet-style government. The whole thing could have been a dress rehearsal for Winnipeg. Meanwhile, in London the subway motormen, railway engineers, and restaurant employees went on strike, and the electrical workers threatened to turn off the lights. On February 8, Prime Minister David Lloyd George hurried home from the peace conference to deal with the deteriorating situation on the homefront.

For all the industrial unrest that was plaguing Britain, Lloyd George's greatest challenge was actually across the Irish Sea. He had been returned to power in a general election the previous December as head of a coalition government of Liberals and Conservatives. But in Ireland, where less than three years earlier an uprising in Dublin had been put down ruthlessly by British soldiers, seventy-three of the 105 seats were won by candidates from the republican Sinn Féin party, despite the fact that almost half of them, including their leader Éamon de Valera, were in jail for sedition. In January, these MPs refused to take their seats in

Parliament, instead convening an independent Irish assembly, the Dáil Éireann. Sinn Féin hoped to convince the peace conference at Versailles to endorse an independent Irish Republic, but their hopes were dashed. Delegates from the Allied countries wanted no part of what they preferred to think were internal British politics, and they ignored the Irish. Meanwhile, Lloyd George's government responded with military repression, and the Irish countryside degenerated into low-grade civil war. The militant wing of the republican movement, led by Michael Collins, maintained a general state of unrest with a campaign of robbery and assassination, while the intransigent British poured troops into the country to conduct their own campaign of bloody reprisals. (The violence continued for three years until finally, in 1922, the British acknowledged an independent Irish Free State, now the Republic of Ireland.)

But dramatic as they were, the events unfolding in Great Britain were overshadowed for most Canadians by the alarming situation right next door in the United States, just south of the border.

The spark that ignited the American version of the Red Scare was the Seattle General Strike.[8] In January 1919, about 35,000 shipyard workers in the Pacific port, just a few hours south of Vancouver, walked off the job. The strike won support from other unions in the city, and one by one they voted in favour of a sympathy strike, which began on February 6. It was the first general strike in US history, and employers and the city government had no trouble convincing themselves that it meant Red revolution. They were encouraged in their paranoia by an article by socialist journalist Anna Louise Strong. Titled "No One Knows Where," Strong's sensational piece predicted that the various public services in the city would be taken over by labour. "And that is why we say that we are starting on a road that leads—NO ONE KNOWS WHERE!" she concluded.

As Seattle ground to a halt with several tens of thousands of workers out on strike, federal troops rushed in to maintain the peace. Mayor Ole Hanson, who turned out to be a demagogue waiting for a cause, threatened to "shoot on sight anyone causing disorder." According to the mayor, the strike was a "sympathetic revolution" led by "traitors and anarchists," and he warned that "death will be their portion if they start anything. Law and order are supreme in our city." He told strikers to end the walkout "or else."

With the press and public backing the mayor's bellicose posturing, the resolve of the unions began to crumble, and on February 11 the strike ended. In its aftermath, twenty-seven people, mainly members of the IWW, were charged with sedition. When the first to go to trial was acquitted, charges against the others were dropped. There was no violence during the strike, and never any evidence found afterward that its leaders planned to establish a Seattle Soviet, but that did not stop Hanson from riding a wave of anti-Red anxiety to national prominence. Posing as the man who stopped a Bolshevik revolution in its tracks, he resigned the mayoralty and embarked on a cross-country speaking tour to fan the flames of the Red Scare. He published a book, *Americanism Versus Bolshevism*, and for a while entertained visions of winning the Republican nomination for president in 1920. But long before then the air went out of his campaign, and Hanson retired to obscurity in California.

In Canada, anti-Red hardliners read their own lessons into the events in Seattle. According to *Saturday Night* magazine, the general strike was an attempt to establish a "Soviet Government" led by a few conspirators who had filled the minds of the workers with false hopes and ludicrous ideas. It praised authorities for putting on a show of force to intimidate strikers into backing down. "The incident is a lesson for every city on this continent," said *Saturday Night*. "Prompt action to assert government authority is absolutely necessary; redress of grievances, if they exist, can come later. Toleration of Bolshevism, even in its most incipient stages, bears incalculable consequences."[9]

In the United States, fears generated by events in Seattle intensified at the end of April when a parcel bomb delivered to the home of a former Georgia senator exploded, seriously injuring the family maid. A similar parcel arrived at Mayor Hanson's office, but the homemade bomb inside was detected and disarmed. The post office intercepted thirty-four more parcel bombs over the next couple of days, addressed to prominent government officials and industrialists. The people behind the plot were never identified—it now seems probable that they were a group of Italian anarchists—but there was little doubt in the public mind that a Red conspiracy was targeting the country's leadership. On May 1, labour's annual day of solidarity, demonstrations in several major cities erupted into violent confrontations between police and marchers. These clashes were "dress rehearsals" for revolution, claimed many of the nation's newspapers. Then, on June 2, more bombs exploded at selected homes and offices in eight different cities. In Washington, DC, one of the bombers accidentally blew himself up on the front steps of Attorney General A. Mitchell Palmer's home. Once again the plotters were never identified; once again it was widely assumed that they were anarchists and Bolshevists. None of this was lost on Canadian authorities as they contemplated the events that were unfolding in the streets of Winnipeg that spring.

American politicians responded to the public unease by

compounding it. In February and March, a subcommittee of the US Senate, chaired by Senator Lee Overman, held a series of hearings into Bolshevik propaganda. The committee had been created during the war to investigate links between German propaganda and American brewing interests, but with the war at an end it was happy to ride off in a new direction. In January, a New York lawyer named Archibald Stevenson appeared before the committee. Like Charles Cahan in Canada, Stevenson, who had links to the intelligence community, had conducted an investigation into the Bolshevik threat in the United States. He reported to the committee that Bolshevism represented a grave threat to the country and he presented a list of sixty-two prominent Americans whom he considered to be dangerous radicals, including the pioneering social worker Jane Addams, the editor of the *Nation* magazine and head of the national civil liberties association Oswald Villard, and various liberal university professors. It was Stevenson's sensational testimony that convinced the Senate to extend the mandate of the Overman inquiry.

At the same time, New York State initiated its own legislative inquiry, chaired by state Senator Clayton Lusk and assisted by Stevenson, who was fast becoming the number one "Red hunter" in the US. Searching for evidence, the Lusk Committee authorized police raids on the Soviet Bureau in New York City, the supposed clearing house for the coming American revolution, and on various left-wing organizations such as the IWW and the Rand School of Social Science. The committee became the source of many of the most outlandish scare stories about supposed Red plots, and Senator Lusk passed information across the border to Colonel J.B. Maclean for use in his magazine and to the Dominion Police.

Much of the raw material for Lusk's witch hunt came from raids by agents of the Bureau of Investigation, later the Federal Bureau of Investigation (FBI), an agency of the department of justice. The BI had been created in 1909 mainly to investigate financial frauds. During the war its agents had hounded the IWW, and by early 1919 they were concentrating on the Red threat. Following the parcel bombs and the charges emanating from the two legislative committees, the justice department created a General Intelligence Division, led by a twenty-five-year-old lawyer named J. Edgar Hoover. Just as the Red Scare in Canada revitalized the fortunes of the Mounted Police and led to the creation of the modern RCMP, so in the US the FBI and Hoover, its future leader, built their reputations on keeping America safe from the Reds. Under Hoover's leadership, the division carried out a carefully planned campaign against radical activists that culminated late in 1919 with the infamous Palmer Raids, named for the Attorney General who authorized them. These were a series of police raids on political groups and union offices which netted hundreds of tons of documents, thousands of suspects, and very few convictions. They mirrored, on a far grander scale, the police raids on Canadian activists in the fall of 1918 under the authority of the federal orders-in-council.

The Palmer Raids marked the climax of the American Red Scare. The public had had enough of the fear-mongering and the finger-pointing. The security agencies kept up their undercover work, but the appetite for "Bolshie-bashing" seemed to have been appeased. Although the American Red Scare was more violent and more repressive, many parallels can be drawn between it and the Scare in Canada.[10] The role of Charles Cahan in sounding the alarm about the extent of the Red conspiracy was analogous to the role played by New York attorney Stepenson. In both countries, enforcement agencies—the nascent RCMP and FBI—used the Scare as an opportunity to make a case for their own importance. In both countries, normal expressions of political opinion were criminalized and police forces used newly minted powers to spy on, muzzle, and arrest their own citizens. With few exceptions, the press in both countries played the part of cheerleaders, stoking the hysteria by exaggerating the threat. Both countries experienced dramatic general strikes in large industrial cities that the authorities chose to interpret as political insurrections, and which had to be put down with force.

Many Canadians at the time recognized these parallels. They felt themselves to be experiencing the same Bolshevik-inspired insurrectionary threat as the Americans. Without the events in the US, middle-class Canadians might have been more skeptical of any attempts to arouse fears about the Reds. Instead, the letter bombs, street riots, and police raids south of the border seemed to confirm the existence of a continent-wide conspiracy that threatened their way of life.

+ + +

It was more than just political systems that were shattered by the catastrophe of World War I. Disillusion and uncertainty spread into every walk of life, including the arts—perhaps especially the arts. This mood had been present before the war, represented most famously by the 1913 premier of *The Rite of Spring*. With music by the Russian composer Igor Stravinsky and choreographed by the sensational young dancer Vaslav Nijinsky, the ballet provoked a riot at its Paris opening, scandalizing the audience with the discordancies of the music and the intentional awkwardness of the dancing. Similarly in the visual arts, Pablo Picasso and Georges Braque had discovered a whole new visual language with the invention of cubism. And in Italy, the poet and controversialist Filippo Tommaso Marinetti, founder of the Futurist movement, declared that "art, in fact, can be nothing but violence, cruelty, and injustice."[11]

The war deepened this conviction that the old truths no longer had any meaning. The Canadian artist Fred Varley was with the troops during the final, brutal, One Hundred Days of the campaign in western Europe. "You in Canada ... cannot realize at all what war is like," he wrote to his wife. "You must see it and live it. You must see the barren deserts war has made of once fertile country ... see the turned-up graves, see the dead on the field, freakishly mutilated—headless, legless, stomachless, a perfect body and a passive face and a broken empty skull—see your own countrymen, unidentified, thrown into a cart, their coats over them, boys digging a grave in a land of yellow slimy mud and green pools of water under a weeping sky."[12] The painting Varley made of this experience appeared at a gallery exhibition in London in January 1919. Titled "For What?", it is a stark depiction of a cartload of corpses at a makeshift graveyard in a blasted landscape in France. The sombre title hints at the pointlessness of war and the sense that, in its aftermath, values of all kinds were in question.

When he returned to Canada, Fred Varley became one of the founding members of the Group of Seven. This group of painters, which held its first exhibition in Toronto in May 1920, defined Canadian modernism in the arts. Taking their inspiration from the landscape of northern Ontario, they developed a new way of seeing the land—raw, wild, virile, empty of people, but full of vitality. Perhaps it was the disillusionment of war that led these painters to seek solace in the healing power of nature. "We are endeavouring to knock out of us all the preconceived ideas," Varley explained to his

FIGURE 19 "For What?" a war painting by Frederick Varley, later a member of the Group of Seven, seemed to express the collapse of confidence in traditional values following World War I. *Source: CWM 19710261-0770, Beaverbrook Collection of War Art, © Canadian War Museum*

sister, "emptying ourselves of everything except that nature is here in all its greatness, and we are here to gather it and understand it ..."

New and disturbing as it was to some Canadians, the art of the Group of Seven was tame by comparison to the shock waves bouncing around the salons and cabarets of Europe. How might staid old Toronto have reacted, for example, to the kind of performance that occurred at Zurich's Saal sur Kaufleuten on the evening of April 9, 1919? [13] The show began calmly enough with a lecture on abstract art, followed by a solo dancer wearing an African mask and moving to the discordant music of Arnold Schoenberg. After a few poems, obscure but well-mannered, the evening got steadily more outrageous. Twenty people took to the stage and began reciting a *poème simultane*, a verse form in which several voices spoke lines at the same time—not necessarily the same lines, not necessarily in unison, not necessarily even in the same language. At this the audience began to shout insults and threats, but just as things threatened to get out of hand, the production halted for intermission.

For those who remained, the show continued in a calmer atmosphere after the break. That is, until the appearance of Dr Walter Serner. The French artist Hans Arp described the mysterious Dr Serner as "an adventurer, detective novel writer, sophisticated dancer, skin specialist and gentleman-burglar." For this particular performance he wore a black coat, striped trousers, a grey tie, and carried a headless tailor's dummy. Placing the dummy in the middle of the stage, Serner produced a bouquet of artificial flowers, which he offered to the dummy to smell, then placed at its feet. Then he sat on a chair with his back to the audience and began a lecture on anarchism. As Serner spoke, angry voices from the crowd berated him until finally several members of the audience charged the stage swinging broken pieces of furniture. They drove Serner from the building, smashed the dummy and the chair, and stamped the flowers underfoot. The evening seemed a shambles. But after twenty minutes order was restored and, astonishingly, the show resumed. Even Walter Serner was welcomed back to recite some poems and Tristan Tzara, the troupe's ringleader, read one of his baffling manifestoes: "We demand the right to piss in different colours! I am neither for nor against and I do not explain because I hate common sense."

This was Dada, a loose assemblage of painters, poets, and cabaret performers dedicated to creating confusion and mayhem. The history of Dada is approximate, fittingly so, for why should a movement that made art of non sequitur be intelligible itself? It is probably safe to say, however, that Dada was a reaction against the unspeakable horrors of the war. "While the guns rumbled in the distance," wrote Hans Arp, one of the original Dadaists, "we sang, painted, made collages and wrote poems with all our might. We were seeking an art based on fundamentals, to cure the madness of the age, and a new order of things that would restore the balance of heaven and hell." It was no accident that wartime Zurich became the home of this enterprise. Zurich was still the centre of the European storm. Because Switzerland was neutral in the conflict, it attracted a ragbag assortment of revolutionaries, pacifists, spies, arms dealers, draft evaders, artists, and intellectuals, all seeking a safe refuge to go on with their work. Lenin was there, waiting for the revolution to call him home. So was James Joyce, at work on *Ulysses*. And so were the Dadaists: Arp; Tzara; Hugo Ball and his girlfriend, cabaret singer Emmy Hennings; the painter and architect Marcel Janco; and Richard Huelsenbeck, a poet and medical student.

The group began staging their performances—committed to what Tzara called "the commotion of the new"—at the Cabaret Voltaire on Spiegelgasse Street. This might include Hugo Ball encased in a cardboard suit and wearing a pointed witch-doctor's hat, declaiming one of his sound poems: "gadji beri bimba/ glandridi lauli lonni cadori/ gadjama bim beri glassala ..." and so on. "I don't want words that other people have invented," he explained. Or Jennings singing in her thin, tuneless voice while Ball tinkled the piano. Or Tzara presenting a "static poem." Sometimes he placed words printed on large cards on a row of chairs and periodically came out onto the stage to rearrange them. Or he would cut up a newspaper article into individual words, place them in a bag, shake it, then extract a "poem" word by word. And no cabaret evening was complete without someone declaiming a manifesto of Dada non-principles, some of it comprehensible, much of it not. For example: "Ventilator of cold examples will serve as a cavalcade to the fragile snake and I never had the pleasure of seeing you my dear rigid the ear will emerge of its own accord from the envelope like all marine confections..." (This particular excerpt is from "Manifesto of mr aa the anti-philosopher" and ended with "Give yourself a poke in the nose and drop dead. Dada.")

The burlesque of the Cabaret Voltaire and other Dada spectacles might seem a quixotic response to what Ball called "the paralyzing background of events," but it was meant to be an emphatic gesture against the times. "Every word that is spoken and sung here says at least this one thing," he wrote, "that this humiliating age has not succeeded in winning our respect." Nothing was spared the withering sarcasm of the Dadas. As Berlin artist and sometime Dada sympathizer George Grosz put it: "We derided everything, respected nothing, spat upon everything: that was Dada." Turning away from reason, the Dadas embraced unreason—intuition, impulse, chance. "Logic is always wrong," declared Tzara. In their performances they substituted pure sound for words, they allowed accident to write their poems, they tried to free the unconscious to make its own connections. They did not look for applause or approval. Their purpose was to make their audiences uncomfortable, to get them confused or angry enough to burst free of their smug self-confidence.

The war was crucial to the Zurich Dadas. They were exiles, refugees from a conflict they abhorred and judges of an elite they held responsible. No one captured their intense alienation better than Hugo Ball, who stated: "They cannot persuade us to enjoy eating the rotten pie of human flesh that they present to us. They cannot force our quivering nostrils to admire the smell of corpses. They cannot expect us to confine the increasingly disastrous apathy and cold-heartedness with heroism. One day they will have to admit that we reacted very politely, even movingly. The most strident pamphlets did not manage to pour enough contempt and scorn on the universally prevalent hypocrisy."

The Dadas could not keep it up, of course. It was hard work keeping the bourgeoisie in a perpetual state of outrage, and before long they ran out of steam. The usual rivalries and contrary ambitions asserted themselves, and the Dadas split up. Some crossed over into Surrealism (what one critic called "house-broken Dada"), others dropped out of the art world altogether. By the early 1920s Dada was defunct.

+ + +

Dada stands out as emblematic of this confused, violent period of history in Europe and around the globe. In their strange performances and absurdist proclamations, they represent a world that had lost all sense of direction.

The Dadas acknowledged what many people were afraid to admit, that peace changed nothing. It did not bring justice or democracy, an end to imperialism or even an end to the fighting, not in many parts of the world anyway. In Germany, freelance armies ruthlessly suppressed a socialist revolution, and assassination became the accepted way to change governments. Russia, torn by civil war, was a huge graveyard. In Hungary, an attempt at Bolshevik rule ended in failure. In the Punjab, Indian nationalists seeking independence were slaughtered by British soldiers.

North America was spared the worst of the violence, but authorities there were panicky. As they watched what was happening abroad, they expected their own revolutionaries to rise up and overthrow the governments of the US and Canada. Strident voices called attention to the bankruptcy of familiar nostrums and proclaimed the dawn of a new era.

Even in Canada, it was a Dada kind of world.

FIGURE 20 Most Canadian newspapers portrayed the Russian Bolshevik as a scruffy maniac, a thief, and a mass murderer. Arthur Racey, cartoonist for the *Montreal Star,* was one of the most enthusiastic purveyors of this image. In this drawing from the *Star* dated February 27, 1919, a Bolshevik judge condemns a man to death for the "crime" of taking a bath. By entitling the cartoon, "If We Were Bolshevists," Racey warns that it could happen here. *Source: Trent University Archives, Arthur Racey fonds, 1899–1941, 442*

CHAPTER FIVE

The Image of the Bolshevik

"They announce a doctrine which says that you shall shoot down every man who wears a white collar ..."
—*W.F. Cockshutt, Member of Parliament, February 28, 1919*

The Bolshevik had many faces. There was the cartoon image of the Red—the wild-eyed radical with a bomb in one hand and a political tract in the other—but there were many others as well. In the popular imagination the Reds were usually foreigners; that is, they weren't "like us." They were irresponsible, cowardly, and lazy. They might be misguided dreamers, as the humorist Stephen Leacock argued, or they might be determined terrorists. Some were disrespectful of women, but others were women themselves, feminists who wanted to achieve a dangerous equality between the sexes. Some people even thought that Red ideas were so extreme they were a sign of mental illness. This chapter takes a look at the multiple images of the Bolshevik that evoked so much fear and suspicion among Canadians during the Red Scare.

+ + +

"It is becoming the habit in this country to designate every one a Bolshevist with whom we cannot agree," said wounded war hero and Liberal Member of Parliament Charles "Chubby" Power scolding some of his seatmates in the House of Commons on June 2, 1919.[1] Power was right. The definition of Bolshevism that emerged from all the Red Scare propaganda was infinitely elastic; it could be applied to almost anyone whose political views strayed from the straight and narrow. Some people believed that Bolshevism was essentially an economic doctrine proposing the abolition of the wage system and the transfer of the means of production from employers to workers. Others thought of it as a social doctrine promoting free love and the abolition of the family. To others it was nothing more than organized terrorism on a grand scale. For instance, the federal minister of public works, F.B. Carvell, defined a Bolshevik as "a wild-eyed anarchist looting a bank, shooting down all the Bourgeois or property owners in the country and carrying off their wives and children."[2] And Carvell was a Liberal.

Despite the imprecision, there were certain recurring elements in the image of the Bolshevik that inhabited the collective nightmares of Canadians in the years 1918 to 1919. For one thing, Bolsheviks were usually aliens, immigrants from one of the poorer nations of Europe: Germans, Italians, Finns, and Slavs of all sorts. "The country has been stripped of much of the good old Anglo-Saxon stock," explained Thomas Fraser in his *Maclean's* article of January 1919, "and its place has largely been taken by workmen of foreign extraction, many of them of enemy nationality. That is the root of the whole matter."[3] Even when it was admitted, as it had to be, that most of the radical leaders responsible for widespread labour unrest were from Great Britain, and therefore very much of "Anglo-Saxon stock," it was argued that this leadership only succeeded in spreading its dangerous ideas by exploiting the large immigrant population. It was not solid Canadian working men and women who fell into step behind the radicals, but ignorant "bohunks" and other undesirables from the teeming slums of Europe.

Much of the resentment expressed against Canada's Reds stemmed from the strong animosity against those who were seen as shirkers of their military duty. Supporters of the war despised and ridiculed any able-bodied man who had not gone to fight, and for the most part the labour radicals fit into this category. From their own point of view, radical pacifists had refused to fight the boss's war. But most members of the public did not see it that way. The shirkers were cowards who had remained in the safety of home while others had paid the ultimate price to defend western civilization. As Jonathan Vance points out in his book, *Death So Noble*, the call to service was a test of character, and those who did not answer, or who answered no, had none.[4] Communities took enormous pride in their young men who had answered the call in the affirmative, and took a correspondingly dim view of young men who did not. Part of the image of the Bolshevik, therefore, was that he was a spineless snake in the grass, too cowardly to fight for his country, a man who had done nothing to protect Canada at its moment of peril. Why now, in the post-war world, should they be allowed to have a say in its future development? Much of the vehemence with which the Reds were treated had to do with this sense that they had betrayed Canada's men and women in uniform. To accept that the Reds might have something to contribute to post-war reconstruction was somehow to endorse this betrayal.

Often, Bolsheviks and Germans were confused or conflated in

the public mind. Because they had double-crossed their allies by withdrawing from the war, Russian Bolsheviks were seen as no different than the "Hun." The Allies had defeated Germany on the battlefield, but now it was suspected that German agents were working clandestinely in foreign countries to foment revolution. In some people's minds, the war against the Reds was an extension of the war against Germany. John Newton, vice-president of the Winnipeg branch of the Great War Veterans Association, explained how it worked. The conspirators' plan, he wrote in a newspaper article, was to stir up trouble among labour groups, ignite a series of strikes to disrupt the economy, raise the cost of living, and set social class against social class, all of which would eventually result in civil war and the creation of a Soviet-style government in Canada. The Reds, he said, were "only the cat's-paw of the still worse gang behind the scenes who are carrying out the orders of their overlord, the Hun."[5]

Bolshevism was considered to be an alien philosophy, profoundly un-Canadian, as anyone would know who truly understood the country. "It is time," declared another Member of Parliament, W.F. Cockshutt, "that the laws of Canada should be enforced against those who come over from the old lands, have found sanctuary here and do not appreciate it any more than to preach doctrines so subversive of all law, order and decency as the Bolsheviki have done in Russia, and as they will do here if permitted. In a free country like Canada no such doctrines as those are justified."[6]

What were these alien doctrines which the Reds allegedly would impose on Canada if their revolutionary plans were successful? Some of them were laid out in an editorial in the Toronto *Globe* in April 1919, titled "Bolshevism in Canada." First of all, said the *Globe*, all private property would be seized and given to the state. ("The home, the very foundation of civilization, is swept away

...") Next, all civil liberties, all courts, all laws would be abolished. "Force takes the place of justice." And third, manual workers would take over the government of the country; everyone else would be excluded from positions of power. "The time comes for the taking of defensive measures of a drastic sort against those who would reproduce in Canada the conditions now existing in Russia," warned the *Globe*.[7]

What most alarmed mainstream Canadian opinion-makers was the doctrine of class warfare, and the violence it implied. "They announce a doctrine which says that you shall shoot down every man who wears a white collar, or a white shirt," exclaimed Cockshutt in the House of Commons.[8] By setting one class against another, the Bolsheviks seemed to advocate a complete breakdown of civil authority. The result would be chaos and anarchy, and to prove the point one only had to look at Russia where, according to the stories regularly appearing in the Canadian press, murderers and thieves ran amok. Early in 1919 the *Manitoba Free Press* reported in a front page article that conditions were so bad in Russian cities that peddlers were selling human flesh on the streets to eat.[9] Most middle-class Canadians agreed that there was no need to preach class warfare in Canada. Canada was a democracy, they said, not some brutal dictatorship. Even if revolution might have been necessary in Tsarist Russia, in Canada freedom already existed, guaranteed by the very institutions—the family, private property, elected government—that the Reds sought to destroy. Bolshevism was not simply wrong to propose a reorganization of Canadian society along socialist lines, it was treasonous. It went against everything the country stood for, and as a result had to be suppressed with all the force at the state's disposal.

Sexual licentiousness, indecency, and a lack of respect for women played a large role in the Bolshevik identity as many Canadians imagined it. Garbled reports from Russia described the "socialization of women" that went on there. Respectable opinion warned that the Reds had the same thing in mind for Canada. The "defilement" of women was a constant theme, though it was usually expressed in the allusive manner of this report by a police spy in Brandon, Manitoba: "Another deplorable thing has occurred here on several occasions, when several highly respectable married women have been grossly insulted in their homes by draymen and deliverymen. I could not find out what was said, but I am led to believe that it was of a very immoral nature and about what one might expect to come from men of ignorant Bolshevik ideas."[10]

If the Bolshevik was believed to be gross and uncouth, he was also believed to be devious and ruthless, without any sense of fair play. Russia had proven this, after all, by withdrawing from the war so precipitately early in 1918. Abandoning its allies, it had come close to costing them the war. It was hard for many Canadians to forgive this act of betrayal, and it seemed to indicate how thoroughly all Bolsheviks lacked loyalty and honour. Without these virtues, Bolshevism could be nothing more than the rule of terror. The Reds might talk about the legitimate grievances of working people, but this was a front for their real intentions, plunder and robbery. "Bolshevikism [sic] is a remarkable manifestation of malice and ignorance and murderousness combined," wrote the editor of the Ottawa *Journal*.[11] In theory, the *Montreal Star* explained to its readers, Bolshevism appeared to be a Utopian political theory. In practice, it was nothing but "brigandage," the forcible transfer of wealth from those who had earned it to a small number of idlers, thieves, and murderers.[12] The Winnipeg activist Sam Blumenberg was not exaggerating when he told the audience at the Walker Theatre meeting in December 1918: "Nine-tenths of the people accept the newspaper portrait of a Bolshevist as a man who never had a shave nor a haircut in his life, with a knife in his mouth, a torch in one hand and a bomb in the other, and Bolshevism is considered as something similar to 'Flu' or 'black itch'."[13]

Laziness was another common attribute of the "Imaginary Bolshevik." Reds allegedly wanted to steal from the industrious rich and give to the indolent poor. "Broadly speaking," H.F. Gadsby told the readers of the Toronto weekly, *Saturday Night*, "the Bolshevists in all countries are those who do not fit in with the age-old formula—that man lives by the sweat of his brow. They want to reap where they have not sown. They are the inept, the idle, the vicious—the semi-loafers who are half in and half out of a job, or who prefer no job at all. They have not the get-up to climb the tree and pick the fruit, so they want to shake the tree and bruise everything."[14]

Middle-class Canadians imagined Bolsheviks to be furtive and conspiratorial, meeting in dark basements, sharing secret passwords and handshakes, spreading their poisonous messages in codes and subterfuge. The radical leaders who spoke openly at public meetings were just the tip of the Bolshie iceberg; the majority of the movement carried on its revolutionary work below the surface. This shadowy world of Bolshevik intrigue was evoked in a memo from a police agent on the subject of "secret writing," which reported that when "foreign agitators" communicated with each other they engaged in devious tradecraft. For example, first, the Bolshevik wrote an inoffensive letter on one side of a sheet of paper and then, on the other side, wrote a secret message "with a pointed stick dipped in milk." The result was invisible until the recipient brushed some fresh ash across the page, making the milk writing reappear clearly.[15] The wily Bolshevik was assumed to have many tricks every bit as ingenious as this one to avoid detection by the authorities.

This was the image of the Bolshevik then: a ruthless, secretive terrorist dedicated to the forcible dispossession of the employing classes and the socialization of wealth and property. "Professing to be democrats, the Bolsheviki attack democracies," wrote the Ottawa *Journal*; "professing to be champions of the poor, the Bolsheviki murder the poor; professing to champion the progress of humanity, the Bolsheviki trample on education, the chief hope of humanity."[16] Socialists and labour leaders in Canada did not seem to fit this profile, but it did not matter. They were believed to be either the unwitting dupes of hardcore revolutionaries who created and manipulated social unrest from the background, or dedicated revolutionaries themselves who cleverly disguised their real intentions behind a screen of feigned moderation. Either way, mainstream opinion considered them to be an extreme threat to the Canadian way of life, a threat that had to be stopped by almost any means.

For their part, the Reds engaged in their own stereotyping. For them, every industrialist was a war profiteer, a top-hatted plutocrat, pockets stuffed with cash, living a life of immoral luxury. The wives of the rich draped themselves in silks, furs, and diamonds while the workers starved. Employers were like vampires growing rich from the blood of the fallen soldier and the sweat of the toiling masses. The Red Scare pitted one set of extreme stereotypes against another, narrowing the space where moderate opinion might find room for sensible discussion. Both sides were guilty of outrageous distortions and scare tactics. But if there was a battle of duelling stereotypes, it was a mostly one-sided conflict. It was the frightening images of the Bolshevik, not the Capitalist Boss, which filled the pages of the nation's newspapers. The Reds commanded no police force, had no power to pass laws, and few ways to manipulate public opinion, leaving them demonized in the mainstream press and silenced by the forces of authority.

+ + +

Most newspapers across the country jumped on the Red Scare bandwagon with enthusiasm, but among the most rabid was the *Montreal Star*, the leading English-language daily in Quebec. The *Star* was founded in 1869 as a penny-daily by a twenty-one-year-old journalist named Hugh Graham, who ran the paper for the next four decades. Under Graham's management, the *Star* pioneered the sort of "people's journalism" that the Toronto *Star* would later make popular in Ontario. This meant lots of sensational, entertaining stories that appealed to a mass audience: social news (what today would be called celebrity gossip), crime, disasters, government corruption, hard-luck stories, and stories of the *beau monde*; anything that fascinated, titillated, or outraged. By 1891 the *Star* had parlayed this formula into the largest daily circulation in the country. Graham was a prominent backroom Conservative, but his paper was innovative in its use of the latest printing technology and its appeal to a broad readership. He knew that a newspaper that led crusades attracted readers and he was a flamboyant crusader. He supported close ties to the British Empire, lobbied Laurier to send Canadian troops to the Boer War, and was so vociferously pro-conscription during World War I that anti-conscriptionists dynamited his summer house.

For such a paper, aggressively populist and sensational, the Red Scare was made to order. Early in February 1919, for example, the *Star* devoted a full page to a dispatch from Russia under the headline "Bolshevism More Autocratic than Czarism and As Destructive As Anarchy." The gist of the article, and the editorial which accompanied it, was that the Bolshevik regime was more tyrannical than the tsars and just as despicable as the recently defeated "German autocracy." Bolshevism was a system based on force and terror, wrote the *Star* reporter, unprepared to admit that the chaotic circumstances of revolution and civil war made any difference. In the cities people were starving, fighting over the carcasses of dead horses to stay alive. In response, reported the *Star,* the Reds marched out into the countryside and murdered the farmers to expropriate their crops. Meanwhile, the army under Trotsky was committing unspeakable atrocities to terrorize the population. Bolshevism, declared the paper's editor, "runs counter to the great current of human life," which was that diligence and intelligence must be rewarded and people had to be allowed freedom to pursue their ambitions. "So long as it is faced with Bolshevik aggression, there is no peace for a tortured world."[17]

A leading scaremonger at the *Star* was the paper's cartoonist, Arthur Racey. Racey took the job of the *Star*'s chief illustrator in 1908 (succeeding the legendary Henri Julien) and during his four decades at the paper became one of the best-known caricaturists in Canada. Between January and April, 1919, the *Star* published a series of quite vicious cartoons by Racey that summed up many of the stereotypes associated with the "Bolshevik" in the popular mind. Racey's drawings caught the attention of Ernest Chambers, the press censor in Ottawa, who put together some anti-Bolshevik information from "confidential official reports" and sent it to the cartoonist to use as background material in his work.[18]

In Racey's drawings, the figure of the Bolshevik resembles a wild beast rather than a human being. He has a tangled mop of filthy hair

FIGURE 21 An Arthur Racey cartoon from the *Montreal Star* shows a caveman dragging home a wife and compares it to the modern Bolshevik doing the same, with the approval of the government. Red scaremongers were convinced that Bolshevism represented an assault on the sanctity of the middle-class home and family. *Source: Trent University Archives, Arthur Racey fonds 1899–1941, 607*

and a long scraggly beard, and is usually dressed in rags. Flies circle his head to indicate that he is in need of a bath. In one cartoon, titled "If We Were Bolshevists," a beady-eyed judge, addled by vodka, enquires, "What is the charge?" The answer: "Caught red-handed taking a bath, just like a capitalist." "Traitor!" is the judge's decision. "Shoot him at sunrise."[19] Another in the series shows "a citizen bringing home his government allotted wife" trussed up in the back of a wagon, an obvious allusion to the widespread belief that in Russia the new regime had "nationalized" women. Racey returned to this theme in a subsequent panel titled "Back to Barbarism," showing a caveman dragging his wife home by her hair, followed by a similar scene showing "Mr. Bolshevist" doing the same thing, only the wife is tagged with a government number.

Another of Racey's cartoons, titled "The Beaver and the Smelly Foreigner," reworks one of Aesop's fables. The caption reads: "A foreign, smelly animal [shown in the cartoon as a skunk, labelled "Bolshevism"] travelling about seeking what it could get without working one day spied a busy, happy Beaver. 'Mr. Beaver,' said he, 'why be a slave? Pull out your capitalistic tooth and be free from work. Follow me and we will help ourselves from the farmers' barns. My motto is—free grub, free booze and no work.' The Beaver, unable to stand the evil odor and thieving suggestions of the foreign agitator, replied, 'Miserable thief! Are you not aware that both of us would perish in time if your suggestions were followed? Clear off to where you came from before I use force to make you. I am too busy to listen to foolishness.'"[20]

Racey's caricatures emphasized the "foreignness" of the Bolshevik and drew attention to the xenophobia that played a substantial role during the Red Scare. The hatred and suspicion of the immigrant that was so widespread in Canada during the war only in-

FIGURE 22 (L) This Racey cartoon from the *Star*, April 3, 1919, shows capitalists in jail for being clean. A lack of personal hygiene was considered to be the hallmark of the revolutionary socialist.
Source: Trent University Archives, Arthur Racey fonds, 1899–1941, 605

FIGURE 23 Another Racey cartoon shows a Bolshevik returning home with his government-approved wife. It was widely believed that after the revolution in Canada all women would be "socialized," marriage would disappear, and everything would become the property of the state.
Source: Trent University Archives, Arthur Racey fonds 1899–1941, 606

tensified afterward. It angered people that so-called foreigners had taken jobs that rightly belonged to the native-born, and especially to the veterans. People seemed to forget that the immigrants whom they resented had been enticed to Canada precisely to settle the West and take the underpaid jobs in the work camps and factories that the native-born did not want. Much of the grief and anxiety that Canadians felt about the loss of a generation of young men and women in the war manifested itself as resentment against the immigrants who seemed to be taking the place of the fallen.

+ + +

During the fall of 1919, Stephen Leacock published a series of articles in the *New York Times* newspaper in which he outlined his views on the current political situation, particularly the challenge to the status quo presented by the radical left. "These are troubled times," Leacock began. "As the echoes of the war die away the sound of a new conflict rises in our ears. All the world is filled with industrial unrest. Strike follows upon strike. [...] The wheels of industry are threatening to stop." Making matters worse was the spreading "infection" of Bolshevism, he wrote. "Over the rim of the Russian horizon are seen the fierce eyes and the unshorn face of the [...] Bolshevik, waving his red flag."

It is indicative of Leacock's reputation at the time that America's most prestigious newspaper thought that he was the best person to explain these momentous events to its readers. He was known principally as a humourist, not just in Canada but around the world. His occasional pieces in newspapers and magazines were collected into best-selling books that made him the most popular funnyman writing in the English language. Titles such as *Sunshine Sketches of a Little Town* (1912) and *Arcadian Adventures of the Idle Rich* (1914) established his reputation for gently satirizing the foibles of everyday life.

But for his articles in the *Times*, Leacock put on his academic hat. As well as being a humourist, he was a trained political economist, a graduate of the University of Chicago, where he had studied under the famed social theorist Thorstein Veblen, and a member of the department of economics and political science at Montreal's McGill University. By most accounts Leacock was an indifferent scholar with a surprisingly slight grasp of his speciality. "Humorists, it was said, thought him an economist, and economists thought

FIGURE 24 As well as being Canada's leading humourist, Stephen Leacock was an economics professor and a commentator on current events. In a series of articles in the *New York Times*, Leacock tried to make sense of the challenge from the radical left. *Photo: National Archives of Canada, C-007869*

him a humorist," one of his biographers wrote.[21] He didn't really care that much for academia, preferring to address a broader audience. He was, in modern parlance, a public intellectual. Business and government leaders sought his advice; his essays appeared in all the leading publications. His thoughts on economic and political matters were taken seriously. Today, Leacock's writings are a useful index to the concerns thoughtful conservatives had about the threat of radical social change.

The *Times* articles, which appeared in 1920 in book form as *The Unsolved Riddle of Social Justice*, addressed what Leacock called the "National Hysteria" that was gripping North American society.[22] The demands of labour for a new deal might be just, Leacock conceded, but they were subverted by "the underground conspiracy of social revolution." As a result the forces of extremism were drowning out the voices of moderation, and society was sliding "nearer and nearer to the brink of the abyss." Leacock was sympathetic to the voices of reform. He agreed that economic inequality was rampant and inexcusable, that something had to change. And he worried that government attempts to stifle dissent merely made martyrs of the dissenters. But that is as far as his sympathies went. He was, after all, an uncomplicated conservative. He believed in the virtue of the British Empire and the importance of Canada's role within it. He opposed equal rights for women. He opposed immigration by Asians and blacks. He was suspicious of anyone who did not share his white, Anglo-Saxon background. And he emphatically rejected the calls by radical labour for a fundamental restructuring of the economy. "The blind Samson of labour will seize upon the pillars of society," he warned, "and bring them down in a common destruction." Socialism was "possible only for the angels," for dreamers. "The attempt to establish it would hurl us over the abyss." Without question the present system was flawed, and Leacock did not oppose all societal change, but change had to come slowly and be measured against the more pressing need to maintain stability.

Unsolved Riddle is a manifesto for the meliorist. Of course society was unjust, Leacock admitted. The question was what to do about it. The socialists, the "dreamers," would tear everything down in order to start again. They would, in Leacock's analogy, destroy our eyes in the hope of making new ones, but total blindness would be the result. What society needed was a new pair of spectacles—"the spectacles of social reform"—to improve its vision. Leacock did not indulge in the worst excesses of Red-baiting. While among the socialists there might have been "men of violence," anarchists who wanted only to destroy, he thought these "Bolshevists" were few in number. There was no necessary connection between socialism and violence, he argued; socialism could co-exist quite easily with the rule of law and should not be banned or persecuted. "A man has just as much right to declare himself a socialist as he has to call himself a Seventh Day Adventist or a Prohibitionist, or a Perpetual Motionist." All that was wrong with socialism, Leacock wrote, was that it was completely impractical, largely because it had too rosy a view of human nature and because it entrusted too much power to government. "Socialism is but a dream," Leacock concluded, "a bubble floating in the air." If people made the mistake of taking it seriously, it would lead to chaos.

Having rejected the radical solution to his "unsolved riddle," Leacock had little to suggest to ease the current crisis. He painted a gloomy picture of society poised between two abysses, one the misguided dream of socialism, the other the "slow strangulation" of the status quo. Yet in the end, all he had to propose was a set of conventional nostrums: jobs for everyone; public relief for the aged, the needy, and the infirm; education for the young; a minimum wage; and shorter hours of work: in short, many of the elements of the modern welfare state. These proposals were surprising, coming as they did from a supporter of the Conservative Party, but they were hardly sufficient to bridge the gulf that lay between radicals and mild reformers.

+ + +

The dominant image of the Bolshevik was invariably male. Reds were not women, not in the popular imagination. Quite the reverse, in fact. Women were ladylike and domestic, not unruly rabble-rousers. They had no role to play on the front lines of social conflict, but were one of the foundations on which a stable society was built. Weren't they the victims of the Bolshevik, nationalized by the State and sent into sexual slavery? For the Reds, marriage was a convenience arranged by unfeeling bureaucrats, or so it was said. Ontario Member of Parliament George Nicholson asked his fellow MPs "what they think of the nationalization of women, one of the doctrines of the Bolshevik, under which an innocent girl is torn from her home and turned over to some brute of a man—for what? For no other purpose but the express intention of propagating the species, and that the children born of such an unholy union shall be not the God-given heritage of their parents, but the property of the state, the same as any other animal [...] it gives me a bad taste in the mouth even to utter the word 'Bolsheviki'."[23] Red revolution swept away all semblance of normal, middle-class family life. One of the points of the campaign against the Reds was surely to protect Canadian womanhood from the predatory ideology of free love and socialized marriage.

That said, once the Red Scare got underway, radical women were not spared the attentions of the scaremongers. Emerging into public prominence through the campaign for women's suffrage and then in the struggle against conscription and in support of equal rights for female workers, many articulate, forceful women assumed leadership roles in the social reform movement. Many male socialists and labour leaders seem to have been just as sexist as their more conservative counterparts. Women were not often allowed to occupy prominent positions in left-wing political parties or unions. The doctrinaire Socialist Party of Canada, for instance, had little sympathy for "bourgeois reforms" such as women's suffrage and prohibition. As a result, women often created their own organizations to carry on the struggle for peace and social justice. They were effective enough that the authorities took steps to intimidate, silence, imprison, and persecute them just like radical men. As the main judge at the Winnipeg General Strike trials, Mr Justice Thomas Metcalfe, observed: "In these days when women are taking up special obligations and assuming equal privileges with men, it may be well for me to state now that women [...] can claim no special protection and are entitled to no sympathy."[24] Thanks to the efforts of radical women, the image of the Red had to be expanded to include these Bolsheviks without beards.

World War I brought an unprecedented increase in the involvement of women in the public sphere. It is well-known that tens of thousands of women entered the workplace to take the jobs of men who had gone overseas to fight. More than 30,000 found work in the munitions industry alone, and even more than that took jobs as clerical workers in government and war industry offices. But women's involvement in the war effort took many other forms as well. They joined the army overseas to serve as nurses and ambulance drivers. On the home front, they promoted recruitment, supported families whose fathers were absent at the war, knitted "comforts" for the men in the trenches, organized Victory Bond drives, and generally did anything they could to support the troops. Most Canadian women approved of the war as a Christian crusade against the barbaric German regime. But there were exceptions. Leading pacifists such as Laura Hughes in Toronto and Gertrude Richardson in Manitoba condemned the war. Hughes helped to create a Toronto branch of the International Committee of Women for Permanent Peace (later the Women's International League for Peace and Freedom), and chapters spread across the country. These women endured harassment, even physical intimidation, to get out their message that the war was unjustified, that it brutalized society and led inevitably to profiteering and the exploitation of the working class.

The most important issue for activist women during the war was the suffrage campaign. Aside from the occasional municipal or school board election, Canadian women did not possess the vote prior to World War I, neither federal nor provincial. The corrupt, contentious world of politics, it was argued, was no place for the finer sex. Women's place was in the home, not on the hustings. The suffrage issue had been debated for decades—there were twenty-two different suffrage organizations in Canada between 1877 and 1918[25]—but for a long time the issue lacked urgency. Part of the problem was that the suffrage struggle went on at the provincial level; there was no national organization of any strength to give it vigor. Then, in 1912, a group of Winnipeg activists, including Nellie McClung and Lillian Beynon Thomas, formed the Political Equality League (PEL) to press for the vote. This was the beginning of serious campaigning for women's suffrage in Manitoba, the centre of the struggle, and from then on events moved comparatively quickly right across the country.

A conventional and usually ineffective tactic of the Canadian suffragists was to gather signatures on a petition that a delegation then presented to their provincial legislature. The politicians, smug and unyielding, heard the arguments and dismissed them, and the women went home until the next time. In January 1914, just such a delegation attended a session of the provincial legislature in Winnipeg. "We are not here to ask for a reform, or a gift, or a favor, but for a right," Nellie McClung told the politicians, "not for mercy but for justice." In his response, Premier Rodmond Roblin, oozing condescension, presented the familiar arguments that women's suffrage would destroy the family, corrupt the feminine character, and lead to everything from divorce to prostitution. Little did he realize that McClung was paying less attention to what he said, which was all too predictable, than to how he said it. The next night at the Walker Theatre, she and her colleagues premiered a satiric stage show, the Women's Parliament, to a sold-out house. The women posed as legislators in a place where only they had the vote. A delegation of lowly men arrived pushing a wheelbarrow-load of petitions. McClung, playing the part of an unctuous Roblin to perfection, answered with a speech parroting the same arguments that the premier had used the day before. The crowd hooted and cheered, loving every minute of McClung's caricature, and the whole evening was a great boost for the cause.

In March 1914, thanks to the lobbying efforts of the PEL, the Manitoba Liberal Party adopted female suffrage as a plank in its platform. During the subsequent election campaign McClung and other leading suffragists worked tirelessly to elect the Liberals. Initially they failed and Premier Roblin was returned to office with a reduced majority. But in the spring of 1915, he resigned as a result of a corruption scandal. The Liberals took over and called another election for August. McClung, who had moved to Edmonton, returned to Manitoba to campaign, this time with better success. Led by Tobias Norris, the Liberals formed the government, and on January 28, 1916, Manitoba became the first province in Canada to grant the vote to women—but not without a last-minute hesitation. It turned out that the legislation the government introduced contained a clause excluding women from sitting in the legislature. When they found out about it, the women were furious and threatened to rally public opinion against Norris and his Liberals. The premier backtracked and amended the bill.[26]

Saskatchewan was not far behind. There the Provincial Equal Franchise Board had bombarded the legislature with petitions requesting the vote. When Premier Thomas Scott dithered (despite the fact that his own wife had signed a suffrage petition), a delegation of suffragists attended the legislature on Valentine's Day, 1916, to present their case. "We are your mothers, your sisters and your wives," Mrs C.O. Davidson, president of the Regina chapter of the Franchise Board told the politicians, "and we ask you to honour us as we deserve."[27] But Mrs Davidson was preaching to the converted, as Scott had earlier committed his government to female suffrage, and on this occasion the premier rose in his seat and repeated that promise. Saskatchewan women received the vote on March 14. Alberta followed suit a month later, with the other provinces falling into line until, by the spring of 1922, women everywhere in Canada had the same voting privileges as men (except in conservative, Catholic-dominated Quebec, where the franchise did not become a reality until 1940).

For the most part, the suffrage movement was not considered a

FIGURE 25 Nellie McClung was the most prominent activist in support of women's suffrage in Canada. The struggle for the vote was led by middle-class reformers such as McClung. *Photo: National Archives of Canada, PA-030212*

radical cause. It was led by middle-class reformers—teachers, journalists, and other professional women—who expected that votes for women would purify politics. It was part of a larger reform movement that sought to enhance conditions for children, impose temperance, and improve public health and urban housing. Nellie McClung was a typical suffragist. As a young woman she had taught school, and after she married she turned to writing. Her 1908 novel, *Sowing Seeds in Danny*, was a bestseller, and she went on to become one of the most popular platform speakers in the country, reading from her work and giving speeches about rural life and prohibition. McClung, however, disappointed many of her comrades in the suffrage movement by endorsing the war; for her, it was a struggle between good and evil, and neutrality was unthinkable.

The Wartime Elections Act showed just how far McClung's support for the war would go. Even as the western provinces had granted female suffrage, Prime Minister Borden had dragged his feet on granting women the federal franchise. With the introduction of conscription pending, however, he needed every vote he could get, and so in 1917 he introduced the Military Voters Act, giving the ballot to, among others, female members of the armed forces; then he presented the Wartime Elections Act, extending the vote to female relatives of servicemen (the latter Act took the vote away from conscientious objectors and from naturalized Canadians born in enemy countries). Many suffragists were outraged that the prime minister was manipulating their cause for his own political advantage and to intensify a war they opposed. They were outraged even further when it became known that Nellie McClung, one of their most effective voices, agreed with Borden's attempt to exclude "foreign" women from the voting lists. Under criticism from her colleagues, McClung retracted her position. When the Wartime

Elections Act was introduced in Parliament she opposed it, arguing that it was unjust to deprive naturalized Canadians of the vote. But the incident revealed a cleavage between pro-war, politically mainstream women like McClung and her anti-war, often socialist sisters in the suffrage movement, women like Gertrude Richardson, who wrote, "we desire political power that we may oppose more effectively the terrible onrush of militarism."[28]

It was these latter women whom authorities began to include in their Red paranoia. An example was Vancouver activist Helena Gutteridge.[29] Gutteridge had been introduced to the suffrage cause in her native England where she had taken part with the Pankhursts and other internationally known suffragists in the great London street processions of 1910. In the following year, at age thirty-two, she emigrated to Canada and settled in Vancouver. An experienced tailor and an advocate for working women, Gutteridge found work making clothes and was soon a member of the executive of the Journeymen Tailors' Union and active in the local Trades and Labour Council. Gutteridge saw the vote not just as a step toward political equality but also as a means to force improvements in working conditions and wages for female employees, most of whom received lower salaries and had far fewer workplace rights than their male counterparts. Her experience in England made her impatient with the cautious, middle-class women who ran the local Political Equality League. Eventually she led her own breakaway group of working women who adopted more aggressive strategies, exhorting audiences at street-corner meetings and organizing among shop girls and factory hands. She made common cause with the Social Democratic Party and counted prominent Reds like Victor Midgley and Jack Kavanagh among her friends.

Once suffrage was achieved in British Columbia, Gutteridge

turned her full attention to union organizing and political agitation, lobbying for a minimum wage and the eight-hour day. In the fall of 1918, she led a determined fight by laundry workers seeking higher wages, shorter hours, and a union-only shop, a fight that ended with significant concessions from the employers. In September 1919 she was one of three female delegates to the National Industrial Conference in Ottawa. According to press reports she was the only woman who spoke in the open debate where she stood to challenge financier Melville White. This was nothing new for Gutteridge, who was not intimidated by displays of male power and was used to being the odd woman out, the lone soprano in a choir of bassos.

When it came to the issue of industrial unionism, Gutteridge parted ways with her more radical comrades. She rejected the idea of One Big Union, disliked the tactic of the general strike, and always remained a committed craft unionist, making her more of a Pink than a Red when compared to another leading activist, Sarah Knight in Edmonton. Along with her husband Joe, Sarah Knight took a leading role in the Socialist Party of Canada in Alberta. On a visit to Winnipeg in the fall of 1918, she was arrested for violating the War Measures Act in a speech; police were wielding the federal orders-in-council like a club to silence radical opinion, and she was told that her anti-war views had crossed the line. Although Knight was not convicted, she was warned not to speak publicly about the war.[30] She and her husband later moved further leftward to join the Communist Party.

These three activists—Nellie McClung, Helena Gutteridge, and Sarah Knight—ran the gamut of progressive opinion in Canada from Liberal to Communist during and immediately after the war. Despite their differences, their activism makes obvious the important part women played in the post-war debate about what kind of a society Canada was going to be. Many Canadians could not bring themselves to think of women in this way, as activists, rabble-rousers, and Reds. They preferred the old-fashioned images of women as passive victims, attractive ornaments, or dutiful wives and mothers, but increasingly women were shattering these images and putting a female face on the Red Scare.

+ + +

In 1919 Canada's leading psychiatrist, Dr Charles Clarke, wrote an article in the *Public Health Journal* in which he reflected on "the chaotic state of affairs in Canada." "Bolshevism is not a new world disease," he explained,

> but merely a hot house product imported from the slum centres of Europe, where degeneracy has produced its inevitable results. The specimens of advocates of their doctrines we have met should never have been admitted to this country, as their influence for evil is difficult to estimate, although it is undoubtedly great. Certainly the ideals which have counted so much in the past in keeping this young country sane, and an example of virility, are in danger as a result of the type of immigration that has been fostered of late years. We have been nursing a reptile that may easily prove our undoing when it is fully developed.[31]

It may seem odd that a doctor was making a contribution to the Red Scare. What did medicine, let alone psychiatry, have to do with radical politics? As it turned out, quite a lot. Thanks to the "science" of eugenics, many prominent members of the medical community joined the chorus of concern about the spread of Red ideas.

For these professionals, it was another sign that Canadian society was in poor health, infected by aberrant ways of thinking. Bolshevism was a kind of mental illness; its spread was creating a public health emergency.

A year before his article appeared, Clarke, a professor of psychiatry and dean of the medical school at the University of Toronto, had co-founded the Canadian National Committee for Mental Hygiene (CNCMH). Along with his colleagues Dr Clarence Hincks, medical inspector for the Toronto school system, and Dr Helen MacMurchy, an obstetrician and expert on what were then called the feeble-minded, Clarke used the CNCMH to advocate in support of the fashionable field of eugenics. Conceived in England by the multi-talented Victorian scientist Francis Galton, eugenics proposed that most human deficiencies—mental handicaps, many diseases, physical disability—were inherited and could be eradicated by what were essentially selective breeding practices. Enthusiasts, and Clarke was one, even thought that crime, alcoholism, juvenile delinquency, and other anti-social behaviours were inherited as well.

Eugenics sought to improve the human race by preventing the spread of undesirable characteristics. It was imperative, eugenicists argued, to stop the unfit from reproducing. In Canada before the war, conventional wisdom said that the country faced "national deterioration." The population supposedly was degenerating because the least qualified people were being allowed to reproduce at a faster rate than the more qualified. People spoke openly about the "degeneration of the race," meaning that the fit and the intelligent were being overwhelmed by the genetically inferior, people who were physically, mentally, or morally disabled. The war only made the situation worse. So many of the "best" had lost their lives on the battlefields of Europe. Who was left to keep the population strong?[32]

One response to this perceived public health crisis proposed by eugenics activists was to incarcerate people who were considered "feeble-minded," or "retarded." Feeble-mindedness was thought to be a menace responsible for all manner of social ills. Once identified, victims had to be shut away in institutions for their own good and for the good of the society they threatened. Another solution was sterilization, preferably voluntary but forced if necessary. The weak and the degenerate had to be stopped from passing on their inferiority. This led to calls for the sterilization of the mentally ill and disabled. Sterilization was endorsed by the National Council of Women and leading medical practitioners across the country. (In 1928 Alberta became the first province to pass a law allowing the involuntary sterilization of "mental defectives"; British Columbia followed suit in 1933.)

Eugenicists also targeted immigration as a source of concern. It may have been that too many "unfit" Canadians were giving birth, they argued, but even more crucial was the arrival of large numbers of immigrants from abroad. The huge influx of newcomers that swept into Canada in the years before the war—three million between 1896 and 1914, a sizeable number of whom were non-Anglo-Saxon in origin—provoked anxiety about the kind of "mongrel" society that was emerging. "Foreigners in large numbers are in our midst," wrote the Ontario-born Methodist minister and social democrat, J.S. Woodsworth in his 1909 book *Strangers Within Our Gates*. "More are coming. How are we to make them into good Canadian citizens?" For the most part, British and American immigrants—believed to share the Anglo-Saxon values that dominated mainstream Canadian society—were exempt from these concerns.

But what was to be done about the others, the true "foreigners"? Many observers feared that they were diluting Canada's true, British character in a sea of ethnic diversity. In the words of one Member of Parliament, Canada had become "the dumping ground for the refuse of every country in the world." Another Ontario MP declared that Canadians must resist becoming "a nation of organ-grinders and banana sellers."[33] Others were more circumspect in their language, but basically said the same thing. For instance, Edmonton MP and newspaper publisher Frank Oliver, speaking in the House of Commons in 1903, suggested that many immigrants were "of such class and character as will deteriorate rather than elevate the condition of our people and our country ..." Two years after making this statement, Oliver became minister of immigration in Robert Borden's government.

Eugenics bestowed respectability on these ideas of race prejudice. Eugenicists agreed that Canada was being overwhelmed by the outcasts of Europe, but gave their arguments a scientific gloss. European countries were sending the worst of their people: paupers, slum dwellers, the criminal, the immoral, the mentally defective. Because of the misguided immigration policies of the government, Canada had become, in the words of the Quebec psychiatrist Thomas Burgess, "a 'dumping ground' for the degenerates of Europe,"[34] and this was working to downgrade the quality of the Canadian population. The CNCMH threw its efforts behind attempts to restrict the flow of immigrants into Canada, especially immigrants from non-Anglo-Saxon sources.

Immigrants were blamed for a rising crime rate in the cities and for swelling the populations in jails and asylums. And they were blamed for providing fertile ground for Bolshevik ideas. As the editor of *Saturday Night* magazine wrote, he did not think that the average English-speaking worker would be influenced by the "blood-thirsty ravings" of the Canadian Bolsheviks. "Unquestionably, however, our larger cities have very considerable foreign populations, who came to this continent in the belief that in America men could live without working, and who fairly revel in literature of this kind. If the government does not step in and nip the conspiracy in the bud, there is certain to be serious disorder."[35]

Medical activists like Charles Clarke saw a connection between public health and political radicalism. As Clarke's article in the *Public Health Journal* made clear, he considered Bolshevism to be a disease in itself, similar to other social problems such as alcoholism or insanity. But in addition to that, it was a temptation; so long as the intellectual capability of the population continued to deteriorate, the Reds would be able to attract ill-informed, feeble-minded followers to their cause, people who were too ignorant to tell dangerous social theories from sensible ones. Scaremongers feared that the Reds might be able to whip up this dangerous majority into the kind of revolutionary mob that had toppled governments in Europe.

FIGURE 26 From the beginning, the authorities prepared to use force to bring an end to the Winnipeg General Strike. The militia was mobilized and given vehicles such as this one specially outfitted with machine guns in the back. *Photo: Manitoba Archives, N7549*

CHAPTER SIX

Revolution in Disguise

"Make no mistake about it: This is not a strike at all. It is a conspiracy to subvert the ordered government of this country and put in its place a revolutionary dictatorship."
—*The* Winnipeg Citizen, *May 22, 1919*

"Only fools try to make revolutions, wise men conform to them."
—*William Pritchard*

The Winnipeg General Strike was a prophecy fulfilled. For months beforehand, police spies had been warning that the Reds were planning an insurrection. The mainstream press interpreted similar labour disputes in Seattle and Great Britain as Bolshevik uprisings. When the Winnipeg strike began on May 15, 1919—then quickly snowballed to involve 30,000 workers, bringing the city to a standstill—a government and a public that had convinced themselves to expect a revolt naturally believed that one had broken out. "Surely Canada is not going mad," Senator George Foster wrote in his diary when word of the strike reached him in Paris where Prime Minister Borden had left him in charge of the Canadian delegation to the peace conference. "How much this war has to answer for. The world is sick and full of moods strange and often bitter."[1] Never before had so many workers taken to the streets to protest their working conditions. Never before had a labour dispute escalated to involve people in all sectors of the workforce and in all parts of the country. Canada *must* be on the verge of Red revolution.

Midway through the strike, the *Winnipeg Citizen* newspaper published an analysis that neatly summed up the conspiracy theory that conditioned thinking not just about the General Strike but about the Red Scare in its entirety. Taking as its source a series of articles in the *New York World*, the *Citizen* announced that, according to "information secured in the inner councils of the Bolsheviki of this continent," the "Red Five," the masterminds of the revolutionary movement in Canada, were Winnipeg machinist Dick Johns, William Pritchard and Victor Midgley from Vancouver, Joe Knight from Edmonton, and Joe Naylor from the Vancouver Island mining community of Cumberland. These five men belonged to the inner circle of activists behind the One Big Union, and since the OBU was the Bolshevik conspiracy incarnate, said the *Citizen*, they comprised the sinister cabal that intended to take advantage of labour struggles such as the Winnipeg strike to overturn the government and replace it with a Red regime. These men had at their disposal "2,500 trained and paid agitators" who knew how "to impress and convert the wage earners," warned the *Citizen*, which went on to declare that, "the Bolshevist idea [...] has appealed to a greater number of people in the United States and Canada than is generally believed, and the number of supporters is constantly increasing."[2]

This was the issue at stake in Winnipeg according to the Red

Scare alarmists. It was no mere labour dispute. It was a battle for the loyalties of all Canadians.

+ + +

The bare facts of the Winnipeg General Strike are straightforward enough, though their interpretation has been in dispute down to the present day. On May 1, 1919, after weeks of fruitless negotiation, members of the city's construction trades walked off the job. The next day, workers in the metal trades followed. The issues were collective bargaining rights and higher wages. In the case of the building trades, the employers refused to agree to the pay increase that the workers argued they needed to make up for wartime inflation. As for the metal trades, employers were refusing to negotiate with the newly organized Metal Trades Council, an industry-wide umbrella organization made up of nineteen related unions. Employers wanted to continue dealing with individual unions, as they had always done, but the metal workers recognized there was strength in unity.

At the outset of the conflict, the *Western Labor News*, the official newspaper of the Winnipeg Trades and Labor Council, presented labour's interpretation of the situation:

> Winnipeg is gripped by the biggest strike in its history. Why? Simply because a few employers refuse to recognize the right of Labor to organize. They refuse to consider schedules or to reduce hours. After repeated efforts to have them act in a reasonable manner the men in the Metal Trades struck work. The Building Trades Council was recognized by the Employers' Association and their demands were declared to be just and reasonable, but the

employers said that those reasonable wages could not be
paid. Or, in other words the men involved must work for
less than a living wage. If the workers must starve it may as
well be now as later. This is the reason behind the General
Strike.[3]

On May 6 the Winnipeg Trades and Labor Council (WTLC)
agreed to distribute ballots to local unions so that members could
vote on a general strike in support of the trades that had already
gone out. Premier T.C. Norris and Mayor Charles Gray consulted
with employers, but even with the threat of a general walkout there
was no enthusiasm for renewing negotiations. On Tuesday, May
13, at the Labor Temple on James Street, WTLC secretary Ernest
Robinson announced the results of the strike vote to a jam-packed
meeting: more than 11,000 in favour to 500 opposed. Two days
later at eleven o'clock in the morning, tens of thousands of unionized and non-unionized workers joined the strike. Telephones
stopped ringing. Streetcars stopped running. Movie theatres and
restaurants closed. Firemen did not respond to alarms. Railway
workers downed their hammers, and postal carriers dropped their
mailbags. Elevators were grounded, and uncollected garbage rotted
in the streets. City police unions voted overwhelmingly in favour
of the strike as well, but strike leaders asked them to remain on the
job, fearing the government would use their absence as a pretext to
impose martial law.

Following the walkout, the authorities—the Mounted Police,
the militia, the different levels of government—began to coordin-
ate their response. A group of business and professional leaders in
the city convened the Citizens' Committee of 1,000 to rally support against the strike. (The committee was an expanded version
of the Committee of 100, a similar group that had formed during

FIGURE 27 Placards like this one were distributed by the General Strike committee to businesses providing essential services. Did this mean that strikers were attempting to usurp the powers of the state? The pro-business Citizens' Committee of 1,000 argued that it did. *Photo: Manitoba Archives, N488*

the labour troubles of the previous summer. Whether or not there were actually 1,000 members is anyone's guess. The Committee had a well-earned reputation for secrecy; no list of members was ever made public, and no record was kept of its meetings.) As well as publishing its own newspaper, this group organized volunteers to operate the fire pumps and maintain other services. The commissioner of the RNWMP sent a detachment of officers to Winnipeg from Regina, and Brigadier General Ketchen, the commanding officer of the military district, mobilized the local militia. On the workers' side, a five-member executive committee emerged to take direction of the strike. The five were Bob Russell, Harry Veitch of the typographical union, William Ivens, WTLC secretary Ernie Robinson, and WTLC president James Winning, who was also a city alderman. Their activities included publishing a daily newspaper, encouraging discipline among supporters, and issuing placards that businesses and vehicles displayed to indicate they were operating with the strikers' permission. (Opponents of the strike argued that these permits were proof that the Strike Committee was in reality a "soviet" trying to seize power from the local government; strikers saw them as a practical solution to the problem of providing essential services to the public.)

Initially both sides of the dispute were intransigent as they tested the resolve of their opponents. Strike leaders urged supporters to do nothing that would arouse a backlash from the authorities. "There are those who are very anxious for the workers to do something which would provide an excuse for putting the city under martial law," cautioned the *Western Labor News*. "Therefore [...] do nothing. This is the greatest strike ever put on in Winnipeg and it can be made the greatest victory if every striker does absolutely nothing."[4] Partly as a result of this admonition, the early days of the walkout did not feature much activity in the streets.

Behind the scenes, both sides conspired to turn the conflict to their advantage. Both the Central Strike Committee and the anti-strike forces wanted a victory, not just a resolution of the labour issues. For the strike leaders, this meant that the employers would have to recognize that workers had the right to industry-wide bargaining. This was not a revolutionary demand, but neither was it a form of collective bargaining that had been widely accepted in Canadian labour relations. For the authorities—the direction of the strike was not really in the hands of the employers—the issue was much broader than bargaining rights. The Red Scare had conditioned them to expect a revolution, and they were convinced that the General Strike was the outbreak they had been waiting for. Under these circumstances there was little chance that the two sides would arrive at a negotiated solution to a crisis that one side at least believed was a life and death struggle for control of the Canadian state.

Early in the strike the federal government made it clear that it would not remain a neutral observer. Four days after the walkout began, Arthur Meighen, the acting minister of justice, and Minister of Labour Gideon Robertson left Ottawa on a train for Winnipeg to see for themselves what was going on. The government's attitude was summed up by Meighen, who characterized strike leaders as "revolutionists of various degrees and types, from crazy idealists down to ordinary thieves."[5] When the two federal cabinet ministers reached Fort William, A.J. Andrews of the Citizens' Committee of 1,000 was there to greet them. The fifty-four-year-old Andrews would emerge as a key figure in the strike. A lawyer and a former two-term Winnipeg mayor (he was known as "the boy mayor" because of his youthful appearance), he was a well-connected Conservative with a membership in the city's exclusive social elite. (Coincidentally, he had run for a seat in the legislature in the 1914 Manitoba election and lost to the labour candidate Fred Dixon, who would be arrested for his role in the strike.) The *Toronto Daily Star* called Andrews "the principal human factor opposing the strike movement." He had been "here there and everywhere" during the strike, the paper said.[6] It was Andrews who would draft Mayor Gray's ban on street parades; Andrews who met with visiting federal politicians when they came to town; Andrews who corresponded regularly with Arthur Meighen and consulted with him on legislation aimed at the strike leaders; Andrews who decided whether to keep the arrested strike leaders in jail or not. In short, Andrews was Winnipeg's Wizard of Oz, lurking behind the curtain, manipulating the levers of power.

FIGURE 28 Arthur Meighen was minister of the interior and acting minister of justice in Ottawa. Along with federal minister of labour Gideon Robertson, he spearheaded the federal government's suppression of the strike. *Photo: National Archives of Canada, PA-145060*

At the Fort William meeting, Andrews impressed upon Meighen and Robertson that the government had to take a tough stand against the strikers. Both cabinet ministers accepted the view that they were dealing with a sinister plot aimed at overthrowing the government. As the *Star* reported, the two men "are not preserving neutrality, they are openly opposed" to the strike.[7] A few days later in Winnipeg, Meighen warned that "it is up to the citizens of Winnipeg to stand firm and resist the efforts made here to overturn proper authority."[8] He had already appointed Andrews the justice department's special representative on the ground with the assignment of gathering evidence against the strike leadership that would prove they were engaged in a seditious conspiracy. On his return to Ottawa, Meighen—who had refused to meet with any of the strike leaders while he was in Winnipeg—rose to speak in the House of Commons on June 2 and made it clear that his government saw recent events as what he termed "the perfection of Bolshevism." Meighen argued that by definition a general strike was an insurrection. "A general strike to succeed or, indeed, to continue, must result in the usurpation of governmental authority on the part of those controlling the strike. It did so result in Winnipeg; it must ever so result." This was the crucial issue, said Meighen, not collective bargaining or some other labour issue, and the government must hold firm. "It was essential that the greater issue raised by the assumption of Soviet authority [...] should be once and for all decided and be decisively beaten down ..."[9] From the beginning, then, the federal government made it clear that it was committed to the suppression of the strike, not its resolution.

There was an alternative view of the strike articulated in Parliament that day. It was proposed by Ernest LaPointe, the Liberal member for Kamouraska district in Quebec. A lawyer and future justice minister, LaPointe was one of the Laurier loyalists who had remained true to the old leader during the vote over conscription. He was considered to be one of the bright lights of the party in Quebec. He spoke ahead of Meighen, but in response to the comments of the Conservative member for North Winnipeg, Dr M.R. Blake, who had just told the House that "sedition must be stamped out" and that "radical socialist leaders must be interned or deported." LaPointe argued that the origins of the Winnipeg strike could be found in the high cost of living and the workers' natural resentment against a system "which allows meat trusts, flour trusts, and other dealers in the necessaries of life to pile up their dividends and multiply their millions while the prices of bread, bacon, meat and other commodities are soaring into altitudes heretofore unknown." But what was to be done in the short term to establish peace between labour and capital, LaPointe asked? For one thing, "it is useless to mystify the public by acting a Bolshevist melodrama," he said. These were "wild and stupid accusations." The labour movement was simply acting on its determination to achieve equal power with the employer; the charges of Bolshevism were "slanderous attacks" on reputable labour leaders. In his view, the government was mishandling the situation and Senator Robertson had ended his usefulness as a mediator by siding so recklessly with one side in the dispute. As for Meighen, he was not temperamentally suited to settling disputes. "He stands in Canada as the Apostle of arbitrary enactments and despotic legislation," thundered LaPointe, a reference to Meighen's earlier role in forcing through conscription. In the end, LaPointe did not have any suggestions to offer as to how the government might settle the Winnipeg dispute, though he did recommend a national conference of employers and employees to discuss the larger issues. Meanwhile, the most he had to offer was the usual vague advice from an Opposition MP: "Do something and do it now."[10] In precisely two weeks, the government would take this advice, though not in the way that LaPointe would have imagined.

Back in Winnipeg, Andrews was using his authority with the justice department to plan strategy with police and civic officials. Although he never wavered in his conviction that the strike was a Red conspiracy, he argued behind the scenes for caution. The Reds had to be defeated in such a way that they were discredited in the eyes of their followers and the public and did not become martyrs to government repression. As he wrote to Meighen in early June, "I believe if this strike fails, as I believe it will fail, of itself, and because public opinion is against it, it will be exceedingly difficult at any future time to get the large body of labor to strike. They will have suffered so much that their natural impulse will be to blame the strike leaders. If we arrest the strike leaders now and this results in breaking the strike, labor will always claims [*sic*] that they would have won but for the intervention of the Government controlled by the master class."[11] Andrews believed that if the situation in Winnipeg was handled properly, the government could deal a fatal blow to the Red conspiracy right across Canada.

Nonetheless, the government laid plans to make a dramatic move against the strike leaders when the right moment arrived. Andrews advised Meighen to speed up proposed changes to the Immigration Act that would extend the government's power to deport agitators. When Parliament passed the amendments on June 5, Andrews immediately cabled his disappointment to Ottawa. The new law gave the government the power to deport anyone who promoted public disorder, advocated the overthrow of constituted authority by force, or advocated the destruction of property—but in Andrews' view, it did not go far enough. It covered immigrant "troublemakers," but Canadian citizens were excluded from the amended act. In other words, the British-born Canadian strike leaders were unaffected. Meighen told Andrews he had already seen the shortcomings of the new legislation and was taking steps to remedy them. The next day, June 6, in a mere forty-five minutes, a further amendment was rushed through Parliament extending the provisions of the act to include British-born immigrants. It was "one of the least debated and most hurriedly passed pieces of legislation in the history of Canada," historian David Bercuson wrote in his book on the General Strike.[12] The necessary legislation was now in place to come down hard on the strike leaders.

At the end of May, Winnipeg's returned soldiers began holding parades and suddenly the streets erupted in a flurry of protests and demonstrations, most of them peaceful. Hardly a day passed that a downtown park did not host a large rally of placard-waving supporters or an auditorium was not filled with vehement speeches and demands for action. As historian Ian McKay has pointed out, the strike was "general" not just because it involved a large number of unions, but also because it engaged the general public in political activism on an unprecedented scale.[13] There were 171 mass meetings during the six-week strike, prompting an irritated Mayor Gray to refer to "the obsession and almost fanatical mania for meetings and parades."[14] Many of the outdoor meetings took place in Victoria Park, two blocks from City Hall, where William Ivens could be found on Sunday mornings holding meetings of his Labor Church in support of the strike, and where returned soldiers held open-air sessions that came to be called the "Soldiers' Parliament."

The veterans were active on both sides of the dispute. They have been called "the third force" in the strike because of their pivotal role in deepening the crisis.[15] Prior to the walkout, many veterans had been pressuring the government to deport the so-called "aliens" and confiscate their property. They were angry about the lack of jobs and resentful that so many positions were filled by the aliens. On the other hand, many veterans were sympathetic to the cause of the workers. The strike was an opportunity for both camps to capitalize on the unrest and push forward their own concerns. On a rainy Saturday, May 31, a huge crowd of about 10,000 pro-strike veterans marched on the provincial legislature to confront Premier Norris. When Norris said, somewhat disingenuously, that he preferred to stay out of the dispute, the veterans moved on to City Hall where they booed Mayor Gray when he came out to speak to them on the front steps.

Over the next few days, pro-strike veterans were joined in the streets by parading veterans who opposed the strike. These anti-strike vets formed the Loyalist Returned Soldiers Association and offered their services to the city as volunteer police and firefighters. Authorities worried that when the parading demonstrators met head-on, as they inevitably would, violence might result. On June 6, Mayor Gray issued a proclamation banning all street parades, and three days later he dismissed 240 members of the regular police force, who had resisted taking an oath of loyalty to the city, and replaced them with a force of hired "specials" who were given clubs and sent into the streets to maintain order. The specials were not as brutal as the murderous *Friekorps* "cleansing" the streets of Berlin and other German cities, but their purpose was the same—to assert government control by intimidating the workers and their supporters. Once again the Strike Committee urged calm. "Steady, Boys, Steady," cautioned the *Western Labor News*. "Keep quiet. Do nothing. Keep out of trouble. Don't carry weapons. Leave this to

FIGURE 29 Anti-strike veterans joined a "Loyalist" parade to the legislature on June 4. Marches like this one alarmed the authorities who feared they would lead to violence in the streets. *Photo: Manitoba Archives, N12295*

your Enemies. Continue to prove that you are the friends of law and order."[16] But clearly, the longer the strike went on, the greater was the possibility for violence.

+ + +

A month into the General Strike, the *Free Press* newspaper in London, Ontario, published an interview with W.J. Taylor, a member of the Canadian Press Association who had just returned from western Canada. "The trouble in Winnipeg should not be called a strike," alleged Taylor. "It is nothing more nor less than a determined attempt on the part of the ringleaders to put on a revolution and to set up in the City of Winnipeg a Soviet government, and if the 'Red Fifteen', as the leaders call themselves, had succeeded in Winnipeg, the program would have been extended throughout all western Canada."[17] This fear, that if the situation in Winnipeg was not handled properly it might touch off a spark that would ignite all of Canada, was what kept political leaders awake at night. The authorities judged that, across the nation, labour was in a very volatile mood and that, as May drew to a close, the country was on the verge of an unprecedented social upheaval.

In Amherst, Nova Scotia, where workers formed the Amherst Federation of Labour, an industrial union that looked suspiciously to employers like a One Big Union, most of the town's factory hands and civic employees were out on strike. In Montreal, where shipyard workers led the way, a general strike involving at least 12,000 people in a wide variety of trades would soon threaten to shut down the city. The situation in Toronto was so volatile, with unionists voting two to one in favour of a general walkout and the press talking about "the Red Flag European Socialist Forces in the labour movement," that Prime Minister Robert Borden felt he had to step in.[18] On May 29 Borden invited representatives of the employers, the unions, and the civic government to Ottawa for a meeting to resolve the dispute. But the prime minister had no success, and on May 30 the citizens of Toronto witnessed their first general strike. In Brandon, Manitoba, a sympathetic strike had begun just a few days after the Winnipeg walkout and continued for several weeks. Railway workers, telephone operators, brewery hands, civic employees, and bakers all joined the strike. So did the police and electrical workers but, as in Winnipeg, they remained on the job to provide essential services. In Saskatoon, the Trades and Labor Council initiated a sympathy strike that also lasted until the Winnipeg dispute ended. In Edmonton and Calgary, attempts to rally workers were less successful and resulted in short-lived and not very extensive walkouts, but in Vancouver, where the local Trades and

Labour Council had waited to see how events in Winnipeg would unfold, a sympathetic strike that started on June 3 dragged on for a month, involving shipyard workers, street railwaymen, telephone operators, and all civic employees.

A look at a map of Canada on June 1, 1919, revealed a string of labour strife connecting almost all major metropolitan centres from Nova Scotia through the industrial heartland and across the Prairies to the Pacific Coast. In each of these cities, the strikes had local issues and local causes, but they were all inspired by Winnipeg, and they all contributed to a growing sense of alarm in government that the contagion of Red revolt was spreading like a plague and infecting larger and larger numbers of people. There is evidence to suggest that the organizers of the OBU, whom the government considered to be directing the labour unrest, were actually lukewarm about it because it seemed to be happening before they were fully organized. Carl Berg, a leading OBU supporter in Edmonton, for example, wrote to a comrade: "There are strikes in Winnipeg and Ottawa and it looks as [if] it was going to spread. I hope that we will be able to hold it back until we have our organization perfected, but if the workers decide to go out then we will have to act and do the best we can."[19] This letter suggests that at least some of the so-called Reds were reacting to events, not leading them. But this was not how the government saw things; in the context of the Red Scare, authorities thought they knew who they were dealing with—Bolshevik revolutionaries, agents of Moscow.

And events in the city of Winnipeg were key to this imagined revolution. In the Manitoba capital, strikers were preparing for "The Great Dream of the Winnipeg Soviet," according to the *Manitoba Free Press*; this was where revolution had to be stopped in its tracks. As the days passed and strikers showed no sign of losing their resolve, the anti-strike forces prepared to call in the troops.

+ + +

At the beginning of the strike, typographers and pressmen in Winnipeg had joined the walkout and presses at the city's newspaper had fallen idle. Stepping into the void, the Citizens' Committee of 1,000 began publishing its own paper, the *Citizen*, starting on May 19. The paper claimed to present "the actual facts," but unreservedly took the side of the anti-strike forces. The pro-strike version of events was presented in the special *Strike Bulletin* editions of the *Western Labor News*, the paper of the local Trades and Labor Council. When, after several days, the *Manitoba Free Press* got back into print using management to run the paper, its editor, John Dafoe, was livid at the attempt to silence him and took a strong stand against the strike, as did the other regular dailies, the *Telegram* and the *Tribune*. Dafoe wrote in his first issue back that a "dictatorship of the proletariat" had suppressed his paper, while the *Tribune* thundered that the strike was the work of "lawless, anarchistic agitators."

There was one daily newspaper, however, that broke with the conventional media view that the strike was a Red conspiracy. On May 22 William Plewman arrived in the city from Toronto to cover the story for the *Toronto Daily Star*. Plewman was a British immigrant to Canada who had come to Toronto with his family as a child. Although his politics were Conservative, he joined the liberal-leaning *Star* as an editor in 1903, and during World War I his daily column about events in Europe made him one of the best-read journalists in the city. When the strike broke out in Winnipeg, Joseph Atkinson, the *Star*'s owner, saw an opportunity not just to appeal to his widening readership among Toronto's working class, but also to cause trouble for the Borden government, which he opposed. He immediately dispatched Plewman, the star of his editorial staff, to the strike zone, along with Main Johnson, the paper's labour specialist, who was covering the Mathers Commission as it made its way across Canada. Together with John Conklin, the *Star*'s usual freelance stringer in Manitoba, Plewman and Johnson provided Toronto readers with coverage of the strike unmatched by any other Toronto daily. (Because telegraphers were on strike, Johnson had to take a train south across the border to Thief River Falls, Minnesota, to send his initial stories to Toronto.) Johnson left Winnipeg on another assignment after five days, but Plewman remained there until the end of the strike, filing stories that appeared almost daily on the front page of the *Star*.

Plewman, who was pro-labour in his outlook to begin with, favored a calm assessment of the issues instead of fear-mongering. In his first dispatch, dated May 23, the day after he arrived, Plewman wrote: "The writer came to the city understanding that the Strike Committee of Five had inaugurated a reign of terror, preventing willing workers from serving their employers and the public [...] But the whole thing is a delusion and a figment of the imagination. There is no Soviet. There was little or no terrorism." His conclusion? "The strikers have gone pretty far and they have made some mistakes but they have not perpetrated Bolshevism."[20] Nothing he learned during the more than five weeks that he spent in the city would change his mind. Atkinson accepted his reporter's analysis. "It is becoming more and more clear that the issue is not Bolshevism or any attempt to usurp the government of Canada," a *Star* editorial said a week into the strike, "but a dispute between employers and employed [...] Nothing is to be gained by exaggerating the evil, painting the situation black, and making Winnipeg look like Petrograd."[21]

By contrast, on May 27 the *Winnipeg Telegram*, the most extreme of the anti-strike newspapers, ran a full-page statement under the headline "The Frozen Breath of Bolshevism." "If Bolshevism comes to Canada," said the *Telegram*, "it will do here what it has done in Russia and what it seeks to do in Germany. Liberty will be destroyed ... Property will be confiscated ... Laws will be annulled and the whole social system thrown into chaos ... Women and children will be the property of the state ... Religion will vanish ..."

Plewman gave *Star* readers an intimate view of the unprecedented unrest that was sweeping the city. He marched with the returned veterans, attended open-air meetings of the Labor Church in Victoria Park, and was in the streets to witness the violence of June 21, "Bloody Saturday." He interviewed many of the union leaders, as well as the employers and the key politicians both local and federal when they came to town. Thanks to Plewman and his colleagues, the *Star* was one of the few mainstream newspapers that the strike leaders trusted and one of the few that attempted to convey the strikers' point of view.[22]

+ + +

The Winnipeg General Strike actually began a few hours early. At seven o'clock in the morning on May 15, four hours before the official deadline announced by the Trades and Labor Council, 500 telephone operators shut down the phone system and went home. These women, known as the "Hello Girls," many of them single mothers supporting families on forty dollars a month, remained out for the duration of the strike despite intense pressure from their employer, the provincial government. There were reports that some women received threats that if they continued to strike they would

The Frozen Breath of Bolshevism

If Bolshevism comes to Canada it will do here what it has done in Russia and what it seeks to do in Germany.

LIBERTY will be destroyed, because Bolshevism means that one class shall rule over all other classes.

PROPERTY will be confiscated without payment to its owners. Your house, your household belongings if you do not own a house, your savings in the bank, your Victory Bonds—you will lose all these.

FOOD will be put beyond the reach of all except those who can seize it by brute strength, for Bolshevism takes the farmer's land, eats the food that is in sight and makes no provision for tomorrow.

LAWS will be annulled and the whole social system thrown into chaos. There will be no courts to adjust wrongs; no punishment for wrong-doers.

GOVERNMENT will be transferred from the elected representatives of the people into the hands of committees, or soviets, without any central authority—without legislatures or parliaments.

WOMEN AND CHILDREN will be the property of the state. One of the soviets which set the fashion in Russia—the soviet of Vladimir—has already decreed that all women over 18 must register at a bureau of free love and there hold themselves subject to the will of any man who may order them to follow him.

RELIGION will vanish when respect for law and for women and children vanishes. Bolshevism worships not the God of our fathers, but license.

Russia, after her months of Bolshevism, is almost a desert, with millions of her people dead and other millions dying of famine; her industries paralyzed; her government in the hands of ruthless assassins; her law-abiding men and women either murdered or living in hiding, stripped of everything they possessed.

The Canadian idea guarantees every man a free and open opportunity to share in prosperity and happiness. The workman of today may be the millionaire of tomorrow. Labor to be efficient and productive must co-ordinate with capital; both must live under the laws which are made by the elected representatives of the people.

Our greatest bulwark against Bolshevism must be the intelligence, thrift and patriotism of the Canadian workman

This Article is One of a Series—Be Sure to Read Them All.

FIGURE 30 The *Winnipeg Telegram* warned its readers about the dangers of Red revolution in this full-page spread dated May 27, 1919.

not get their jobs back. Several hundred women who opposed the strike stepped forward to work the phone lines as volunteers. Then, after twelve days, the company started advertising for new, permanent operators at ten dollars a month more than the striking operators had been getting. Some women could not resist their need for an income and returned to work. After the strike was over, many of the "volunteers" received cheques in the mail from the company at a rate that was fifty percent higher than the starting wage had been for regular operators. At the same time, as threatened, many of the striking operators did not get their old jobs back. Those who did lost their seniority and had to promise that they would not take part in any future sympathetic strikes.

The "Hello Girls" were just one group of women who supported the strike. Confectionery workers, store clerks, office stenographers, garment workers, and waitresses all joined them. From the beginning, women played a key role in the labour crisis. They may not have had seats in the unions' inner councils, but they were foot soldiers in the struggle, and many paid a heavy price for their involvement in terms of lost wages and lost jobs.

If the strike was about militancy and protest, it was also about sacrifice and need. With their incomes gone, many of the women could not pay their rent or feed their families. Recognizing the hardship that went along with the walkout, the Women's Labor League organized the Labor Café. Staffed by volunteer cooks and helpers, this food dispensary served three meals a day to women and children who needed them (men were asked to make a donation), as well as giving out rent money and even cash if it was available. Money to pay for the Café was collected from the Trades and Labor Council, as well as at union meetings and the sessions of the Labor Church. Initially the Café was hosted by the Strathcona

FIGURE 31 During the General Strike, women on both sides of the dispute volunteered to keep essential services operating. This duo tended the gas pumps at a local filling station. *Photo: Foote Collection, Manitoba Archives, N2736*

Hotel. When the Citizen's Committee of 1,000 put pressure on the hotel's owner to shut the Café down, the women moved to the Oxford Hotel and then the Royal Albert. The food kitchen served as many as 1,500 meals a day throughout the strike.

The prime mover behind the Labor Café was Helen Armstrong, wife of Socialist Party militant George Armstrong and a union organizer and outspoken advocate of women's equality in her own right. During the war, women's suffrage and opposition to conscription were two of her causes. Once, campaigning against conscription, she had been been roughed up by a gang of returned soldiers who did not want to hear her pacifist opinions. After the end of the war, Armstrong was particularly interested in workplace issues, and when the General Strike broke out, she was front and centre. She spoke from the same platform as the men, and if they tried to stop her, she fought her way onto the podium. She picketed, marched, and organized; a feminist firebrand, Armstrong ridiculed the fat-cat employers in her speeches and called the Borden government "a moribund, last gasp group of incompetents." An indefatigable organizer of unions for women workers, she had been one of the few women delegates to the Western Labor Conference in Calgary where she spoke forcefully in favour of the One Big Union. During the strike, she was arrested more than once for inciting protestors to stand up to the employers. On one occasion, police charged her with counselling to commit a crime in relation to an incident involving two young women who tried to stop newspaper vendors from selling an anti-strike paper. Armstrong was actually in jail the day the strike ended, being held without bail because authorities wanted to keep her off the streets. It was only once the strike was officially over that they decided it was safe to release her.

Armstrong would not be patronized, she would not be silenced, and she would not be still. Even with the strike at an end, she lobbied the Winnipeg Trades and Labor Council to help women who had not been rehired by vindictive employers. She travelled to Ontario to fundraise for the arrested strike leaders and was disappointed in the lack of militancy in what she referred to as the "effete East." The eastern press returned the compliment by calling her "the wild woman of the west." Helen Armstrong scandalized opponents of the strike by not behaving like a well-mannered housewife. Her "masculine" behaviour earned her special attention in the press— one paper even said she was mentally ill—but she was simply one of the most articulate and impassioned of many women activists who rallied to the strikers' cause.[23]

+ + +

Winnipeg was the major junction in Western Canada for both transcontinental rail lines. It appeared likely in early June that the workers who operated the railways might join the strike, effectively shutting down rail service in the country. Fearing that the local situation might escalate into a national emergency, the government decided to decapitate the strike leadership. On Wednesday, June 11, Gideon Robertson returned to Winnipeg. By this point Mayor Gray had issued his ban on public marches. On the previous day, 200 newly hired "specials" had battled demonstrators who were throwing stones and bottles at the corner of Portage and Main. This was the first violent incident of the strike; the injuries suffered by a pair of "specials" seems to have represented a tipping point for the anti-strike forces. The *Telegram* published a call for "a strong hand and a firm policy [...] There can be no middle course with anarchy," and A.J. Andrews wrote to Arthur Meighen that "the time

FIGURE 32 On June 10 a group of police "specials" were surrounded by an angry crowd at the corner of Portage and Main. They were rescued by reinforcements, but it took all afternoon to disperse the crowd. The creation of the specials was a particular sore point with strike supporters. *Photo: Manitoba Archives, N12313*

has arrived to act."[24] On Friday, rumours began to circulate that the government was preparing to declare martial law and make a mass arrest of strike leaders.[25] The rumours turned out to be correct. Robertson had been meeting with members of the Citizens' Committee, employers, and military officials, and had concluded that "the Red element" had to be removed. He wired Prime Minister Borden that he planned to hustle them onto a train bound for the wartime internment camp at Kapuskasing, Ontario.

On Sunday evening just after eight o'clock, a terrific windstorm blew in from the north, and without warning smashed into the city. Newspapers recorded that the gale reached speeds of 84 miles (135 kilometres) an hour. It was the worst hurricane Winnipeg had ever seen. The storm blew the roof off the children's hospital. Telephone and trolley poles snapped like twigs, while trees toppled over and plate-glass windows caved in. Pedestrians who had been out seeking relief from the muggy heat scurried for cover. Electrical wires whipped and fizzled as lightning struck the main power station and cast the city into darkness. The wind tore the roof from a building downtown and dropped it on a passing automobile, injuring two people, then a deluge of rain followed the windstorm and continued all night. It was estimated that damage reached half a million dollars.

While Nature tried to get everyone's attention, the work of the strikebreakers continued. Plans were in place to move against the leadership, but Robertson and Andrews worried about how the strikers would respond. On Saturday, the labour minister managed to convince the employers in the metal trades dispute to accept a modified form of collective bargaining, one that would make it look as if the employers were making concessions and, as importantly, one that would keep the railways running.[26] On Monday evening, the General Strike Committee met to consider the employers' offer. As Robertson and his co-conspirators expected, the offer was rejected, and a few hours later the authorities went into action.

Before dawn on the morning of June 17, police cars pulled up at targeted homes in Winnipeg's North End. Officers rousted six strike leaders out of bed, arrested them, and drove them to a neighbourhood police station where they were processed before being transferred to Stony Mountain Penitentiary north of the city. Those arrested were A.A. Heaps and John Queen, both city aldermen; George Armstrong, a carpenter and indefatigable soap-box orator; Bob Russell, a member of the Central Strike Committee; William Ivens, the editor of the *Western Labor News*; and Roger Bray, a leader of the pro-strike veterans. As well as raiding their homes, police also visited the offices of several labour organizations looking for incriminating documents. Dick Johns was arrested the same day in Montreal, where he was visiting on union business. Two days later, William Pritchard, who had come from Vancouver to observe the strike, was tracked down on a train on his way to Calgary, taken into custody, and transported back to Stony Mountain. On June 23, police picked up J.S. Woodsworth as he stood talking on a street corner. Woodsworth, who had arrived from Vancouver midway through the strike, had taken over editorship of the *Strike Bulletin* following Ivens' arrest. His co-editor, Fred Dixon, went into hiding but surrendered himself to police once the strike ended.

All the members of this group, who became known as the Winnipeg Ten, were of British origin. For the government, it didn't look good that a conspiracy that was supposed to be led by foreign agitators was in fact nothing of the sort. In order to give the impression of alien involvement, police also arrested four "foreign" strike leaders. Sam Blumenberg, the outspoken socialist orator, had already been the target of anti-Red street disturbances back in January when he was assaulted. Michael Charitinoff, editor of *Robotchny Narod*, the Ukrainian newspaper, had been arrested the previous year for possession of seditious literature. Twenty-two-year-old Oscar Schoppelrie was an American citizen and an unemployed musician, and Moses Almazoff, another Russian socialist, was a bookkeeper and a student at the University of Manitoba who was arrested just four days after his final exams. The four "foreigners," three of whom—Blumenberg, Almazoff, and Charitinoff—were Jews, were held at Stony Mountain without bail, then brought in front of an Immigration Board of Inquiry which considered their deportation. The case of Sam Blumenberg, the eldest of the four, aged thirty-three, was the first to be heard on July 14. An undercover military spy testified that at the Walker Theatre meeting the previous December, Blumenberg had spoken from the stage in defence of Bolshevism. Another witness who attended the later meeting at the Majestic Theatre told the inquiry that Blumenberg "was trying, with others, to organize a revolution to overthrow the government."[27] It was clear from the testimony that the government's intention was to broaden the inquiry beyond the events of the general strike in order to prove that Blumenberg and the others were involved in a wide conspiracy dating back many months. The board ruled that Blumenberg should be deported to Europe; instead he was allowed to leave for the US where he lived for the rest of his life. At Almazoff's hearing in August, a RNWMP spy named Harry Daskalud broke cover to testify. He reported that at a May meeting of the Jewish Labor League, Almazoff had advocated violent revolution. Almazoff's defense counsel, Marcus Hyman, was able to find two witnesses who contradicted Daskalud, testifying that at the meeting in question Almazoff had said just the opposite, that he opposed bloodshed. Hyman was also able to show that Daskalud, a native of Austria who had been in Canada for six years, did not understand English well enough to be a reliable witness to what Almazoff had or hadn't said. In the end, the inquiry decided that the evidence produced by the government was not sufficient to warrant deportation. Almazoff was released, and he too left for the US. A similar board hearing for Michael Charitinoff ruled that he should be deported, but this decision was later overturned on appeal. Oscar Schoppelrie was deported back to the US because it was shown that he had crossed the border into Canada illegally.

Meanwhile, on the morning of June 21, four days after they were taken into custody, the six men who had been whisked away from their homes in the pre-dawn raids were released on bail. Initially, authorities had intended to spirit the strike leaders out of town and summarily deport them. The changes to the Immigration Act earlier in the month had prepared the way for such a strategy, but then Andrews changed his mind. He remained intent on breaking the strike without any backlash, and he was concerned that the leaders might be seen as martyrs to their cause. At a meeting of the pro-strike Soldiers' Parliament in Victoria Park later on the day of the arrests, speakers cautioned the crowd not to overreact. Ernest Robinson of the WTLC warned that the arrests were an attempt by the government to incite protest so that martial law could be imposed. "Keep calm and let ideas triumph over force," Robinson urged.[28] But in spite of this mild reaction, Andrews preferred to avoid any unrest in the streets. To this end he decided to use the arrested leaders as a bargaining chip and obtained from the Strike Committee a promise that if they were released, the men would sit out the rest of the strike. "A.J. Andrews, K.C., representative of the federal department of justice, has changed the plan of action against the alleged revolutionary leaders," reported the *Telegram*. "The men under the new course will be tried in the ordinary criminal courts ..."[29]

Andrews took this decision on his own. The Citizens Committee of 1,000 was opposed, as was opinion in the press. But the government had put Andrews in charge of the operation. Accordingly, early on the morning of June 21, six strike leaders—Russell, Armstrong, Heaps, Bray, Ivens, and Queen—left Stony Mountain on bail.

As events turned out, Andrews' tactic did not work. Later that morning he met at the Royal Alexandra Hotel with a delegation of pro-strike veterans, along with Mayor Gray, Gideon Robertson, and A.B. Perry of the RNWMP. The veterans asked for permission to march to protest "the denial of free speech" and "the Russian methods adopted by the present government."[30] When Gray refused, they served notice that they would do so anyway. As thousands of marchers gathered in the downtown core, Gray asked the Mounties to support the special police in the event of trouble. The march began and, at 2:35 p.m., Gray read the Riot Act from the steps of City Hall. At which point the violence of "Bloody Saturday" began.

The next day, Mayor Gray issued his unapologetic description of the events, ending defiantly: "Winnipeg is determined to shake off these fetters of lawlessness and Bolshevism festering here for some time, and if it means sterner measures yet they will be taken with dispatch in the sure knowledge that we are acting in the best interests of all and are determined to see that the British flag, now as in the past, shall be the sole banner of authority."[31]

"Bloody Saturday" destroyed what was left of the strikers' resolve. There were no more demonstrations, and dispirited workers began drifting back to their jobs. One by one, public services were restored. The strike committee offered to call off the strike if Premier Norris appointed a royal commission into the conditions that had caused it. Norris agreed, and at 11 a.m. on Thursday morning, June 26, the Winnipeg General Strike ended.[32]

+ + +

Following the General Strike, its opponents remained certain that they had nipped a Red revolution in the bud. "The attempt to make a Bolshevist revolution disguised as a general strike has failed," boasted the *Telegram*. "It has terminated, as was inevitable from the first that it must terminate when once the true citizens of Winnipeg grasped the significance of the dastardly attack that was made upon them and their liberties."[33] Certainly the employers, including the government, turned out to have won a victory on the labour issues. The strikers gave in almost without concessions. Metal workers received a reduction in their work week but no increase in pay. Public employees who had joined the strike—telephone operators, postal workers, firefighters, and police—did not win automatic reinstatement and many lost their jobs.

Members of the Winnipeg business elite who had led the campaign to defeat the strike considered that they had won a battle but not the war. They continued to believe that Canada faced an imminent threat from the Reds, only a glimpse of which had been seen in Winnipeg. One thing they wanted was a federal inquiry to investigate and reveal the conspiracy. But Arthur Meighen, who remained acting justice minister until the end of July, would not agree. He thought that Charles Cahan had already done this work the previous autumn. He also believed that enough steps had been taken to defuse and control the Reds. The Mathers Commission was reporting on industrial unrest, and Manitoba had asked provincial judge Hugh Robson to prepare a report on the General Strike. Although the province showed no interest in prosecuting the ringleaders, the various security agencies were maintaining their clandestine watch on suspected Reds. As far as Meighen was concerned, all this was sufficient. It was a time to mend fences with labour, not to build them.

As historian Tom Mitchell has shown, the acting justice minister was even reluctant to proceed with the legal cases against the arrested strike leaders. Meighen used to be considered the prime mover behind the breaking of the strike—and that was true enough. But Mitchell's research reveals that after the strike was over, the future leader of the Conservative Party tried to keep A.J. Andrews and his friends in the Citizens' Committee of 1,000 from pursuing their vendetta against its leaders.[34] In fact, for several weeks it seemed probable that the men would be released. Certainly the federal government was hearing from labour groups across the country demanding that the arrestees go free. Andrews repeatedly requested authority from Ottawa to proceed with sedition charges, and repeatedly Meighen turned him down.

The situation changed late in July when the actual justice minister, Charles Doherty, returned to Ottawa from Europe and resumed his duties. (Prime Minister Borden was also back from Europe, but poor health kept him from involving himself much in his own government's business.) Doherty had shown himself to be much more concerned about the Reds than Meighen. He had been justice minister when Cahan submitted his threat assessment the previous September and had accepted Cahan's analysis that radicalism posed a serious challenge to public security. Now he agreed with Andrews that prosecution would send a strong message to the Reds that the government would not tolerate their activities. As the manifesto of the Citizens' Committee of 1,000 stated: "Feeling as we do that nothing less than Bolshevism has raised its ugly head, it is the duty of loyal citizens to band themselves together and [...] wherever this vile serpent appears hit it and hit it hard."[35]

In August, Doherty gave the green light for Andrews to proceed against the strike leaders. Canada would have its show trials after all.

CHAPTER SEVEN

The Most Infamous Conspiracy

"The Canadian people are in the process of having their rights and liberties stolen from them by the shabbiest pack of political jackals that ever harassed a civilized country."
—*Fred Dixon*, Manitoba Free Press, *July 10, 1919*

For the Red scaremongers, it was all a matter of connecting the dots. The first dot was the meeting at Winnipeg's Walker Theatre on December 22, 1918, when militants predicted the "coming revolution," attacked capitalism, praised Lenin and his gang of Russian Bolsheviks, and generally stirred up class resentment amongst the members of the audience, or so it was said. The second dot was the meeting at the Majestic Theatre three weeks later when several of the Winnipeg Ten advocated the destruction of the current economic system and so inflamed the passions of the mob that the streets of the city erupted into violence. The plot thickened with the third dot, the Western Labor Conference in Calgary in March 1919, when the conspirators made plans to seize control of all

FIGURE 33 The strike leaders arrested in the pre-dawn police raids of June 17 were whisked away to Stony Mountain Penitentiary where this photograph was taken. Back row (L–R): Roger Bray, George Armstrong, John Queen, Bob Russell, Dick Johns, and Bill Pritchard; front row: William Ivens, and Abe Heaps. J.S. Woodsworth was never brought to trial; Fred Dixon was tried separately. *Photo: Manitoba Archives, N 12322*

industry in the country and put an end to private property. And the last dot was back in Winnipeg where in May and June the General Strike, "the perfection of Bolshevism" as Arthur Meighen called it, aimed to spark a series of mass uprisings across the country that would result in the overthrow of constituted authority.

This was the case that the prosecution attempted to make at the show trials of the Winnipeg strike leaders. When the charges were finally agreed upon after the preliminary hearings, it took almost an hour to read the indictment, but basically the accused were charged with forming a conspiracy to overturn the government of

Canada and replace it with a "Soviet" system. The objective of the trials was not just to put a few Reds in jail; rather, it was to reveal the extent of the nefarious Red plot and, by exposing it to the full light of public knowledge, to destroy it.

Like Stalin's show trials in the 1930s, the trials of the Winnipeg strike leaders took place in a glare of publicity. Both sides realized their importance. Dramatic accounts of the court proceedings filled the news columns of the daily papers. Two of the defendants' closing speeches were published as pamphlets and sold to raise money to pay for court costs. Rallies and marches took place to publicize the plight of the accused. It was the final act of the Red drama that Canadians had been caught up in since the end of the war.

The prosecution of the strike leaders skirted the boundaries of illegality and sometimes may have crossed over. It was led by A.J. Andrews and his allies at the Citizens' Committee, enabled by the province, and funded clandestinely by the federal government. Technically there was no reason why a private party could not undertake a criminal prosecution; it was legal under the Criminal Code. But it would not have happened unless someone agreed to pay the lawyers, and that someone was the federal justice minister, Charles Doherty. Historian Tom Mitchell has revealed that at a meeting in Ottawa in August, Doherty told Andrews that the government would find the money to finance his crusade.[1] Normally it would have been the responsibility of the province to prosecute the strike leaders, but Premier Norris made it clear that he had no interest in doing so. Still, Norris could have stopped Andrews if he had wanted to, but he did not. The funds came eventually from money set aside by the government to pay for post-war reconstruction. Ottawa paid $196,000 (the equivalent of about $2.3 million in today's dollars) to Andrews and other Winnipeg lawyers, all of them members of the Citizens' Committee, as well as to a private detective agency that carried out investigations related to the case. Additionally, the prosecution was able to obtain access to names of prospective jurors and used that information to investigate their political views so as to choose a jury most likely to convict. If there was a conspiracy going on in Winnipeg, it appears to have been a conspiracy to subvert the normal course of legal proceedings to obtain a verdict agreeable to the state.

+ + +

Preliminary legal proceedings against the arrested strike leaders began in Winnipeg on July 21. On August 14, the court committed all ten accused to trial later that fall. Eight stood accused of seditious conspiracy, while Fred Dixon and J.S. Woodsworth, who had been arrested as interim editors of the *Western Labor News*, faced the lesser charge of seditious libel. In late November, Mr Justice Thomas Metcalfe agreed to the prosecution's request to proceed with the case against Bob Russell first and separately. Russell was the only one of the fifteen-member Central Strike Committee to be arrested and charged, largely because he was the only one who could be tied to the wider conspiracy that the prosecution intended to prove. The chief prosecutor was the ubiquitous A.J. Andrews, who felt that the case against Russell was strongest and might pave the way for convictions in the other cases. The trial began on November 25 and lasted twenty-three days, much of them spent choosing a jury and then in angry sparring between attorneys over the admissibility of different pieces of evidence. Robert Cassidy, Russell's lead attorney, argued repeatedly that his client was merely a labour leader acting on behalf of his members as part of a perfectly legal organization. There was no evidence of revolutionary intent, claimed Cassidy, no cadre of armed rebels, no plans to set up a new government; in a phrase, no smoking gun.

The prosecution was less interested in what Russell had done during the strike and more interested in his long history as a prominent Red and a promoter of discontent among the working class. As Andrews told the court, he was going to prove that Russell intended "1) to stir up strife; 2) to set class against class with the object of stirring up a revolution; 3) to bring about in Canada a Soviet form of government by means of a general strike."[2] Given the penchant of the accused strike leaders for using inflammatory rhetoric, Andrews had little trouble producing evidence out of Russell's own mouth that his ambitions went beyond a mere strike. At one point, he piled a table with socialist literature that had been seized in the various police raids across the country. "See the masses of it," he told the jury with a calculated mix of disbelief and disgust.[3]

Contemporaries and historians have agreed that Russell was one of the leading Reds in the country. "Well Bob," one of his union comrades wrote slyly to him in a letter, "I see by the press reports that you are Chairman of the SOVIET in Winnipeg, more power to you."[4] Another called him "the real brains in the conduct of the strike." D.C. Masters, in his history of the Winnipeg strike, identified Russell and Dick Johns as "the two most influential" leaders.[5] More recently, historian Peter Campbell calls him "the key figure, not just in Winnipeg but in western Canada as a whole."[6] To call him "the brains" behind the strike was to downplay the contributions made by many others, and Russell himself told the court, "there are no leaders but only mouthpieces," but there was no denying his influence.[7]

He was a plain-looking man with a long face, a high forehead, and fleshy lips that made him look a bit like the screen actor Charles Laughton, but he had a commanding presence. Russell's intelligence and drive had been evident since his arrival in Canada from his native Scotland in 1911 when he was twenty-three years old. Within five years he was on the national executive of his union, the International Association of Machinists. He played a leading role in the so-called "western labor revolt" against the national Trades and Labor Congess in 1918, and by the following spring he belonged to the inner circle of OBU organizers. His debating style was direct and belligerent; he saw no need to pull his punches. There was no question that his views were radical; Russell was a member of the militant Socialist Party of Canada and over the years, in speeches and in print, he had made clear his opposition to capitalist forms of production. "The present system of capitalism, or production for profits, is the cause of all the evils in present-day society," he wrote in 1915, "and only by abolishing capitalism can the cooperative commonwealth be realized."[8] His views did not change, and it was easy for prosecutors to find evidence of his apparent support for revolution. "We have passed into the most important stage of Capitalistic development," he declared at the beginning of 1919, "namely the period of Revolution."[9]

This made Russell a threat to the status quo—but did it make him a criminal? And what did he mean by revolution? Russell would say he was only stating a fact, not issuing a call to arms. He insisted there was no need for violence, believing that history was moving inexorably in the direction of profound social change. "The movement is a peaceful one," he wrote during the winter of 1918–19; "it accepts the civilized weapons of political and industrial action, propaganda and agitation."[10] But for the prosecution, the seditious intent consisted in Russell's eloquence in arousing opposition to the government. It was no crime, said Andrews, to stand up in public and praise the Bolshevik regime. The crime was in doing so in a manner that encouraged discontent and revolt. That was sedition.[11]

One of the most dramatic moments of Russell's trial occurred on the morning of December 5, when the prosecution called Frank Zaneth as a witness. Into the courtroom marched the man known to his fellow labour organizers as Harry Blask, a trusted comrade. But he was all decked out in the red serge of the Royal North-West Mounted Police. Zaneth had broken cover to testify against Russell, and it was revealed that "Harry Blask" was an undercover spy for the Mounted Police. He had infiltrated right to the heart of the radical labour movement, working as a Wobbly organizer and acting as secretary to a prominent union leader in Calgary. As Blask, he had been part of the Western Labor Conference in Calgary; he'd appeared in front of the Mathers Commission; he had attached himself to the inner circle of Calgary's Socialist Party and the organizers of the sympathetic strike; he'd even been arrested and thrown in jail. And now he was ready to reveal everything he had learned from his months undercover.

Zaneth testified for an afternoon and part of the next day. The prosecution received wide latitude from the judge to ask questions about meetings and activities that had little if anything to do with Bob Russell. In fact, though Zaneth had met Russell at the Western Labor Conference, his activities as an undercover agent had not brought the two men together. Rather, Zaneth's testimony referred more to contacts in Calgary and was intended to flesh out the theory of a wide conspiracy. At one point Zaneth even told the jury how Joe Knight, an Edmonton OBU organizer, had told him about a cache of rifles owned by the military, and had said to Zaneth that "we should keep our eyes on them as we might need them some day." This was damaging testimony that got headlines in all the newspapers the next day. It had nothing at all to do with Bob Russell, but it was effective in playing on fears that the Reds were armed and dangerous. After his appearance in court, A.J. Andrews wrote to Zaneth's superior officer that "there is nothing I can now say which would be too flattering to this young chap. His evidence in this case was most clear cut and decisive ..."[12] With his cover blown, Zaneth's usefulness as an undercover officer in labour circles in Canada was over, but he went on to have a long career in the RCMP, retiring as an assistant commissioner in 1951.

On December 24, the jury found Bob Russell guilty on all counts. He was sent home to be with his family for the holiday, then on Boxing Day the police drove him away in handcuffs to Stony Mountain to begin a two-year prison term. Neither Russell nor any of the other strike leaders ever admitted to any wrongdoing. In their view, there were no wrongs to admit to; they had been railroaded by the machinery of the state. According to Harry and Mildred Gutkin in their book on the strike leaders, after Russell was released from jail at the end of 1920, Judge Metcalfe, who was then dying, asked to speak with him. "Let him die with his guilty conscience," Russell said, and refused to meet.[13]

+ + +

The government of Manitoba had created a royal commission to investigate "the causes and effects of the General Strike" in its immediate aftermath. Hugh Robson, a provincial judge and sole commissioner, held eleven days of hearings in Winnipeg and delivered his report in early November, not long before the Russell trial began.

Robson concluded that the underlying cause of the strike was "a state of discontent" among a majority of workers that their leadership was able to exploit to mobilize mass action in support of collective bargaining. He did not deny that socialist activists attached themselves to the concerns of the labour movement and tried to take control of the strike to perpetrate fundamental changes in society—but he did not think they had succeeded. He found no evidence that "the great mass of workers, intelligent and loyal to British institutions" were attempting "to elevate Labour into a state of dictatorship." Nor did he implicate the strike's leaders in any of the street parades and demonstrations. In fact, he said, they had tried to prevent them. The strike was a strike, and a protest against unemployment, the cost of living, war profiteering, and inequality; it was not a revolution.[14]

In other words, an official inquiry appointed by the provincial government said that there was no Bolshevik conspiracy. This conclusion directly contradicted the basic presumption behind the prosecution of the strike leaders. The province might have stepped in at this point and withdrawn the permission it had given to allow the trials to take place, but instead Premier Norris kept the findings of the Robson report secret. He did not release it to the public until the following March, after the trials were at an end. Once again the premier made himself an instrument of the anti-strike forces while appearing to maintain a public stance of impartiality.

+ + +

The joint trial of the seven other strike leaders began on January 22, 1920, after the Manitoba Court of Appeal had turned down Bob Russell's final appeal. Three of the defendants—Bray, Johns, and Armstrong—had lawyers; the other four—Queen, Heaps, Pritchard, and Ivens—defended themselves. Once again Justice Metcalfe was on the bench and A.J. Andrews was the lead prosecutor.

The defendants found themselves pitted against the full force of the Winnipeg country-club set. Judges and prosecutors all belonged to the exclusive elite that ran the city. They lived within a few blocks of one another in the upscale Crescentwood neighbourhood. They dined together, partied together, curled, played golf, and rode horses together. They worshipped at the same churches. Their wives had tea and went shopping together. (Judge Metcalfe was even, it was later revealed, the lover of Andrews' wife.) As leading members of the Liberal or Conservative parties, they ran for election against one another and directed civic development as members of the Board of Trade. Naturally they had rallied to the banner of the Citizens' Committee —which Roger Bray called "that shameless bunch of profiteers"—to help put down the General Strike, and in its wake they believed they were protecting society from a dangerous gang of Bolshevik thugs. For example, Hugh Macdonald, local police magistrate and pillar of the Winnipeg establishment, wrote to Arthur Meighen just before he took the bench as the presiding judge at the preliminary hearings for the strike leaders. Macdonald wanted to congratulate the government for its resolute stand against "the extremists" and urged Meighen to deport as many of the "undesirable aliens" as he could. They had to be shown, Macdonald argued, that the government would enforce the law firmly. "Fear is the only agency that can be successfully employed to keep them within the law," he wrote.[15] The members of the Winnipeg legal establishment clearly saw their role as providing punishment, not justice.

Sitting at the defence table on the other side of the courtroom, the seven defendants came from a completely different background. Except for Ivens, a Methodist minister, they had all left school before the age of fifteen to apprentice in a trade. Abe Heaps was an upholsterer, John Queen a cooper, Bill Pritchard a longshoreman, George Armstrong a carpenter, Roger Bray a butcher, and Dick Johns a metal worker. Ivens was forty-one years old and Armstrong was forty-nine; the rest were all in their thirties—young men of intelligence and energy

FIGURE 34 William Ivens was the founder of the Labor Church and editor of the *Western Labor News*. He spoke in his own defence in court for two and a half days. Unconvinced, the jury convicted him, and he served a year in the penitentiary, during which time he was elected to the provincial legislature. *Photo: Manitoba Archives, N10452*

who held respected positions in their unions and in their communities. The defendants were not the semi-literate rabble-rousers depicted in the popular press. Self-educated, they had honed their rhetorical skills in the union hall and on the election platform and could entertain an audience for hours, without notes or hesitation, quoting John Stuart Mill, Karl Marx, or Henry George as fluently as they could the Bible. The public meetings at which they spoke were tutorials in political theory; they could parse the meaning of socialist texts as knowledgably as most university professors. They were in no way intimidated by the legal proceedings against them. Quite the opposite; they used the courtroom as a pulpit to shout their defiance of the business leaders who, they said, were trying to muzzle them.

William Ivens, who was born in Warwickshire, England, had come to Manitoba at the age of eighteen in 1896, the first year of the immigrant boom to Western Canada. Like so many single immigrant men, he went to work as a farm labourer with thoughts of one day getting his own piece of land. Instead he became a theology student at Winnipeg's Wesley College where he became a convert to the social gospel, the social justice wing of the Methodist Church. In 1916 he took over as minister at McDougall Methodist Church, but his preaching became increasingly radical. Ivens opposed the war and conscription, a position that effectively placed him outside the law, and in the summer of 1918 church officials removed him from the pulpit. Ivens established the Labor Church and began holding meetings at the Winnipeg Labor Temple. According to its membership card, the Labor Church was "independent and creedless," taking as its aim "the establishment of justice and righteousness among men of all nations." In other words, it was not really much of a church at all, more a progressive social movement. Anyone could belong, Ivens said, "who believes in the need and possibility of a better day for human society." Later that summer he took on the job of editor of the weekly *Western Labor News*, in whose pages he warned the business leaders of Winnipeg: "Your system will fall down about your ears with a suddenness and thoroughness that will surprise you." During the General Strike he edited the *Strike Bulletin*, the special daily edition of the *Labor News*, as well as holding regular meetings of the Labor Church in Victoria Park, prompting the Manitoba Methodist Conference to revoke his ordination.

Abe Heaps had grown up in a working-class Jewish neighbourhood in Leeds, England. After he emigrated to Canada he found work in the Canadian Pacific Railway shops in Winnipeg and joined the upholsterers' union. He first ran for political office for the Social Democratic Party in the 1916 civic election and won election to city council the following year. He had a soft-spoken manner and a wry wit that perhaps at times belied his political commitment. "He told funny stories in a very serious way," was how his fellow defendant Bill Pritchard described

ALD. A. A. HEAPS

FIGURE 35 Abe Heaps was acquitted on all charges. He was also a member of city council and later held a Winnipeg seat in the federal House of Commons for fifteen years. *Photo: Manitoba Archives, N14329*

him.[16] As a member of city council and a supporter of labour, Heaps worked tirelessly during the General Strike to bring the warring sides together.

John Queen was Heaps' colleague on city council. Queen had emigrated to Winnipeg from Scotland in 1906 at the age of twenty-four and got a job as a barrel maker with an oil company. He was known as "Silent John" because he exhibited a rare trait for a politician—he only spoke when he had something to say. Like Heaps, he was a Social Democrat—and hardly a radical; on council he devoted most of his energies to bread-and-butter issues such as housing, transportation, and the cost of living. But Queen had chaired the Walker Theatre meeting and had exhorted the crowd there to give three cheers for the Russian Revolution, so he was on the Citizens'

FIGURE 36 John Queen was a barrel maker by trade and a city alderman. While serving his sentence he was elected to the provincial legislature. Later he served two terms as mayor of Winnipeg. *Photo: Manitoba Archives, N14996*

Committee's radar. When police arrived at Heaps' house on the morning of June 17 to arrest him, they found Queen asleep there as well. The two aldermen were staying together while Queen's wife and children were away at their summer cottage.

Bill Pritchard was from Vancouver, where he had emigrated to from England in 1911, joining his father James who was already deeply involved in socialist politics. Within two weeks of his arrival, Bill was a member of the Socialist Party of Canada. During the war he served as editor of the *Western Clarion*, the party paper. He was a vocal opponent of conscription, promising that if he was called up he would not go. He only visited Winnipeg briefly during the General Strike, but he was known to police as one of the leading organizers of the OBU and as such got his name on the government's enemies list.

George Armstrong, who was born in 1870 on a farm in Ontario, was the only one of the defendants who was a native Canadian. Perhaps the best orator of them all, certainly the most long-winded, he was an implacable Marxist with little time for mere reformers. But his wife Helen had played a more central role in the General Strike than he did. Once again, it was his activism with the Socialist Party and his prominence at the Walker and Majestic Theatre meetings that marked him down for the attention of the authorities.

Roger Bray, who was born in Sheffield, England, was the only one of the accused who had served in the army during the war. He was one of the many young men who volunteered to go overseas because they had no prospects at home. He managed to avoid front-line action and returned to Winnipeg too late to take part in the winter unrest, but when the General Strike began, he emerged as a leader of the veterans who supported the workers. At one point, a police spy called him "the most dangerous person in the City," presumably because of his influence over the thousands of pro-strike returned soldiers he could call into the streets. In fact, though Bray belonged to the General Strike Committee, he really wasn't involved in any of the strike planning, as Judge Metcalfe would admit during the trial.

FIGURE 37 George Armstrong was a founding member of the Winnipeg chapter of the Socialist Party of Canada. His wife Helen was a tireless activist who played a significant role in the strike and was also arrested for her efforts. *Photo: Manitoba Archives, N22184*

"Dickie" Johns was born in Cornwall in 1888. When he was twenty-one years old, he left England to find work, first in the United States and then in Winnipeg where he got a job as a machinist in the CPR shops. He was absent in Montreal on union business as the General Strike unfolded, and that is where police caught up with and arrested him. To his prosecutors, it was enough

FIGURE 38 Fred Dixon was charged with seditious libel and was tried separately from the others. The jury acquitted him. Already a member of the Manitoba legislature, he was re-elected following the trial. *Photo: Manitoba Archives, N21098*

that he had spoken at the Majestic Theatre meeting and was one of the organizers of the OBU; his role at Winnipeg was immaterial.

While the proceedings against the seven strike leaders were underway, Fred Dixon went on trial by himself in a separate court, charged with seditious libel. The case against Dixon was weak. He was a moderate reformer—committed to the single-tax theories of Henry George and to the parliamentary system—not a revolutionary. He had been elected to the provincial legislature as an independent in 1915, defeating George Armstrong, one of the other defendants with whom he was supposedly in league. He did not attend the Western Labor Conference or the Majestic Theatre meeting, and he had nothing to do with planning the General Strike. But he supported it, and took over for a short while as editor of the *Western Labor News*, which was enough to damn him in the eyes of Mr Justice Alexander Galt who more or less instructed the jury to find Dixon guilty. "The evidence is uncontradicted," Galt said; "there is nothing against it; and it clearly shows, to my mind, the creation of the most infamous conspiracy I have ever heard of in Canada ..."[17]

Dixon's closing remarks to the court contained a passionate defence of freedom of expression. The *Manitoba Free Press*, no friend of the strikers, called it "one of the most impressive speeches ever made in a court of law in Manitoba."[18] Dixon told the jury: "In your decision either you will give liberty to public opinion, the right of free speech, or you will send it down into a black abyss. Remember that you are to decide whether the right to free speech is to be yours, and your children['s], and if it is to belong to me and my children."[19] The jury responded by returning on Monday morning, February 16, with a verdict of not guilty. The courtroom, jammed with Dixon supporters, erupted in jubilation. Reluctantly Justice Galt dismissed Dixon, whose closing address was rushed into print to raise money for the defence fund. Having failed to convict Dixon, the prosecution immediately dropped similar charges against J.S. Woodsworth.

That left the seven, whose trial was proceeding in another courtroom. The prosecution repeated the arguments it had used in the case against Bob Russell and brought forward many of the same witnesses. It did not seem to matter that some of the defendants were in Winnipeg during the strike while others were not, or that some were members of the Strike Committee while others were not, or that some endorsed the OBU while others did not, or that some appeared on stage at the crucial meetings in December and January while others did not. In the opinion of the prosecution, they were all Reds together, linked in a wide-ranging conspiracy to bring down the government.

The defendants called no witnesses, preferring to make their case in their own words, arguing that everything they were accused of was perfectly legitimate political activity. They were simply being persecuted, they said, for ideas that challenged the status quo. Ivens was the first to address the jury, laying out his own defence for two and a half days. His leadership of the Labor Church had made him a gifted sermonizer; "Ivens the Terrible" one newspaper called him. At one point he approached the prosecution table and taunted the four lawyers seated there for their membership in the Citizens' Committee of 1,000. "I look them in the eyes," he said, "and tell them that I would rather be here defending myself than one of you here prosecuting me."[20]

Next came Pritchard. He spoke for two days, from ten o'clock in the morning until ten o'clock at night, keeping his strength up with large glasses of buttermilk. When it was printed after the trial, his speech ran to 216 pages. The *Winnipeg Tribune* called him "the most brilliant of the galaxy of star orators who have so far addressed the jury" and said that his performance "would astound the average individual whose mental picture of a labour leader is a horny-handed, unread, ungrammatical toiler." The paper reported that Pritchard "seemed to hold the entire court through the sheer force of his personality and the power of his logic."[21] The *Free Press* reporter described him "leaning over the table between him and the jury box, looking into the eyes of the twelve men who are between him and the penitentiary, holding his right hand aloft dramatically, and declaring in ringing tones, 'I have done nothing of which I am ashamed, nothing for which I feel I need to apologize'."[22]

Abe Heaps spoke last. The presentation was less dramatic, though his calm demolition of the case against him went so well that when he began to wind down, one of the defence attorneys told him to "Keep it up, son," and he continued for another half day. When the jury returned with their verdicts on March 27, it turned out that Heaps' presentation had been effective. Five of the defendants were convicted on all counts and later received sentences of one year in the penitentiary. War veteran Roger Bray was convicted on only one charge and got six months. Alone among the defendants, Heaps was acquitted. But this was not a moment to celebrate.

Despondent at the verdict for his comrades, he told a reporter, "I would rather have been convicted along with the rest."[23]

The large crowd that came to hear the verdict filled the courthouse and spilled out into the surrounding streets. Initially the people thought they heard that the defendants had been declared "not guilty," and a loud celebration began. When the actual verdicts became clear, the crowd turned ugly and police had to sneak the members of the jury out the back entrance to avoid trouble. Then the convicted prisoners were taken away to serve their terms at the provincial prison farm. (Russell, having received a two-year sentence, did his time at the penitentiary.)

As a sad footnote to the whole dreary affair, the infant son of William and Louisa Ivens caught diphtheria and died just two weeks after his father went to jail. Ivens was allowed home to see the child shortly before his death. J.S. Woodsworth conducted the funeral at the Ivens' home. A crowd of several thousand mourners turned out, wishing to acknowledge the sacrifice not just of the Ivens but of the families of all the jailed strike leaders.

+ + +

The convictions of the Winnipeg strike leaders marked the winding down of the Red Scare. In truth, the court cases were anticlimactic; not for the men who went to jail and their families, obviously, but for Canadian public opinion. By early 1920, not many people, except for members of the Citizens' Committee, still believed that the country was poised on the brink of revolution. The seeming urgency of the previous year's events had faded. The benign conclusions contained in Hugh Robson's report on the General Strike were one indication of this new mood, and they were echoed that winter in Quebec, where the Department of Labour sponsored its own investigation into the reality of the Red Scare, only to come to the conclusion that "neither revolution nor socialism is arousing the working classes today." The department's report went on to say:

> No doubt there are ardent theorists and partisans of these dangerous doctrines in our province but the masses are ignorant of them. What the working class wants is improvement in their lot, fair remuneration for work and, above all, that living may not be unjustly made too dear for them [...]
>
> They were told that the country's greatest interests were at stake and they were asked to consent to such a sacrifice, the better to ensure the Allies success. But the war has ended and there is no change. Far from dropping, the cost of living is soaring to heights more and more inaccessible to the masses.
>
> The people seek a remedy for the evil [...] but nothing is done. They become irritated, for they rightly or wrongly suspect the authorities of having allowed a band of profiteers to make large fortunes out of labour. The authorities have had enquiry after enquiry made but they only show more clearly the gravity of the evil.[24]

If anyone was looking for proof that the Red Scare had waned, they needed to look no further than the election platform where voters were showing that they had no fear of the so-called rabid Bolsheviks and dangerous revolutionaries. In Winnipeg, seven of the ten men charged with sedition subsequently were elected to public office. John Queen, George Armstrong, and William Ivens all won seats in the provincial legislature in the June 1920 election, while they were still in prison. Queen was later a multi-term mayor of Winnipeg. A.A. Heaps was elected to the House of Commons in 1925 and served as a Member of Parliament for fifteen years. After a long career in education, Dick Johns became an elected member of the Winnipeg school board. Fred Dixon, who was already a member of the Manitoba legislature when he was arrested, was re-elected as one of the labour candidates in 1920. J.S. Woodsworth won election to Parliament as the member for Winnipeg North Centre in 1921 and went on to be the founding leader of the Co-operative Commonwealth Federation (CCF), the forerunner of today's New Democratic Party.

While electors were apparently willing to forgive the Reds their excesses, they were not so generous to the government that had encouraged the scare. In July 1920 Arthur Meighen, notorious for his role in suppressing the General Strike, took over leadership of the Conservative Party and in the fall of 1921 he led it into a general election. The result was a disaster for the Conservatives, who lost all their seats in the prairie provinces, including Meighen's own, while finishing in third place overall behind Mackenzie King's resurgent Liberals and the newly formed Progressive Party. It was a stinging rebuke for a man who just two years earlier was riding high as one of his party's leading Red scaremongers.

All across the country, left-wing candidates did well in elections following the Red Scare. In Ontario in October 1919, eleven Independent Labour Party candidates won election and joined with the United Farmers in a coalition government. In Nova Scotia a labour-farmer coalition took eleven seats in the 1920 provincial election, enough to form the official opposition. In Alberta the United Farmers swept to power in the July 1921 provincial election with labour support. Four labour candidates won seats in the legislature, and one joined the United Farmers cabinet. For all the hysteria of the Red Scare, the voters turned out to be less frightened of change than their leaders.

The Red Scare did not evaporate completely, and many newspapers continued to editorialize about the Reds. Businessmen still nodded in agreement at after-dinner speeches warning about subversion and insurrection. Authorities remained vigilant. In November 1919, Parliament merged the Royal North-West Mounted Police with the Dominion Police to form a reorganized Royal Canadian Mounted Police, and the Mounties went from a small, regional police force of 303 members to a national, 2,500-member force with responsibility for keeping a close watch on radical labour and political groups. "They have sustained a temporary setback," reported RCMP commissioner Bowen Perry, referring to the Reds, "but to think that we have heard the last of them is only resting in a false sense of security." And Perry had previously assured his superiors that "we have operatives who are members of practically every known organization in the west which has been in any way connected with or influenced by the present wave of Bolshevik and socialistic propaganda."[25] A simmering anxiety about the Red threat would characterize Canadian political life for decades to come.

Still, the obsession that gripped the country in the spring of 1919 eased as the year wore on and the revolution failed to materialize. It would be another decade before the panic about Red revolution re-emerged with anything like the same intensity.

CHAPTER EIGHT

Nothing to Fear but Fear-Mongering Itself

"The voice of dissent in Canada may be stopped, but it will be a fearful and irresolute people who do it."
—*Thomas Berger,* Fragile Freedoms

During the winter of 1918–19, the Canadian bourgeoisie, unsettled by the war and alarmed at the success of the Bolsheviks in Russia, believed it was facing a revolution. There was plenty of reason to think so. Labour unrest had increased dramatically, and the overheated rhetoric of the Reds was promising a dictatorship of the proletariat. General strikes were threatening to bring major urban centres to a standstill. An "alien" ideology, successful in other countries, seemed to have won the allegiance of important elements of the working class.

With the benefit of hindsight, we can see that there was no serious chance that Canada would have experienced an insurrection in 1919. Revolutionary ideas had wide currency, but even within the labour movement itself they appealed to a minority of workers.

While the unrest associated with Winnipeg's general strike did spread to other major cities, nowhere else did it disturb much more than the complacency of the employers. Despite what the fear-mongers said, there was never a large appetite in Canada for violent social change. This does not deny that working people felt disenfranchised and were making unprecedented demands for greater control of their own lives. Nor was this effort confined to the workplace. Women, for example, were agitating for equality on the job and wanting to play a larger role outside the home. Farmers had grievances about tariff policy, freight rates, and the power of the banks. In short, there was a broad desire for change. If peaceful change, brought about through the ballot box, can be called revolutionary, then perhaps there *was* a revolution going on in post-war Canada. But even so defined, it was not a revolution that threatened the stability of the state. Rather, it was the government itself that did most damage to democratic institutions by wielding its power in such an arbitrary manner.

But the Red Scare was not about reality. Because of its power and its access to the media, Canada's ruling elite—the government and the business leaders that supported it—was able to stir up a scare without producing much in the way of hard evidence that a threat actually existed. Under the pretext that the country was threatened by "an enemy within," and using the powers of the War Measures Act, the government launched a campaign of repression against its own citizens, aimed at left-wing political parties, ethnic organizations, and labour unions, supported by a propaganda campaign magnifying the threat posed by Red revolutionaries. Ottawa banned a variety of progressive organizations and periodicals. It became illegal to use certain foreign languages or to read publications from banned organizations. Police forces were asked to infiltrate unions and political groups to gather information that could be used to discredit their leaders as "Bolshevik." The modern RCMP emerged at this time as an internal surveillance agency with operatives across the country spying on Canadian citizens. Federal election laws were manipulated to exclude voters who might oppose the government and enfranchise those who might support it. The mainstream press was fed information—and misinformation—to stoke the fear of Red revolution. Members of the radical left were dismissed as "aliens" who had no rights of citizenship. Parliament hurried laws into effect that were unprecedented in their infringement on civil liberties. In Winnipeg, armed militia joined police in the streets to put down a public demonstration with force. Show trials were orchestrated to expose the extent of the conspiracy against the state and to punish its supposed leaders.

The government, or at least significant elements in the government, were genuinely convinced that a threat existed. They were spooked by the rhetoric of the radicals and the revolutionary events that they saw unfolding around the world. At the same time, it served their interests not to question too deeply the extent of Bolshevik influence in Canada. It was easier to portray all demands for a new economic order as "Bolshevism." Scaremongers believed in the threat of revolution, but they wouldn't have believed if it hadn't served their ideological agenda to do so—and that agenda was to discredit radical change and control the terms of the debate about the emerging post-war world. Much of the information that inflamed the Scare came from the police, which also had its own an agenda. It served the interests of the police to inflate the Red threat because it gave them a rationale for expanding their own activities. For example, in the case of the RN-WMP, it is probable that the force would not have survived if the

Scare had not come along to give it a new reason for existing.

In the end, the so-called Reds did pose a threat to the establishment. Their vision of an empowered working class challenged the unbridled power of government and business to run things the way they always had. Attempts to obtain better pay, improved working conditions, and perhaps most of all a meaningful voice in the management of the economy were considered threatening to the state and to employers. In this sense the threat was real, and the Red Scare was less an illogical outbreak of paranoia than it was a response by the power elite to a challenge to its hegemony.

+ + +

The triumph of repression over the forces of radical change was symbolized by the infamous Section 98, an amendment to the Criminal Code passed by Parliament in early July 1919 in the wake of the General Strike. Section 98, intended to replace the provisions of the War Measures Act, which was ready to expire, banned all organizations advocating "any governmental, industrial or economic change in Canada by the use of force, violence, or injury to persons and property." Anyone found to be a member of such an "unlawful association" could be sent to prison for up to twenty years, and membership was defined to include anyone who attended a meeting or handed out a piece of literature. This was the legacy of the Red Scare at the beginning of the 1920s: the abrogation of free speech and freedom of association for all Canadians.

In many ways, the Red Scare was a harbinger of things to come. It provided the government with tested strategies for coping with future threats to internal security when they arose. For instance, the government used Section 98 to suppress the Communist Party of Canada (CPC), which had formed at a secret meeting at a barn near Guelph, Ontario, in 1921 and surfaced to become a legal organization three years later. During the early 1930s, Prime Minister R.B. Bennett promised to grind communism under "the heel of ruthlessness." In 1931 police raided the headquarters of the CPC in Toronto and, in a reprise of the Winnipeg show trials, seven party members, including its leader Tim Buck, were sentenced to five-year terms in the Kingston Penitentiary. The following year the government decided to get rid of foreign-born radicals. Police identified several men who had not yet become naturalized citizens, rounded them up in coordinated raids, took them by train to Halifax where they were condemned by secret hearings, and deported them to Europe. It was all reminiscent of the proposal to "disappear" radical leaders during the first Red Scare in 1919. At that time the idea had seemed too extreme; by the 1930s the government was so spooked by communism that forced deportation came to seem like prudent public policy. Once again the mainstream press unleashed a barrage of anti-Red propaganda, fanning the public fear of "foreign agitators" and "Red troublemakers." Communism, like Bolshevism in 1919, was portrayed as an alien, un-Canadian philosophy spread by outsiders. Finally, in 1936, with the Liberal Party back in power, Parliament responded to complaints that peaceful political activity was being criminalized and repealed Section 98, replacing it with new provisions on sedition in the Criminal Code.

During World War II, widespread anxiety about the intentions of Japanese-Canadians living on the Pacific Coast touched off another scare. This one led to the forced removal of people of Japanese origin from the coast, many of whom were Canadian citizens. Authorities seized their possessions and removed them to camps in the interior of British Columbia or across the mountains to Alberta, Manitoba, and Ontario. Men who refused to be separated from their families were interned in prison camps. When the war ended, several thousand were pressured to accept repatriation to Japan, and several thousand others were sent to eastern Canada. It was not until 1949 that people of Japanese ancestry were allowed back to live on the BC coast.

Just as World War I contributed to the first Red Scare, so the post-World War II era saw another outbreak of Red paranoia. Before dawn on February 15, 1946, in a series of choreographed raids that were remarkably similar to the Winnipeg General Strike arrests, government agents descended on the homes of several Ottawa civil servants, arresting suspects and carting away evidence. Eleven men and two women were held incommunicado under the terms of the War Measures Act, invoked hurriedly by Prime Minister Mackenzie King's government. The civil servants were part of a Russian spy ring operating in Canada, the details of which had been revealed by the Soviet cipher clerk Igor Gouzenko, who had defected to Canada the previous year. The government appointed a special royal commission to investigate. It reported a widespread network of Soviet spies operating in the country, motivated by their sympathy with the communist system. Eventually eleven conspirators were convicted, including a Communist Member of Parliament from Montreal, Fred Rose. Once again a wave of concern about communist subversion swept the country. And once again secret agents of the RCMP were deployed to infiltrate and spy on labour unions, political groups, and other left-wing organizations in order to root out the dangerous ideas that supposedly threatened the Canadian way of life.

During the 1960s, militant Quebec separatists replaced the communists as the most feared threat to the Canadian state. Members of the *Front de Libération du Québec* (FLQ), which advocated an independent, socialist Quebec, carried out more than 200 bombings during the decade, mostly in and around Montreal. In October 1970 different cells of the FLQ kidnapped James Cross, a British diplomat, and Pierre Laporte, a provincial cabinet minister, and demanded the release of two dozen "political prisoners." By the middle of the month, 6,000 soldiers were on the streets of Montreal and Prime Minister Pierre Trudeau, at the urging of Quebec Premier Robert Bourassa and Montreal Mayor Jean Drapeau, invoked the War Measures Act (WMA). The country, said Trudeau, was in a state of "apprehended insurrection." There were also rumours—as in Winnipeg in 1919—of a plot to set up an alternative provincial government. Soldiers and police used the extraordinary powers conferred by the WMA to conduct raids on suspected FLQ members and sympathizers, mainly artists, nationalists, and known left wingers; close to 500 people were arrested without warrant. The day after Trudeau invoked the WMA, police found Laporte's body in the trunk of a car. The public, traumatized by the kidnappings and the unprecedented use of violent terror tactics in Canada, supported the government, just as people had supported the use of extraordinary measures against the Reds in 1919. Eventually, in December, the FLQ released Cross, and in a moment of nationally televised drama his abductors were allowed to fly into exile in Cuba. Laporte's murderers were found, convicted, and sent to jail. It was the first time since World War I that authorities had used the War Measures Act to deal with a domestic crisis and, in retrospect, it was generally considered to have been overkill. In 1988 the Act was replaced by new, less sweeping, legislation, the Emergencies Act.

During the 1970s, the activities of the RCMP's internal security service, which dated back to the Red Scare of 1919, came under intense scrutiny. In 1977 the Trudeau government appointed a royal commission to investigate an array of allegations that the force was straying beyond the law in its zealous search for subversives. Mail tampering, break-ins, burglary, monitoring of politicians, spying on Aboriginal and black activists; the list of dirty tricks went on and on. Among other things, the commission recommended that the RCMP lose its responsibility for internal security, and so in 1984 the government created a new, civilian agency, the Canadian Security Intelligence Service (CSIS). Canadians suspected of subversion might still be spied on, but it would no longer be by members of the RCMP.

+ + +

Canadian soldiers have invaded foreign soil to defeat terrorism and to install a regime considered friendly to the West. Almost without debate, Parliament has introduced laws giving the police broad new powers of arrest and detention. Undercover agents are deployed to spy on shadowy "alien" enemies accused of plotting acts of violence against the Canadian government. South of the border, the Americans feel themselves to be under siege from foreign-sponsored subversives and launch a war on terror. Border security has been tightened to ensure that terror suspects cannot pass easily between the two countries. There is widespread alarm in the media about the possibility of catastrophic assaults on domestic targets. Trials take place revealing a sensational conspiracy to strike at the heart of the Canadian state.

This scenario is a description of Canada in 1919. Yet it sounds remarkably like a description of Canada today; all the elements of the first Red Scare are also part of the government response to the al-

Qaeda-backed attacks on the United States on September 11, 2001. Sometimes it seems as if the modern war on terror has followed a script written almost a century ago.

In the aftermath of the attacks on the World Trade Center and the Pentagon, American President George W. Bush launched his infamous "war on terror," and Canada signed on as an enthusiastic junior partner. By the end of 2001, Parliament had passed the Anti-Terrorism Act (Bill C-36), expanding police powers of surveillance, arrest, and detention. Most controversially, the new act allowed authorities to hold terrorism suspects without charge. Amid misinformed allegations that the people responsible for 9/11 had somehow used Canada as a backdoor to enter the US (they hadn't), new regulations were imposed at the borders. At airports, a confusing set of security requirements were driving travellers mad with frustration. Early in 2002, the Liberal government of Jean Chretien contributed Canadian troops to a multinational invasion of Afghanistan aimed at destroying the al-Qaeda terrorist organization, removing the Taliban from power, and securing the country for a new, democratic regime. This intervention took place under the auspices of the UN, then NATO. The Chretien government stopped short of joining the Americans in their 2003 invasion of Iraq, but, generally speaking, Canada has been a willing ally in the US-led war on terror.

As in 1919, the obsession with security from terror threats came with many possibilities for abuse, as illustrated by the notorious case of Maher Arar. A Syrian-born Canadian, Arar was detained in September 2002 in New York on his way home to Canada from a holiday. American authorities, suspecting Arar of links to al-Qaeda, held him incommunicado for ten days, then deported him to Syria where he was tortured before being released in September 2003.

Subsequent inquiries cleared Arar of any connection to terrorist activity and the Canadian government ended up giving him an official apology and a substantial cash settlement. Arar's case was an object lesson in what can happen during a time of panic when security concerns outweigh civil rights and due legal procedures.

By 2004 the Canadian government's initial panicky response to 9/11 had passed. Just as the Red Scare of 1919 eventually gave way to a calmer assessment of the Bolshevik threat in Canada, so the government of then-Prime Minister Paul Martin abandoned the rhetoric of the war on terror in favour of a more measured response to national security threats. As an example of this calmer approach, in 2007 Parliament repealed the most extreme emergency powers granted under Bill C-36. And in 2008 Prime Minister Stephen Harper put a time limit on Canada's military involvement in Afghanistan, announcing that Canadian soldiers would leave the country by 2011.

Nonetheless, it is discouraging to note the comparisons between the war on terror and the Red Scare of 1918–19 (and the government's other anxious responses to subversive threats, both real and imagined, throughout the intervening decades). If there is a lesson to be learned from the Red Scare, it is that it—or something like it—will almost certainly happen again. When faced with perceived threats to security over the years, the Canadian government, with the support of the press and much of the public, has responded time after time with Robert Borden's stern hand of repression. Admittedly there is a distinction between maintaining the nation's internal peace and security and preserving its democratic procedures and principles. But if history teaches us anything, it is that in Canada we will cross the line whenever it feels as if the country is threatened, regardless of our commitment to freedom of expression and the rule of law.

This is the lesson, and the warning, of the 1918–19 Red Scare.

ACKNOWLEDGMENTS

As readers will discover for themselves, this book relies heavily on the work of many academic scholars who have been active in the field longer than I. Their books and articles are listed in the sources, but I should single out the work of Gregory Kealey, David Bercuson, Craig Heron, Linda Kealey, Barbara Roberts, and Tom Mitchell for special mention. I'd like to thank especially Mark Leier of Simon Fraser University who read the manuscript and made many important suggestions that clarified both the presentation and the argument. The subject of the Red Scare has been niggling at me for a long time. My own research has spanned many years, off and on, and took me to libraries and archives in Ottawa, Toronto, Winnipeg, Peterborough, and Vancouver. The dedicated librarians and archivists there are too numerous to mention individually; as a group they made the research possible and, as always, I am grateful for their assistance. Lastly, thanks to my friend Frank Mackey in Montreal for his help and to my editor at Arsenal Pulp, Susan Safyan, who saved me from numerous embarrassing blunders, both grammatical and historical.

Notes

PROLOGUE

1 Doug Smith and Michael Olito, *The Best Possible Face: L.B. Foote's Winnipeg* (Winnipeg: Turnstone Press, 1985), 4.

2 George Foster Papers, National Archives of Canada, MG27 II D7, Diary, vol. 8, June 23, 1919.

3 A. Ross McCormack, *Reformers, Rebels and Revolutionaries: The Western Canadian Radical Movement, 1899–1919* (Toronto: University of Toronto Press, 1977), 169.

4 Stephen Leacock, *Social Criticism: the Unsolved Riddle of Social Justice and Other Essays*, edited by Alan Bowker (Toronto: University of Toronto Press, 2nd edition, 1996), 75.

CHAPTER ONE

1 O.D. Skelton, "Current Events," *Queen's Quarterly* (July–September 1919): 127.

2 Quoted in Desmond Morton and Glenn Wright, *Winning the Second Battle* (Toronto: University of Toronto Press, 1987), 106.

3 *Canadian Annual Review of Public Affairs for 1918*, 602–03.

4 Royal Commission in Industrial Relations, Evidence, volume 1, Calgary, 3 May 1919, 786. (Hereafter RCIR.)

5 Charles Gordon, *Postscript to Adventure* (Toronto: McClelland & Stewart, 1975), 286–87.

6 Canada. Parliament. *Debates*. House of Commons, 4th session, 8th Parliament, July 1899.

7 Quoted in Mary Hallett and Marilyn Davis, *Firing the Heather* (Saskatoon: Fifth House, 1993), 145.

8 The best account is F. Murray Greenwood, "The Drafting and Passage of the War Measures Act in 1914 and 1927: Object Lessons in the Need for Vigilance" in W. Wesley Pue and Barry Wright, eds., *Canadian Perspectives on Law & Society* (Ottawa: Carleton University Press, 1988), 291–327.

9   See Desmond Morton, "Sir William Otter and Internment Operations in Canada during the First World War," *Canadian Historical Review* 55, no. 1 (March 1974): 32–58.

10 The following account is based on William Rodney, "Broken Journey: Trotsky in Canada, 1917," *Queen's Quarterly* (December 1967): 649–65 and Hans Werner, "And what, exactly, was Leon Trotsky doing in Nova Scotia in 1917?," *Saturday Night*, August 1974, 26–29.

11 For a history of the Wobblies, see Melvyn Dubofsky, *We Shall Be All: A History of the Industrial Workers of the World* (New York: Quadrangle Press, 1969).

12 See Mark Leier, *Where the Fraser River Flows* (Vancouver: New Star Books, 1990).

13 *Province*, April 3, 1912.

14 Quoted in A. Ross McCormack, *Reformers, Rebels and Revolutionaries: The Western Canadian Radical Movement, 1899–1919* (Toronto: University of Toronto Press, 1977), 109.

15 Ibid., 131.

16 Greg Kealey, "The Surveillance State: The Origins of Domestic Intelligence and Counter-Subversion in Canada, 1914–21," *Intelligence and National Security* 7, no. 3 (July 1992): 193.

17 These files have been published in Gregory Kealey and Reg Whitaker, eds., *RCMP Security Bulletins: The Early Years, 1919–1929* (St. John's: Canadian Committee on Labour History, 1994).

18 R.B. Russell Papers, Archives of Manitoba, MG10 A14-2, Box 3, File 7, December 26, 1918, Chris Stephenson to R.B. Russell.

19 Ibid., Box 3, file 9, November 30, 1918, Chris Stephenson to Tom Beattie.

20 Desmond Morton and J.L. Granatstein, *Marching to Armageddon: Canadians and the Great War, 1914–1919* (Toronto: Lester and Orpen Dennys, 1989), 87.

21 Robert Craig Brown and Ramsay Cook, *Canada 1896–1921: A Nation Transformed* (Toronto: McClelland & Stewart, 1974), 232.

22 Statistics Canada. *Historical Statistics of Canada*, 1983. Table E248-267a/b, http://www.statcan.gc.ca/pub/11-516-x/sectione/4147438-eng.htm#7.

23 Quoted in Tim Cook, *At the Sharp End: Canadians Fighting the Great War, 1914–1916* (Toronto: Viking Canada, 2007), 131.

24 Norman Penner, ed. *Winnipeg 1919: The Strikers' Own History of the Winnipeg General Strike* (Toronto: James Lorimer & Co., 1975), 14.

25 Michael Bliss, *A Canadian Millionaire: The Life and Times of Sir Joseph Flavelle* (Toronto: Macmillan, 1978), 53.
26 For a discussion of this strike see Meyer Siemiatycki. "Munitions and Labour Militancy: the 1916 Hamilton Machinists' Strike," *Labour/Le Travail*, vol. 3 (1978): 131–51.
27 This discussion is based on Bliss, *A Canadian Millionaire*.
28 Ian Milligan, "Sedition in Wartime Ontario: The Trials and Imprisonment of Isaac Bainbridge, 1917–1918," *Ontario History* C, no. 2 (Autumn 2008): 164–65.
29 *Canadian Forward*, October 12, 1917.
30 Quoted in Joseph Schull, *Laurier: The First Canadian* (Toronto: Macmillan of Canada, 1966), 590.
31 Quoted in Gerald Friesen, "Bob Russell's Political Thought: Socialism and Industrial Unionism in Winnipeg, 1914 to 1919," in *River Road: Essays on Manitoba and Prairie History* (Winnipeg: University of Manitoba Press, 1996), 126.
32 *The Voice*, December 7, 1917.
33 John Herd Thompson, *The Harvests of War: The Prairie West, 1914–19.* (Toronto: McClelland & Stewart, 1978), 139.
34 Ibid., 141.
35 Quoted in Barbara Roberts, *A Reconstructed World: A Feminist Biography of Gertrude Richardson* (Montreal: McGill-Queen's University Press, 1996), 207.
36 Skelton, "Current Events," 128.

CHAPTER TWO

1 Robert Borden, *Robert Laird Borden: His Memoirs*, Vol. 2 (New York: Macmillan, 1938), 972.
2 Library and Archives Canada, Sir Robert Borden Papers, MG26 H, Gideon Robertson to Borden, February 20, 1918 (Henceforth Borden Papers).
3 Borden Papers, Cawdron to Minister of Justice, March 5, 1918, March 21, 1918.
4 Borden Papers, Borden to C.H. Cahan, May 19, 1918.
5 R. Craig Brown, *Robert Laird Borden*, Vol. 1 (Toronto: Macmillan, 1975), 29ff.

6   Borden Papers, C.H. Cahan to Charles Doherty, Minister of Justice, July 20, 1918.

7   See Susan Mayse, *Ginger: The Life and Death of Albert Goodwin* (Madeira Park, BC: Harbour Publishing, 1990) and Roger Stonebanks, *Fighting for Dignity: The Ginger Goodwin Story* (St. John's: Canadian Committee on Labour History, 2004).

8   *Vancouver Province*, August 3, 1918; Peter Campbell, *Canadian Marxists and the Search for a Third Way* (Montreal: McGill-Queen's University Press, 1999), 44; Irene Howard, *The Struggle for Social Justice in British Columbia: Helena Gutteridge, the Unknown Reformer* (Vancouver: University of British Columbia Press, 1992), 119.

9   Borden Papers, Cahan to Doherty, September 14, 1918.

10 Borden Papers, James Calder to Borden, September 20, 1918.

11 George Foster Papers, vol. 7, September 27, 1918.

12 Borden Papers, Cahan to Borden, October 21, 1918.

13 Ian Mackay, *Reasoning Otherwise: Leftists and the People's Enlightenment in Canada, 1890–1920* (Toronto: Between the Lines, 2008), 449ff.

14 Newton Rowell Papers, MG27 IID13, Rowell to Doherty, October 18, 1918.

15 Borden Papers, Crerar to Borden, October 31, 1918.

16 *Globe*, October 26, 1918.

17 *Ottawa Citizen*, November 19, 1918.

18 Borden papers, Cahan to Doherty, October 22, 1918.

19 Eileen Pettigrew, *The Silent Enemy: Canada and the Deadly Flu of 1918* (Saskatoon: Western Producer Prairie Books, 1983), 33; Esyllt W. Jones, *Influenza 1918: Disease, Death, and Struggle in Winnipeg* (Toronto: University of Toronto Press, 2007), 6.

20 Mary-Ellen Kelm, "British Columbia First Nations and the Influenza Pandemic of 1918–19," *BC Studies* 122 (Summer 1999): 25.

21 *Vancouver Sun*, October 19, 1918.

22 Gregory Kealey, "State Repression of Labour and the Left in Canada, 1914–20: the Impact of the First World War," *Canadian Historical Review* 73, no. 3 (September 1992): 301–02.

23 *Globe*, January 16, 1919.

24 Ibid., July 6, 1918.

25 *Toronto Daily Star*, October 21, 1918; see Ian Milligan, "Sedition in Wartime Ontario: The Trials and Imprisonment of Isaac Bainbridge, 1917–1918," *Ontario History* 100, no. 2 (Autumn 2008): 150–77.

26 *Toronto Daily Star*, January 14, 1919.

27 Ibid., January 16, 1919.

28 George Fetherling, *The Rise of the Canadian Newspaper* (Toronto: Oxford University Press, 1990), 98.

29 *Saturday Night*, December 28, 1918.

30 Borden Papers, Borden to White, December 2, 1918.

31 NAC, Dept. of National Defence, RG24, vol. 2543, C.H. Cahan to Charles Doherty, January 8, 1919.

32 David Ricardo Williams, *Call in the Pinkertons: American Detectives at Work in Canada* (Toronto: Dundurn Press, 1998), 164.

33 Dept. of National Defence, RG24, vol. 4527, A.P. Sherwood circular letter, December 1918.

34 Dept. of National Defence, RG24, vol. 2543, F.J. Chambers to Robert Falconer, Jan. 11, 1919; Robert Falconer to E.J. Chambers, Jan. 16, 1919; Chief Press Censor, RG6 E1, vol. 613, Chambers to Falconer, January 18, 1919.

35 *Canadian Annual Review of Public Affairs, 1918* (Toronto: Canadian Annual Review Ltd., 1919), 42, 315–18

36 Ibid., 324.

37 National Archives of Canada, John S. Willison Papers, MG30 D29, vol. 2, file 20, Sir Edward Beatty to Willison, June 23, 1919.

38 Gregory Kealey, "The Surveillance State," *Intelligence and National Security*, 191; Borden Papers, C.H. Cahan to Borden, May 28, 1919.

39 C.H. Cahan, "Socialistic Propaganda in Canada: Its Purposes, Results and Remedies," speech given to the St. James Literary Society, Montreal, December 12, 1918.

40 *Maclean's*, September 1919.

41 Ibid., December 1918.

42 Ibid., January 1919.

43 Archives of Ontario, Maclean Hunter Ltd. Records, F-138, series B, E.J. Chambers to J.B. Maclean, January 10, 1919.

44 *Maclean's*, June 1919.

45 Ibid., August 1919.

46 Quoted in Todd J. Pfannestiel, *Rethinking the Red Scare: The Lusk Committee and New York's Crusade Against Radicalism, 1919–1923* (New York: Routledge, 2003), 40.

CHAPTER THREE

1 Mathers Commission, Hearings, Halifax, N.S., June 4, 1919.

2 McKay, *Reasoning Otherwise: Leftists and the People's Enlightenment in Canada, 1890–1920* (Toronto: Between the Lines, 2008), 431.

3 *Manitoba Free Press*, December 23, 1918.

4 Norman Penner, ed., *Winnipeg 1919: The Strikers' Own History of the Winnipeg General Strike* (Toronto: James Lorimer & Co., 1975), 11.

5 Benjamin Isitt, "Mutiny from Victoria to Vladivostok, December 1918," *Canadian Historical Review* 87, No. 2 (June 2006): 244.

6 *Manitoba Free Press*, December 23, 1918.

7 Robert Russell Papers, PAM, MG10 A14, Box 3, file 7, 5, Russell to Joe Knight, January 3, 1919.

8 Toronto *Star*, January 13, 1919.

9 Penner, *Winnipeg 1919*, 17–20.

10 *Free Press*, January 27, 1919.

11 NAC, RCMP records, RG18, vol. 3314, Winnipeg Strike files, Transcript of Immigration Board of Inquiry, July 15, 1919.

12 *Free Press*, January 28, 1919.

13 Winnipeg *Telegram*, January 29, 1919.

14 RG6 E1, vol. 613, F292-2, Norman Smith to E.J. Chambers, January 28, 1919.

15 See Gerald Tulchinsky, *Canada's Jews: A People's Journey* (Toronto: University of Toronto Press, 2008); also Alan Davies, ed., *Antisemitism in Canada: History and Interpretation* (Waterloo, ON: Wilfrid Laurier University Press, 1992); Yaacov Glickman, "Anti-Semitism and Jewish Social Cohesion in Canada" in Ormond McKague, ed., *Racism in Canada* (Saskatoon: Fifth House, 1991), 45–63.

16 Tulchinksy, 126.

17 *Toronto Daily Star*, February 17, 1919.

18 Quoted in Brown and Cook, *Canada 1896–1921*, 337.

19 Quoted in John English, *The Decline of Politics* (Toronto: University of Toronto Press, 1977), 113.

20 *Star*, February 17, 1919.

21 Toronto *Globe*, February 18, 1919.

22 A.E. Smith, *All My Life* (Toronto: Progress Books, 1949), 66.

23 James Dubro with Robin Rowland, *Undercover: Cases of the RCMP's Most Secret Operative* (Markham, Ont.: Octopus Publishing Group, 1991), 44.

24 Mark Leier, *Rebel Life: The Life and Times of Robert Gosden, Revolutionary, Mystic, Labour Spy* (Vancouver: New Star Books, 1999), 31.

25 Ibid., 86. This discussion of Gosden relies on Leier's book.

26 Borden Papers, vol. 96, pt.1, file Oc485, Perry to A.A. McLean, June 30, 1919.

27 Ian Angus, *Canadian Bolsheviks* (Montreal: Vanguard Publications, 1981), 35.

28 O.D. Skelton, "Current Events," *Queen's Quarterly* 27, no. 1 (July–September 1919): 122.

29 Montreal *Daily Star*, March 18, 1919; Calgary *Daily Herald*, March 18, 1919.

30 Borden Papers, Report of Agent 10 on the Western Labor Conference, March 19, 1919.

31 This discussion of Zaneth is based on James Dubro, *Undercover.*

32 S.W. Horrall, "The Royal North-West Mounted Police and Labour Unrest in Western Canada, 1919," *Canadian Historical Review* 61, no. 2 (June 1980): 176.

33 Borden Papers, A.B. Perry, "Report re. Western Labor Conference," April 2, 1919.

34 NAC, Dept. of National Defence, RG24, vol. 3985, file NSC1055-2-21, vol. 1, "Memo on Revolutionary Tendencies in Western Canada," April 1919.

35 Borden Papers, Thomas White to Borden, April 16, 1919.

36 R. Craig Brown, *Robert Laird Borden*, vol. 2 (Toronto: Macmillan, 1980), 165.

37 Quoted in Craig Heron and Myer Siemiatycki, "The Great War, the State, and Working-Class Canada" in Craig Heron, ed., *The Workers' Revolt in Canada, 1917–1925* (Toronto: University of Toronto Press, 1998), 37.

38 NAC, Royal Commission on Industrial Relations, Hearings, Victoria, BC, April 28, 1919, 172.

39 Ibid., Halifax, June 4, 1919, 4355.

40 Ibid., Vancouver, April 29, 1919, 280, 434.

41 Ibid., 469.

42 Ibid., Calgary, May 3, 1919, 718–20.

43 Ibid., Vancouver, April 29, 1919, 525, 602.

44 Ibid., Regina, May 8, 1919, 1124.

45 Quoted in Harry and Mildred Gutkin, *Profiles in Dissent: The Shaping of*

Radical Thought in the Canadian West (Edmonton: NeWest Publishers, 1997), 63.

46 RCIR, Winnipeg, May 10, 1919, 1465.

47 Canada, *Report of the Royal Commission on Industrial Relations* (Ottawa, 1919), 6.

48 *Globe*, September 16, 1919.

49 Gregory Kealey, "1919: The Canadian Labour Revolt," *Labour/Le Travail*, 13 (Spring 1984): 17.

50 *La Patrie*, March 26, 1919.

CHAPTER FOUR

1 Quoted in Richard M. Watt, *The Kings Depart: The Tragedy of Germany: Versailles and the German Revolution* (London: Weidenfeld and Nicolson, 1968), 322.

2 NAC, George Foster Papers, MG27 II D7, Political Diaries, vol. 8, May 2, 1919.

3 Quoted in Arno Mayer, *Politics and Diplomacy of Peacemaking: Containment and Counterrevolution at Versailles, 1918–19*, (New York: Alfred A. Knopf, 1967), 148.

4 Quoted in Ian Angus, *Canadian Bolsheviks: The Early Years of the Communist Party in Canada* (Montreal: Vanguard Publications, 1981), 20.

5 Smith, *All My Life*, 44.

6 Quoted in Margaret MacMillan, *Paris 1919: Six Months That Changed the World* (New York: Random House, 2001), 67.

7 *Globe*, January 18, 1919.

8 See Robert L. Friedheim, *The Seattle General Strike* (Seattle: University of Washington Press, 1964).

9 *Saturday Night*, February 22, 1919.

10 For the American Red Scare, see Theodore Draper, *The Roots of American Communism* (New York: The Viking Press, 1957); Robert K. Murray, *Red Scare: A Study in National Hysteria, 1919–1920* (Minneapolis: University of Minnesota Press, 1955); Todd J. Pfannestiel, *Rethinking the Red Scare: the Lusk Committee and New York's Crusade Against Radicalism, 1919–1923* (New York: Routledge, 2003); Regin Schmidt, *Red Scare: FBI and the Origins of Anticommunism in the United States, 1919–43* (Copenhagen: Museum Tusculanum Press, 2000).

11 *Le Figaro*, February 20, 1909, available at http:// www.italianfuturism.org.

12 Charles C. Hill, *The Group of Seven: Art for a Nation* (Toronto: McClelland and Stewart, 1995), 65.

13 This section is based on Hugo Ball, *Flight out of Time: A Dada Diary* (New York: Viking Press, 1974); Richard Huelsenbeck, *Memoirs of a Dada Drummer* (New York: Viking Press, 1974); Robert Motherwell, *The Dada Painters and Poets* (New York: Wittenborn, 1951); Hans Richter, *Dada, Art and Anti-Art* (London: Thames & Hudson, 1997; orig. published 1965); Michel Sanouillet, *Dada in Paris* (Cambridge, Mass,: The MIT Press, 2009).

CHAPTER FIVE

1 *Debates House of Commons* (hereafter *Debates*), 2nd session, 13th Parliament, vol. 1, June 2, 1919, 3034.

2 *Debates*, vol. 1, February 26, 1919, 42.

3 Thomas Fraser, "Is Bolshevism Brewing in Canada?," *Maclean's*, January 1919, 34.

4 Jonathan F. Vance, *Death So Noble: Memory, Meaning, and the First World War* (Vancouver: University of British Columbia Press, 1997), 115.

5 *The Manitoba Veteran*, June 21, 1919, in NAC, Meighen Papers, MG26-I, reel C-3214, 287.

6 *Debates*, vol. 1, February 28, 1919, 127.

7 Toronto *Globe*, April 15, 1919.

8 *Debates*, vol. 1, February 28, 1919, 127.

9 *Manitoba Free Press*, March 12, 1919.

10 NAC, RG18, RCMP records, Winnipeg General Strike files, vol. 3314, Inspector F.H. French to RNWMP Commissioner, May 26, 1919.

11 *Ottawa Journal*, January 3, 1919.

12 *Montreal Star*, February 1, 1919.

13 Norman Penner, ed. *Winnipeg 1919: The Strikers' Own History of the Winnipeg General Strike* (Toronto: James Lorimer & Co., 1975), 15.

14 *Saturday Night*, January 25, 1919.

15 NAC, Dept. of National Defence, RG 24, vol. 3985, file NSC 1055-2-21, vol. 1, "Memo re. secret writing," May 5, 1919.

16 *Ottawa Journal*, January 3, 1919.

17 *Montreal Star*, February 2, 1919.

18 NAC, RG6 E1, vol. 613, F292-2, E.J. Chambers to Arthur Racey, February 13, 1919.

19 *Montreal Star,* February 27, 1919.

20 *Montreal Star,* March 7, 1919.

21 Margaret MacMillan, *Stephen Leacock* (Toronto: Penguin Canada, 2009).

22 Stephen Leacock, *Social Criticism: The Unsolved Riddle of Social Justice and Other Essays,* Alan Bowker, ed. (Toronto: University of Toronto Press, 2nd edition, 1996).

23 *Debates,* vol. 1, March 3, 1919, 145.

24 Quoted in Linda Kealey, *Enlisting Women for the Cause: Women, Labour and the Left in Canada, 1890–1920* (Toronto: University of Toronto Press, 1998), 219.

25 Carol Lee Bacchi, *Liberation Deferred? The Ideas of the English-Canadian Suffragists, 1877–1918* (Toronto: University of Toronto Press, 1983), 3.

26 Barbara Roberts, *A Reconstructed World: A Feminist Biography of Gertrude Richardson* (Montreal: McGill-Queen's University Press, 1996), 146.

27 Regina *Leader,* February 15, 1916, quoted in James Pitsula, *For All We Have and Are: Regina and the Experience of the Great War* (Winnipeg: University of Manitoba Press, 2008), 92.

28 Roberts, *A Reconstructed World,* 146.

29 For Gutteridge, see Irene Howard, *The Struggle for Social Justice in British Columbia: Helena Gutteridge, the Unknown Reformer* (Vancouver: University of British Columbia Press, 1992).

30 Kealey, *Enlisting Women for the Cause,* 211.

31 C.K. Clarke, "Immigration," *Public Health Journal* 10, (1919), quoted in Ian Robert Dowbiggin, *Keeping America Sane: Psychiatry and Eugenics in the United States and Canada, 1880–1940* (Ithica, NY: Cornell University Press, 1997), 173

32 For eugenics in Canada, see Angus McLaren, *Our Own Master Race: Eugenics in Canada, 1885–1945* (Toronto: McClelland & Stewart, 1990).

33 *Debates,* January 23, 1914, 140.

34 Dowbiggin, 153.

35 *Saturday Night,* December 7, 1918.

CHAPTER SIX

1 NAC, George Foster Papers, MG27 II D7, Political Diaries, vol. 8, May 25, 1919.

2 *The Winnipeg Citizen,* June 7, 1919.

3 *Western Labor News,* May 17, 1919.

4 Ibid., May 20, 1919.

5 Quoted in David J. Bercuson, *Confrontation at Winnipeg: Labour, Industrial Relations and the General Strike* (Montreal: McGill-Queen's University Press, 1974), 136.

6 *Toronto Daily Star*, June 27, 1919.

7 Ibid., May 26, 1919.

8 *Winnipeg Citizen*, May 24, 1919.

9 *Debates*, June 2, 1919, 3036–43.

10 *Debates*, June 2, 1919, 3010–15.

11 Tom Mitchell, ed., "A.J. Andrews to Arthur Meighen: Winnipeg General Strike Correspondence," *Manitoba History*, no. 24 (Autumn, 1992).

12 Bercuson, *op. cit.*, 163.

13 Ian McKay, *Reasoning Otherwise: Leftists and the People's Enlightenment in Canada, 1890-1920* (Toronto: Between the Lines, 2008), 481.

14 Tom Mitchell and James Naylor, "The Prairies: In the Eye of the Storm," in Craig Heron, ed., *The Workers' Revolt in Canada, 1917–1925* (Toronto: University of Toronto Press, 1998), 187; Winnipeg *Telegram*, June 23, 1919.

15 See Uduak Idiong, "The Third Force: Returned Soldiers in the Winnipeg General Strike of 1919," *Manitoba History*, 34 (Autumn 1997).

16 *Western Labor News*, June 6, 1919.

17 *London Free Press*, June 19, 1919.

18 James Naylor, "Toronto 1919," *Historical Papers 1986* (Toronto: Canadian Historical Association, 1987), 49.

19 PAM, Robert Russell Papers, MG10 A14, box 3, file 11, Carl Berg to William Kolling, May 2, 1919.

20 *Toronto Daily Star*, May 23, 1919.

21 Ibid., May 23, 1919.

22 For the role of the *Toronto Star* in Winnipeg, see Michael Dupuis, "A Unique Career in Canadian Journalism: William R. Plewman of the *Toronto Daily Star*," *Canadian Journal of Media Studies*, 2, no. 1 (April 2007), 109–29 and "Main Johnson: Reporting the Winnipeg General Strike for the *Toronto Star*," *Prairie Forum*, 32, no. 2 (Autumn 2007), 273–98.

23 For more on Armstrong, see Harry and Mildred Gutkin, *Profiles in Dissent: The Shaping of Radical Thought in the Canadian West* (Edmonton: NeWest Publishers, 1997) and Linda Kealey, *Enlisting Women for the Cause* (University of Toronto Press, 1998), chapter 7.

24 Winnipeg *Telegram*, June 13, 1919; quoted in Tom Mitchell, "'To Reach the Leadership of this Revolutionary Movement': A.J. Andrews, the Canadian State and the Suppression of the Winnipeg General Strike," *Prairie Forum*, 18, no. 2 (Autumn 1993), 246.

25 *Western Labor News*, June 13, 1919.

26 Mitchell, "'To Reach the Leadership'," 247.

27 NAC, RG18, RCMP records, vol. 3314, Winnipeg General Strike files, "Transcript of Immigration Board of Inquiry," August 1, 1919.

28 *Western Labor News*, June 18, 1919.

29 *Telegram*, June 20, 1919.

30 *Western Labor News*, June 20, 1919.

31 *Telegram*, June 23, 1919.

32 A good overview of the strike is found in J.M. Bumsted, *The Winnipeg General Strike of 1919: An Illustrated History*. Winnipeg: Watson & Dwyer, 1994.

33 *Telegram*, June 25, 1919.

34 Tom Mitchell, "'Repressive Measures': A.J. Andrews, the Committee of 1000 and the Campaign Against Radicalism After the Winnipeg General Strike," *Left History*, 3, no. 2 (Fall 1995), 141.

35 Quoted in Tom Mitchell, "'Legal Gentlemen Appointed by the Federal Government': the Canadian State, the Citizens' Committee of 1000, and Winnipeg's Seditious Conspiracy Trials of 1919-1920," *Labour/Le Travail*, 53 (Spring 2004), 24.

CHAPTER SEVEN

1 Tom Mitchell, "'Legal Gentlemen Appointed by the Federal Government': the Canadian State, the Citizens' Committee of 1000, and Winnipeg's Seditious Conspiracy Trials of 1919–1920," *Labour/Le Travail* 53 (Spring 2004): 9–46.

2 *Manitoba Free Press*, December 5, 1919.

3 Ibid., December 24, 1919.

4 Quoted in Gutkin, *Profiles in Dissent*, 155.

5 D.C. Masters, *The Winnipeg General Strike* (Toronto: University of Toronto Press, 1950), 8.

6 Peter Campbell, *Canadian Marxists and the Search for a Third Way* (Montreal: McGill-Queen's University Press, 1999), 181.

7 *Manitoba Free Press*, December 29, 1919.

8 Quoted in Gerald Friesen, "Bob Russell's Political Thought: Socialism and Industrial Unionism in Winnipeg, 1914 to 1919," in *River Road: Essays on Manitoba and Prairie History* (Winnipeg: University of Manitoba Press, 1996), 130.

9 Ibid., 136.

10 Ibid., 135.

11 Tom Mitchell, "'Repressive Measures': A.J. Andrews, the Committee of 1000 and the Campaign Against Radicalism After the Winnipeg General Strike," *Left History* 3, no. 2 (Fall 1995): 158.

12 Dubro, *Undercover*, 86.

13 Gutkin, *Profiles*, 166.

14 *Royal Commission to Enquire into and Report Upon the Causes and Effects of the General Strike....* (Winnipeg: Government of Manitoba, 1919), 5, 10, 17.

15 NAC, Meighen Papers, MG26-1, Hugh J. Macdonald to Arthur Meighen, July 3, 1919.

16 Quoted in Gutkin, 314.

17 Quoted in Gutkin, 41–42.

18 *Manitoba Free Press*, February 16, 1920.

19 *Manitoba Free Press*, February 16, 1920.

20 *Manitoba Free Press*, March 23, 1920.

21 *Winnipeg Tribune*, March 23, 1920, March 25, 1920.

22 *Manitoba Free Press*, March 25, 1920.

23 Gutkin, 315.

24 Quoted in Terry Copp, *The Anatomy of Poverty: The Condition of the Working Class in Montrreal, 1897–1929* (Toronto: McClelland and Stewart, 1974), 134.

25 Gregory Kealey, "The Surveillance State: The Origins of Domestic Intelligence and Counter-Subversion in Canada, 1914–21," *Intelligence and National Security*, 7, no. 3 (July 1992), 202.

SOURCES

PRIVATE PAPERS
National Archives of Canada
Sir Robert Borden Papers, MG26 H.
Sir George Foster Papers, MG27 II D7.
Arthur Meighen Papers, MG26-I.
Newton Rowell Papers, MG27 IID13.
John S. Willison Papers, MG30 D29.

Provincial Archives of Manitoba
Robert Russell Papers, MG10 A14-2.

UNPUBLISHED GOVERNMENT RECORDS
National Archives of Canada
Department of the Chief Press Censor, RG6 E1.
Department of Justice, RG 13.
Department of National Defence, RG 24.
Royal Canadian Mounted Police, RG 18.
Royal Commission on Industrial Relations, 1919, Evidence, RG33-95.

Provincial Archives of Manitoba
Winnipeg General Strike Collection, MG14 A18.

Archives of Ontario
Maclean-Hunter Ltd. Records, F-138.

PUBLISHED REPORTS
Canada. *Report of the Royal Commission appointed to enquire into Industrial Relations in Canada.* Ottawa, 1919.
Manitoba. *Royal Commission to Enquire into and Report Upon the Causes and Effects of the General Strike Which Recently Existed in the City of Winnipeg for a Period of Six Weeks, 1919.* Winnipeg, 1919.

BOOKS AND ARTICLES
Altman, Morris. "New Estimates of Hours of Work and Real Income in Canada from the 1880s to 1930: Long-Run Trends and Workers'

Preferences." *Review of Income and Wealth*, Series 45, no. 3 (Sept. 1999): 353–372.

Andrews, A.J. "A.J. Andrews to Arthur Meighen: Winnipeg General Strike Correspondence." *Manitoba History* 24 (Autumn 1992): http://www. mhs.mb.ca/docs/mb_history/24/generalstrikecorrespondence.shtml.

Angus, Ian. *Canadian Bolsheviks: The Early Years of the Communist Party in Canada*. Montreal: Vanguard Publications, 1981.

Artibise, Alan. *Winnipeg: An Illustrated History*. Toronto: James Lorimer and Co., 1977.

Avery, Donald. "The Radical Alien and the Winnipeg General Strike of 1919." In *The West and the Nation*, edited by Carl Berger and Ramsay Cook: 209–231. Toronto: McClelland & Stewart, 1976.

———. *"Dangerous Foreigners": European Immigrant Workers and Labour Radicalism in Canada, 1896–1932*. Toronto: McClelland & Stewart, 1979.

Bacchi, Carol Lee. *Liberation Deferred? The Ideas of the English-Canadian Suffragists, 1877–1918*. Toronto: University of Toronto Press, 1983.

Ball, Hugo. *Flight out of Time: A Dada Diary*. New York: Viking Press, 1974.

Bercuson, David J. *Confrontation at Winnipeg: Labour, Industrial Relations and the General Strike*. Montreal: McGill-Queen's University Press, 1974.

———. *Fools and Wise Men: The Rise and Fall of the One Big Union*. Toronto: McGraw-Hill Ryerson, 1978.

Berger, Thomas. *Fragile Freedoms: Human Rights and Dissent in Canada*. Toronto: Irwin Publishing, 1981.

Bliss, Michael. *A Canadian Millionaire: The Life and Times of Sir Joseph Flavelle*. Toronto: Macmillan, 1978.

———. *Right Honourable Men: The Descent of Canadian Politics from Macdonald to Mulroney*. Toronto: HarperCollins, 1994.

Borden, Robert. *Robert Laird Borden: His Memoirs*. Vol. 2. Edited by Henry Borden. New York: Macmillan, 1938.

Brown, Robert Craig. *Robert Laird Borden*. 2 vols. Toronto: Macmillan, 1975, 1980.

Brown, Robert Craig, and Ramsay Cook. *Canada 1896–1921: A Nation Transformed*. Toronto: McClelland & Stewart, 1974.

Bumsted, J.M. *The Winnipeg General Strike of 1919: An Illustrated History*. Winnipeg: Watson & Dwyer, 1994.

Cahan, Charles H. *Maclean's*, September 1919.

————. *Ottawa Citizen*, November 19, 1918.

————. "Socialistic Propaganda in Canada: Its Purposes, Results and Remedies." Speech given to the St. James Literary Society, Montreal, December 12, 1918. (printed as a pamphlet).

Calgary Daily Herald, March 18, 1919.

Campbell, Peter. *Canadian Marxists and the Search for a Third Way.* Montreal: McGill-Queen's University Press, 1999.

————. "Understanding the Dictatorship of the Proletariat: The Canadian Left and the Moment of Socialist Possibility in 1919." *Labour/Le Travail* 64 (Fall 2009): 51–73.

Chalmers, Floyd. *A Gentleman of the Press: The Story of Colonel John Bayne Maclean and the Publishing Empire He Founded.* Toronto: Doubleday, 1969.

Cook, Tim. *At the Sharp End: Canadians Fighting the Great War, 1914–1916.* Toronto: Viking Canada, 2007.

————. *Shock Troops: Canadians Fighting the Great War, 1917–1918.* Toronto: Viking Canada, 2008.

Cook, Ramsay. *The Politics of John W. Dafoe and the "Free Press."* Toronto: University of Toronto Press, 1963.

Copp, Terry. *The Anatomy of Poverty: The Condition of the Working Class in Montreal, 1897–1929.* Toronto: McClelland and Stewart, 1974.

Craven, Paul. *"An Impartial Umpire": Industrial Relations and the Canadian State, 1900–1911.* Toronto: University of Toronto Press, 1980.

Dowbiggin, Ian Robert. *Keeping America Sane: Psychiatry and Eugenics in the United States and Canada, 1880–1940.* Ithica, NY: Cornell University Press, 1997.

Draper, Theodore. *The Roots of American Communism.* New York: The Viking Press, 1957.

Drolet, Benjamin. *La Patrie*, March 26, 1919.

Dubofsky, Melvyn. *We Shall Be All: A History of the Industrial Workers of the World.* New York: Quadrangle Press, 1969.

Dubro, James with Robin Rowland. *Undercover: Cases of the RCMP's Most Secret Operative.* Markham, Ont.: Octopus Publishing Group, 1991.

Dupuis, Michael. "A Unique Career in Canadian Journalism: William R. Plewman of the *Toronto Daily Star*." *Canadian Journal of Media Studies* 2, no. 1 (April 2007): 109–129.

————. "Main Johnson: Reporting the Winnipeg General Strike for the *Toronto Star.*" *Prairie Forum* 32, no. 2 (Autumn 2007): 273–298.

English, John. *The Decline of Politics: The Conservatives and the Party System.* Toronto: University of Toronto Press, 1977.

Fetherling, Douglas. *The Rise of the Canadian Newspaper.* Toronto: Oxford University Press, 1990.

Forbes, Ernie. *Maritime Rights: The Maritime Rights Movement, 1919– 1927.* Montreal: McGill-Queen's University Press, 1979.

Fraser, Thomas. "Is Bolshevism Brewing in Canada?" *Maclean's*, January 1919.

Friedheim, Robert L. *The Seattle General Strike.* Seattle: University of Washington Press, 1964.

Friesen, Gerald. "'Yours In Revolt': The Socialist Party of Canada and the Western Canadian Labour Movement." *Labour/Le Travail* 1 (1976): 139–157.

————. "Bob Russell's Political Thought: Socialism and Industrial Unionism in Winnipeg, 1914 to 1919." In *River Road: Essays on Manitoba and Prairie History.* Winnipeg: University of Manitoba Press, 1996: 121– 146.

Gadsby, H.F. *Saturday Night*, January 25, 1919.

Globe, "Bolshevism in Canada," April 15, 1919.

————, July 6, 1918.

————, October 26, 1918.

————, January 16, 1919.

————, January 18, 1919.

————, February 18, 1919.

————, September 16, 1919.

Goldstein, Robert Justin. *Political Repression in Modern America: From 1870 to the Present.* New York: Schenkman Publishing/Two Continents Publishing, 1978.

Gordon, Charles. *Postscript to Adventure.* Toronto: McClelland and Stewart, 1975.

Grant, Hugh. "Revolution in Winnipeg." *Labour/Le Travail* 60 (Fall 2007): 171–179.

Gray, Charles Frederick. *Winnipeg Telegram*, June 23, 1919.

Greenwood, F. Murray. "The Drafting and Passage of the War Measures Act in 1914 and 1927: Object Lessons in the Need for Vigilance." In

Canadian Perspectives on Law & Society, edited by W. Wesley Pue and Barry Wright, 291–327. Ottawa: Carleton University Press, 1988.

Gutkin, Harry, and Mildred Gutkin. *Profiles in Dissent: The Shaping of Radical Thought in the Canadian West.* Edmonton: NeWest Publishers, 1997.

Hagedorn, Ann. *Savage Peace: Hope and Fear in America, 1919.* New York: Simon & Schuster, 2007.

Hallett, Mary, and Marilyn Davis. *Firing the Heather: the Life and Times of Nellie McClung.* Saskatoon: Fifth House, 1993.

Harkness, Ross. *J.E. Atkinson of the Star.* Toronto: University of Toronto Press, 1963.

Heron, Craig, ed. *The Workers' Revolt in Canada, 1917–1925.* Toronto: University of Toronto Press, 1998.

Higham, John. *Strangers in the Land: Patterns of American Nativism, 1860–1925.* New Brunswick, NJ: Rutgers University Press, 1955.

Hill, Charles C. *The Group of Seven: Art for a Nation.* Toronto: McClelland and Stewart, 1995.

Hopkins, J. Castell. *The Canadian Annual Review of Public Affairs, 1918.* Toronto: Canadian Annual Review Ltd., 1919.

Horodyski, Mary. "Women and the Winnipeg General Strike of 1919." *Manitoba History* 11 (Spring 1986): 28–37.

Horrall, S.W. "The Royal North-West Mounted Police and Labour Unrest in Western Canada, 1919." *Canadian Historical Review* LXI, 2 (June 1980): 169–190.

Howard, Irene. *The Struggle for Social Justice in British Columbia: Helena Gutteridge, the Unknown Reformer.* Vancouver: University of British Columbia Press, 1992.

Huelsenbeck, Richard. *Memoirs of a Dada Drummer.* New York: Viking Press, 1974.

Idiong, Uduak. "The Third Force: Returned Soldiers in the Winnipeg General Strike of 1919." *Manitoba History* 34 (Autumn 1997): 15–22.

Isitt, Benjamin. "Mutiny from Victoria to Vladivostok, December 1918." *Canadian Historical Review* 87, no. 2 (June 2006): 223–264.

———. "Searching for Workers' Solidarity: The One Big Union and the Victoria General Strike of 1919." *Labour/Le Travail* 60 (Fall 2007): 9–42.

Jones, Esyllt W. *Influenza 1918: Disease, Death, and Struggle in Winnipeg.* Toronto: University of Toronto Press, 2007.

Katz, Leslie. "Some Legal Consequences of the Winnipeg General Strike." *Manitoba Law Journal* 4, No. 1 (1970): 39–52.

Kealey, Gregory S. "1919: The Canadian Labour Revolt." *Labour/Le Travail*, 13 (Spring 1984): 11–44.

———. "The Surveillance State: The Origins of Domestic Intelligence and Counter-Subversion in Canada, 1914–21." *Intelligence and National Security* 7, no. 3 (July 1992): 179–210.

———. "State Repression of Labour and the Left in Canada, 1914–20: the Impact of the First World War." *Canadian Historical Review* 73, no. 3 (September 1992): 281–314

———. "Spymasters, Spies, and their Subjects: the RCMP and Canadian State Repression, 1914–39." In *Whose National Security?: Canadian State Surveillance and the Creation of Enemies*, edited by Gary Kinsman, Dieter K. Buse and Mercedes Steedman. Toronto: Between the Lines, 2000. 18–33.

Kealey, Gregory S. and Reg Whitaker, eds. *RCMP Security Bulletins: The Early Years, 1919–1929*. St. John's: Canadian Committee on Labour History, 1994.

Kealey, Linda. *Enlisting Women for the Cause: Women, Labour and the Left in Canada, 1890–1920*. Toronto: University of Toronto Press, 1998.

Kelly, Paula. "Looking for Mrs. Armstrong." *The Beaver* 82, no. 3 (June/July 2002): 20–26.

Kelm, Mary-Ellen. "British Columbia First Nations and the Influenza Pandemic of 1918–19." *BC Studies* 122 (Summer 1999): 23–47.

Keshen, Jeffrey A. *Propaganda and Censorship During Canada's Great War*. Edmonton: University of Alberta Press, 1996.

Klingaman, William K. *1919: The Year Our World Began*. New York: Harper & Row, 1987.

Kordan, Bohdan S. *Enemy Aliens, Prisoners of War: Internment in Canada during the Great War*. Montreal: McGill-Queen's University Press, 2002.

Larivière, Claude. *Albert Saint-Martin, Militant D'Avant-Garde (1865–1947)*. Laval, Que.: Les Éditions coopératives Albert Saint-Martin, 1979.

Leacock, Stephen. *Social Criticism: the Unsolved Riddle of Social Justice and Other Essays*. Alan Bowker, ed. Toronto: University of Toronto Press, 2nd edition, 1996.

Leier, Mark. *Where the Fraser River Flows: The Industrial Workers of the World in British Columbia*. Vancouver: New Star Books, 1990.

———. *Rebel Life: The Life and Times of Robert Gosden, Revolutionary, Mystic, Labour Spy*. Vancouver: New Star Books, 1999.

Lincoln, W. Bruce. *Passage Through Armageddon: the Russians in War and Revolution, 1914–1918*. New York: Simon and Schuster, 1986.

———. *Red Victory: A History of the Russian Civil War*. New York: Simon & Schuster, 1989.

Maclean, John Bayne. *Maclean's*, December 1918.

———. *Maclean's*, June 1919.

Maclean's, August 1919.

Manitoba Free Press, December 23, 1918.

———, January 27, 1919.

———, January 28, 1919.

———, March 12, 1919.

———, December 5, 1919.

———, December 24, 1919.

———, December 29, 1919.

———, February 16, 1920.

———, March 23, 1920.

———, March 25, 1920.

McCormack, A. Ross. *Reformers, Rebels and Revolutionaries: The Western Canadian Radical Movement, 1899–1919*. Toronto: University of Toronto Press, 1977.

McGinnis, Janice P. Dickin, "The Impact of Epidemic Influenza: Canada, 1918–1919." In *Medicine in Canadian Society: Historical Perspectives*, edited by S.E.D. Shortt. 447–478. Montreal: McGill-Queen's University Press, 1981.

McKay, Ian. *Reasoning Otherwise: Leftists and the People's Enlightenment in Canada, 1890–1920*. Toronto: Between the Lines, 2008.

Mackenzie, David, ed. *Canada and the First World War*. Toronto: University of Toronto Press, 2005.

McLaren, Angus. *Our Own Master Race: Eugenics in Canada, 1885–1945*. Toronto: McClelland & Stewart, 1990.

MacLaren, Roy. *Canadians in Russia, 1918–1919*. Toronto: Macmillan, 1976.

MacMillan, Margaret. *Paris 1919: Six Months That Changed the World*. New York: Random House, 2001.

———. *Stephen Leacock*. Toronto: Penguin Canada, 2009.

Masters, D.C. *The Winnipeg General Strike*. Toronto: University of Toronto Press, 1950.

Mawdsley, Evan. *The Russian Civil War*. Boston: Allen & Unwin, 1987.

Mayer, Arno J. *Politics and Diplomacy of Peacemaking: Containment and Counterrevolution at Versailles, 1918–19*. New York: Alfred A. Knopf, 1967.

Mayse, Susan. *Ginger: The Life and Death of Albert Goodwin*. Madeira Park, BC: Harbour Publishing, 1990.

Miller, Ian Hugh Maclean. *Our Glory and Our Grief: Torontonians and the Great War*. Toronto: University of Toronto Press, 2002.

Milligan, Ian. "Sedition in Wartime Ontario: The Trials and Imprisonment of Isaac Bainbridge, 1917–1918." *Ontario History* C, no. 2 (Autumn 2008): 150–177.

Mills, Allen. "Single Tax, Socialism and the Independent Labour Party of Manitoba." *Labour/Le Travail* 5 (Spring 1980): 33–56.

———. *Fool for Christ: The Political Thought of J.S. Woodsworth*. Toronto: University of Toronto Press, 1991.

Mitchell, Tom. "Brandon, 1919: Labour and Industrial Relations in the Wheat City in the Year of the General Strike." *Manitoba History* 17 (Spring 1989): 2–13.

———. "'To Reach the Leadership of this Revolutionary Movement': A.J. Andrews, the Canadian State and the Suppression of the Winnipeg General Strike." *Prairie Forum* 18, no. 2 (Autumn 1993): 239–255.

———. "'Repressive Measures': A.J. Andrews, the Committee of 1000 and the Campaign Against Radicalism After the Winnipeg General Strike." *Left History* 3, no. 2 (Fall 1995): 133–167.

———. "'Legal Gentlemen Appointed by the Federal Government': the Canadian State, the Citizens' Committee of 1000, and Winnipeg's Seditious Conspiracy Trials of 1919–1920." *Labour/Le Travail* 53 (Spring 2004): 9–46.

Mitchell, Tom, ed. "A.J. Andrews to Arthur Meighen: Winnipeg General Strike Correspondence." *Manitoba History* 24 (Autumn 1992): 29–35.

Montreal Daily Star. "Soviet Plotters Busy in Canada," March 18, 1919.

———, February 1, 1919.

———, February 2, 1919.

Morgan, Ted. *Reds: McCarthyism in Twentieth-Century America*. New York: Random House, 2003.

Morton, Desmond. "Sir William Otter and Internment Operations in Canada during the First World War." *Canadian Historical Review* 55, no. 1 (March 1974): 32–58.

———. *A Peculiar Kind of Politics: Canada's Overseas Ministry in the First World War.* Toronto: University of Toronto Press, 1982.

Morton, Desmond, and Glenn Wright. *Winning the Second Battle: Canadian Veterans and the Return to Civilian Life, 1915–1930.* Toronto: University of Toronto Press, 1987.

Morton, Desmond, and J. L. Granatstein. *Marching to Armageddon: Canadians and the Great War, 1914–1919.* Toronto: Lester and Orpen Dennys, 1989.

Morton, W.L. *The Progressive Party in Canada.* Toronto: University of Toronto Press, 1950.

Motherwell, Robert. *The Dada Painters and Poets.* New York: Wittenborn, 1951.

Murray, Robert K. *Red Scare: A Study in National Hysteria, 1919–1920.* Minneapolis: University of Minnesota Press, 1955.

Naylor, James. "Toronto 1919." *Historical Papers* 21, no. 1 (1986): 33-55.

———. *The New Democracy: Challenging the Social Order in Industrial Ontario, 1914–1925.* Toronto: University of Toronto Press, 1991.

Oliver, Peter. *Public and Private Persons: The Ontario Political Culture, 1914–1934.* Toronto: Clarke Irwin, 1975.

Ottawa Citizen, November 19, 1918.

Ottawa Journal, January 3, 1919.

Penner, Norman, ed. *Winnipeg 1919: The Strikers' Own History of the Winnipeg General Strike.* Toronto: James Lorimer & Co., 1975.

Pettigrew, Eileen. *The Silent Enemy: Canada and the Deadly Flu of 1918.* Saskatoon: Western Producer Prairie Books, 1983.

Pfannestiel, Todd J. *Rethinking the Red Scare: The Lusk Committee and New York's Crusade Against Radicalism, 1919–1923.* New York: Routledge, 2003.

Pitsula, James M. *For All We Have and Are: Regina and the Experience of the Great War.* Winnipeg: University of Manitoba Press, 2008.

Plewman, William. *Toronto Daily Star*, May 23, 1919.

Preston, William Jr. *Aliens and Dissenters: Federal Suppression of Radicals, 1903–1933.* Cambridge, Mass.: Harvard University Press, 1963.

Province, April 3, 1912.

———, August 3, 1918.

Racey, Arthur. "The Beaver and the Smelly Foreigner." *Montreal Star*, March 7, 1919.

———. "If We Were Bolshevists." *Montreal Star*, February 27, 1919.

Reilly, Nolan. "The General Strike in Amherst, Nova Scotia, 1919." *Acadiensis* 9 (1980): 56–77.

Reimer, Chad. "War, Nationhood and Working-Class Entitlement: The Counterhegemonic Challenge of the 1919 Winnipeg General Strike." *Prairie Forum* 18, no. 2 (Autumn 1993): 219–237.

Richter, Hans. *Dada, Art and Anti-Art*. London: Thames & Hudson, 1997; orig. pub. 1965.

Rigg, Dick. *The Voice*, December 7, 1917.

Roberts, Barbara. *"Why Do Women Do Nothing to End the War?" Canadian Feminist-Pacifists and the Great War*. Ottawa: Canadian Research Institute for the Advancement of Women, 1985.

———. *Whence They Came: Deportation from Canada, 1900–1935*. Ottawa: University of Ottawa Press, 1988.

———. *A Reconstructed World: A Feminist Biography of Gertrude Richardson*. Montreal: McGill-Queen's University Press, 1996.

Robin, Martin. *Radical Politics and Canadian Labour, 1880–1930*. Kingston, Ont.: Industrial Relations Centre, Queen's University, 1968.

Rodney, William. "Broken Journey: Trotsky in Canada, 1917." *Queen's Quarterly* (December 1967): 649–665.

———. *Soldiers of the International: A History of the Communist Party of Canada, 1919–1929*. Toronto: University of Toronto Press, 1968.

Rutherdale, Robert. *Hometown Horizons: Local Responses to Canada's Great War*. Vancouver: University of British Columbia Press, 2004.

Aanouillet, Michel. *Dada in Paris*. Cambridge, Mass.: The MIT Press, 2009.

Saturday Night, December 7, 1918.

———, December 28, 1918.

———, February 22, 1919.

Schmidt, Regin. *Red Scare: FBI and the Origins of Anticommunism in the United States*. Copenhagen: Museum Tusculanum Press, University of Copenhagen, 2000.

Schull, Joseph. *Laurier: The First Canadian*. Toronto: Macmillan of Canada, 1966.

Sharp, Paul F. *Agrarian Revolt in Western Canada*. New York: Octagon

Books, 1971 [orig. pub. Minneapolis: University of Minnesota Press, 1948].

Siemiatycki, Meyer. "Munitions and Labour Militancy: the 1916 Hamilton Machinists' Strike." *Labour/Le Travail* 3 (1978): 131–151.

Skelton, O.D. "Current Events." *Queen's Quarterly* 27, no. 1 (July–September 1919): 101–128.

Smith, A.E. *All My Life*. Toronto: Progress Books, 1949.

Smith, Doug, and Michael Olito. *The Best Possible Face: L.B. Foote's Winnipeg*. Winnipeg: Turnstone Press, 1985.

Socknat, Thomas P. *Witness Against War: Pacifism in Canada, 1900–1945*. Toronto: University of Toronto Press, 1987.

Stonebanks, Roger. *Fighting for Dignity: the Ginger Goodwin Story*. St. John's: Canadian Committee on Labour History, 2004.

Stubbs, Roy St. George. *Prairie Portraits*. Toronto: McClelland & Stewart, 1954.

Taylor, W.J. *London Free Press*, June 19, 1919.

Thompson, John Herd. *The Harvests of War: The Prairie West, 1914–1918*. Toronto: McClelland & Stewart, 1978.

———. "The Enemy Alien and the Canadian General Election of 1917." In *Loyalties in Conflict: Ukrainians in Canada During the Great War*, edited by Frances Swyripa and John H. Thompson: 25–45. Edmonton: Canadian Institute of Ukrainian Studies, University of Alberta, 1983.

Toronto Daily Star, October 21, 1918.

———, Jaunary 13, 1919.

———, January 14, 1919.

———, January 16, 1919.

———, February 17, 1919.

———, May 23, 1919.

———, May 26, 1919.

———, June 27, 1919.

Traves, Thomas. *The State and Enterprise: Canadian Manufacturers and the Federal Government, 1917–1931*. Toronto: University of Toronto Press, 1979.

Vance, Jonathan F. *Death So Noble: Memory, Meaning, and the First World War*. Vancouver: University of British Columbia Press, 1997.

Vancouver Sun, October 19, 1918.

Watt, Richard M. *The Kings Depart: The Tragedy of Germany: Versailles and the German Revolution*. London: Weidenfeld and Nicolson, 1968.

Werner, Hans. "And what, exactly, was Leon Trotsky doing in Nova Scotia in 1917?" *Saturday Night* (August 1974): 26–29.

Western Labor News, May 17, 1919.

——, June 6, 1919.

——, June 13, 1919.

——, June 18, 1919.

——, June 20, 1919.

Williams, David Ricardo. *Call in the Pinkertons: American Detectives at Work in Canada*. Toronto: Dundurn Press, 1998.

Winnipeg Citizen, May 24, 1919.

——, June 7, 1919.

Winnipeg Telegram, January 29, 1919.

——, June 20, 1919.

——, June 23, 1919.

——, June 25, 1919.

Winnipeg Tribune, March 23, 1920.

——, March 25, 1920.

INDEX